# COMING OF AGE

**VOLUME TWO**

**To Karin and Julie, For Countless Inspirations**

Thanks to the following people, for ideas, suggestions, and help in various ways with this book: Svea Barrett-Tarleton, Andrew Dunn, Karin Emra, Nancy Kern, Nancy McGrath, Pat Riccobene, Don Ryan, Jeannie Ryan, Rubee Scrivani, and Mel Weinstein. Special thanks to the staff of the Ramsey, New Jersey, Public Library. And a very special tribute to my editor, Marianne Quinn, who was also a creative force in the content and structure of this book.

**About the Author**

Bruce Emra supervises the English Department and teaches English at Northern Highlands Regional High School in Allendale, New Jersey. He is the author of NTC/Contemporary's *Sports in Literature* and *Coming of Age, Volume One*.

# COMING OF AGE

**VOLUME TWO**

# Literature

## About Youth and Adolescence

Bruce Emra

National Textbook Company
*a division of* NTC/CONTEMPORARY PUBLISHING GROUP
Lincolnwood, Illinois USA

**Cover Illustration:** Diana Ong/Superstock

ISBN (student edition): 0–8442–0359–9 (hardbound); 0358–0 (softbound)

ISBN (teacher's edition): 0–8442–0357-2 (hardbound); 0490-0 (softbound)

Acknowledgments begin on page 319, which is to be considered an extension of this copyright page.

# COMING OF AGE

## CONTENTS

## PART 1   Searching

*(An asterisk identifies student writers.)*

# PART 2  Competing

# PART 3  Realizing

# PART 4 Loving

# PART 5    Separating

# PREFACE

The first volume of *Coming of Age* was limited to fiction about growing up. In *Coming of Age, Volume Two*, there are short stories and excerpts from novels, but also poetry and various forms of nonfiction, including memoirs, journals, essays, and articles. While the pieces of writing in this collection will help you learn about literary terms and techniques such as plot, point of view, imagery, diction, rhyme and meter, and many others, what will impress you most is the fact that these pieces are *about you*. They are about the same situations and the same feelings that you face and experience every day. As we move through our adolescent years, we are involved in the broad activities of Searching, Competing, Realizing, Loving, and Separating. These are the section headings for this collection.

As in *Coming of Age, Volume One*, each section of this book includes writing by someone your age. Scott Margolin, Melva Prahl, Paula Dan, Angela Patrick, and Richard Hartman all began with blank pieces of paper, or an empty computer screen, just as you do. Then Scott, Melva, Paula, Angela, and Richard all gave form to their experiences in life. My hope is that you can do that, too. Both the student writing and the professional writing in this collection should inspire your own writing.

Annie Dillard in *An American Childhood* speaks of waking "in bits, like all children, piecemeal over the years." She states, "[I] predicted with terrifying logic that one of these years not far away I would be awake continuously and never slip back, and never be free of myself again." *Coming of Age, Volume Two* is guaranteed to help you on that difficult but necessary journey of self-discovery.

**Bruce Emra**

## Jules Feiffer

Jules Feiffer, who was born in 1929, has been a commenter on society and on people's idiosyncrasies and neuroses since he was in his teens. But he got an even earlier start: a drawing he did at age five won a gold medal. His first "steady work in print" was a children's cartoon strip called "Clifford." This strip, as Feiffer tells the story, "ran until 1951, when I was drafted away from it and into the army, the shock of which so enraged me that I was inspired to write my first satire, *Munro*, a children's book for adults about a four-year-old draftee." An animated version of *Munro* won an Academy Award as a short subject. Feiffer drew cartoons for years for *The Village Voice*. Recently his cartoons have appeared on the Op-Ed page of *The New York Times*.

# I Didn't Want to Be Me

EVER SINCE I WAS A LITTLE KID I DIDN'T WANT TO BE ME. I WANTED TO BE BILLIE WIDDLEDON. AND BILLIE WIDDLEDON DIDN'T EVEN **LIKE** ME.

I WALKED LIKE **HE** WALKED. I TALKED LIKE **HE** TALKED. I SIGNED UP FOR THE HIGH SCHOOL **HE** SIGNED UP FOR—

WHICH WAS WHEN BILLIE WIDDLEDON CHANGED. HE BEGAN TO HANG AROUND HERBY VANDEMAN. HE **WALKED** LIKE HERBY VANDEMAN. HE **TALKED** LIKE HERBY VANDEMAN.

HE MIXED ME UP! I BEGAN TO WALK AND TALK LIKE BILLIE WIDDLEDON WALKING AND TALKING LIKE HERBY VANDEMAN.

AND THEN IT DAWNED ON ME THAT HERBY VANDEMAN WALKED AND TALKED LIKE JOEY HAVERLIN AND JOEY HAVERLIN WALKED AND TALKED LIKE CORKY SABINSON.

SO HERE I AM WALKING AND TALKING LIKE BILLIE WIDDLEDON'S IMITATION OF HERBY VANDEMAN'S VERSION OF JOEY HAVERLIN TRYING TO WALK AND TALK LIKE CORKY SABINSON.

AND **WHO** DO YOU THINK CORKY SABINSON IS ALWAYS WALKING AND TALKING LIKE? OF **ALL** PEOPLE— DOPEY KENNY WELLINGTON—

THAT LITTLE PEST WHO WALKS AND TALKS LIKE ME.

# Searching

All of us are continually searching—for answers to problems small and big, for the meaning of things, for something better.

In Part One you will meet adolescents looking for missing parents and not knowing how to cope. You will meet people straying from who they really are as they try to create new self-images. You will meet a boy and girl searching for romantic mates yet hesitating to speak to each other.

Searching for one's identity is at the heart of every piece of writing in this section of the book. Are you on that search yourself?

## Peter Cameron

Contemporary writer Peter Cameron has published two novels, *Leap Year* and *The Weekend*, and two short story collections, including the highly praised *One Way or Another*, from which the following story comes. Born in 1959, he started writing poetry, then turned to prose, as a student at Hamilton College in upstate New York. *The New Yorker* magazine has said of his writing, "Cameron's prose is neat without being fastidious; it is full of observations that ring like porch chimes and flicker like fireflies, evanescent yet indelible." Cameron himself says, "I write about relationships between people, and the more interesting relationships or the more meaningful relationships tend to happen at home rather than out in the world." His stories have been included in three editions of the O. Henry prize stories.

*"The more meaningful relationships tend to happen at home . . . ."*
*But how can any relationship survive the silent treatment?*

# Memorial Day

**I** am eating my grapefruit with a grapefruit spoon my mother bought last summer from a door-to-door salesman on a large three-wheeled bike. My mother and I were sitting on the front steps that day and we watched him glide down the street, into our driveway, and up our front walk. He opened his case on the handlebars, and it was full of fruit appliances: pineapple corers, melon ballers, watermelon seeders, orange-juice squeezers, and grapefruit spoons. My mother bought four of the spoons and the man pedaled himself out of our lives.

That was about a year ago. Since then a lot has changed, I think as I pry the grapefruit pulp away from the skin with the serrated edge of the spoon. Since then, my mother has remarried, my father has moved to California, and I have stopped talking. Actually, I talk quite a lot at school, but never at home. I have nothing to say to anyone here.

Across the table from me, drinking Postum, is my new stepfather. He wasn't here last year. I don't think he was anywhere last year. His name is Lonnie, and my mother met him at a Seth Speaks seminar. Seth is this guy without a body who speaks out of the mouth of this lady and tells you how to fix your life. Both Lonnie and my mother have fixed their lives. "One day at a time," my mother says every morning, smiling at Lonnie and then, less happily, at me.

Lonnie is only thirteen years older than I am; he is twenty-nine but looks about fourteen. When the three of us go out together, he is taken to be my brother.

"Listen to this," Lonnie says. Both Lonnie and my mother continue to talk to me, consult with me, and read things to me, in the hope that I will forget and speak. "If gypsy moths continue to destroy trees at their present rate, North America will become a desert incapable of supporting any life by the year 4000." Lonnie has a morbid sense of humor and delights in macabre newspaper fillers. Because he knows I won't answer, he doesn't glance up at me. He continues to stare at his paper and says, "Wow. Think of that."

I look out the window. My mother is sitting in an inflated rubber boat in the swimming pool, scrubbing the fiberglass walls with a stiff brush and Mr. Clean. They get stained during the winter. She does this every Memorial Day. We always open the pool this weekend, and she always blows up the yellow boat, puts on her Yankee hat so her hair won't turn orange, and paddles around the edge of the pool, leaving a trail of suds.

Last year, as she scrubbed, the diamond from her old engagement ring fell out and sank to the bottom of the pool. She was still married to my father, although they were planning to separate after a last "family vacation" in July. My mother shook the suds off her hand and raised it in front of her face, as if she were admiring a new ring. "Oh, Stephen!" she said. "I think I've lost my diamond."

"What?" I said. I still talked then.

"The diamond fell out of my ring. Look."

I got up from the chair I was sitting on and kneeled beside the pool. She held out her hand, the way women do in old movies when they expect it to be kissed. I looked down at her ring and she was right: the diamond was gone. The setting looked like an empty hand tightly grabbing nothing.

"Do you see it?" she asked, looking down into the pool. Because we had just taken the cover off, the water was murky. "It must be down there," she said. "Maybe if you dove in?" She looked at me with a nice, pleading look on her face. I took my shirt off. I felt her looking at my chest. There is no hair on my chest, and every time my mother sees it I know she checks to see if any has grown.

I dove into the pool. The water was so cold my head ached. I opened my eyes and swam quickly around the bottom. I felt like one of those Japanese pearl fishers. But I didn't see the diamond.

I surfaced and swam to the side. "I don't see it," I said. "I can't see anything. Where's the mask?"

"Oh, dear," my mother said. "Didn't we throw it away last year?"

"I forget," I said. I got out of the pool and stood shivering in the sun. Suddenly I got the idea that if I found the diamond maybe my parents wouldn't separate. I know it sounds ridiculous, but at that moment, standing with my arms crossed over my chest, watching my mother begin to cry in her inflatable boat—at that moment, the diamond sitting on the bottom of the pool took on a larger meaning, and I thought that if it was replaced in the tiny clutching hand of my mother's ring we might live happily ever after.

So I had my father drive me downtown, and I bought a diving mask at the five-and-ten, and when we got home I put it on—first spitting on the glass so it wouldn't fog—and dove into the water, and dove again and again, until I actually found the diamond, glittering in a mess of leaves and bloated inchworms at the bottom of the pool.

I throw my grapefruit rind away, and go outside and sit on the edge of the diving board with my feet in the water. My mother watches me for a second, probably deciding if it's worthwhile to say anything. Then she goes back to her scrubbing.

Later, I am sitting by the mailbox. Since I've stopped talking, I've written a lot of letters. I write to men in prisons, and I answer personal ads, claiming to be whatever it is the placer desires: "an elegant educated lady for afternoon pleasure," or a "GBM." The mail from prisons is the best: long letters about nothing, since it seems nothing is done in prison. A lot of remembering. A lot of bizarre requests: Send me a shoehorn.

Send me an empty egg carton (arts and crafts?). Send me an electric toothbrush. I like writing letters to people I've never met.

Lonnie is planting geraniums he bought this morning in front of the A & P when he did the grocery shopping. Lonnie is very good about "doing his share." I am not about mine. Every night I wait with delicious anticipation for my mother to tell me to take out the garbage: "How many times do I have to tell you? Can't you just do it?"

Lonnie gets up and walks over to me, trowel in hand. He has on plaid Bermuda shorts and a Disney World T-shirt. If I talked, I'd ask him when he went to Disney World. But I can live without the information.

Lonnie flips the trowel at me and it slips like a knife into the ground a few inches from my leg. "Bingo!" Lonnie says. "Scare you?"

I think when a person stops talking people forget that he can still hear. Lonnie is always saying dumb things to me—things you'd only say to a deaf person or a baby.

"What a day," Lonnie says, as if to illustrate this point. He stretches out beside me, and I look at his long white legs. He has sneakers and white socks on. He never goes barefoot. He is too uptight to go barefoot. He would step on a piece of glass immediately. That is the kind of person Lonnie is.

The Captain Ice Cream truck rolls lazily down our street. Lonnie stands up and reaches in his pocket. "Would you like an ice pop?" he asks me, looking at his change.

I shake my head no. An ice pop? Where did he grow up—Kentucky?

Lonnie walks into the street and flags down the ice-cream truck as if it's not obvious what he's standing there for.

The truck slows down and the ice-cream man jumps out. It is a woman. "What can I get you?" she says, opening the freezer on the side of the truck. It's the old-fashioned kind of truck, with the ice cream hidden in its frozen depths. I always thought you needed to have incredibly long arms to be a good Captain Ice Cream person.

"Well, I'd like a nice ice pop," Lonnie says.

"A Twin Bullet?" suggests the woman. "What flavor?"

"Do you have cherry?" Lonnie asks.

"Sure," the woman says. "Cherry, grape, orange, lemon, cola, and tutti-frutti."

For a second I have a horrible feeling that Lonnie will want a tutti-frutti. "I'll have cherry," he says.

Lonnie comes back, peeling the sticky paper from his cherry Bullet. It's a bright pink color. The truck drives away. "Guess how much this cost," Lonnie says, sitting beside me on the grass. "Sixty cents. It's a good thing you didn't want one." He licks his fingers and then the ice stick. "Do you want a bite?" He holds it out toward me.

Lonnie is so patient and so sweet. It's just too bad he's such a nerd. I take a bite of his cherry Bullet.

"Good, huh?" Lonnie says. He watches me eat for a second, then takes a bite himself. He breaks the Bullet in half and eats it in a couple of huge bites. A little pink juice runs down his chin.

"What are you waiting for?" he asks. I nod toward the mailbox.

"It's Memorial Day," Lonnie says. "The mail doesn't come." He stands up and pulls the trowel out of the ground. I think of King Arthur.[1] "There is no mail for anyone today," Lonnie says. "No matter how long you wait." He hands me his two Bullet sticks and returns to his geraniums.

I have this feeling, holding the stained wooden sticks, that I will keep them for long time, and come across them one day, and remember this moment, incorrectly.

After the coals in the barbecue have melted into powder, the fireflies come out. They hesitate in the air, as if stunned by dusk.

Lonnie and my mother are sitting beside the now clean pool, and I am sitting on the other side of the "natural forsythia[2] fence" that is planted around it, watching the bats swoop from tree to tree, feeling the darkness clot all around me. I can hear Lonnie and my mother talking, but I can't make out what they are saying.

I love this time of day—early evening, early summer. It makes me want to cry. We always had a barbecue on Memorial Day with my father, and my mother cooked this year's hamburgers on her new barbecue, which Lonnie bought her for Mother's Day (she's old enough to be his mother, but she isn't, I would have said, if I talked), in the same dumb, cheerful way she cooked last year's. She has no sense of sanctity, or ritual. She would give Lonnie my father's clothes if my father had left any behind to give.

---

1. **pulls the trowel out . . . King Arthur:** The legendary King Arthur pulled the sword Excalibur out of the rock in which it was stuck, thereby proving himself rightful king of England.
2. **forsythia:** bush with dense branches that produces yellow flowers in early spring.

My mother walks toward me with the hose, then past me toward her garden, to spray her pea plants. "O.K.," she yells to Lonnie, who stands by the spigot. He turns the knob and then goes inside. The light in the kitchen snaps on.

My mother stands with one hand on her hip, the other raising and lowering the hose, throwing large fans of water over the garden. She used to bathe me every night, and I think of the peas hanging in their green skins, dripping. I lie with one ear on the cool grass, and I can hear the water drumming into the garden. It makes me sleepy.

Then I hear it stop, and I look up to see my mother walking toward me, the skin on her bare legs and arms glowing. She sits down beside me, and for a while she says nothing. I pretend I am asleep on the ground, although I know she knows I am awake.

Then she starts to talk, as I knew she would. My mother says, "You are breaking my heart." She says it as if it were literally true, as if her heart were actually breaking. "I just want you to know that," she says. "You're old enough to know that you are breaking my heart."

I sit up. I look at my mother's chest, as if I could see her heart breaking. She has on a polo shirt with a little blue whale on her left breast. I am afraid to look at her face.

We sit like that for a while, and darkness grows around us. When I open my mouth to speak, my mother uncoils her arm from her side and covers my mouth with her hand.

I look at her.

"Wait," she says. "Don't say anything yet."

I can feel her flesh against my lips. Her wrist smells of chlorine. the fireflies, lighting all around us, make me dizzy.

---

## Responding to the Story

1. Why does the narrator stop speaking at home? Do you agree with his decision? Why or why not?
2. Why do you think the narrator likes "writing letters to people I've never met?" What does this activity tell you about him?

3.  What does Stephen mean when he says that his mother has no "sense of sanctity, or ritual"? Do you understand why this aspect of his mother bothers him? Explain.
4.  Why do you think that when Stephen is about to speak, his mother "uncoils her arm from her side and covers [his] mouth with her hand" and says, "Wait, don't say anything yet"?

## Exploring the Author's Craft

Writers often mean more than what they seem to say. For example, they will often use something concrete—an object, place, character, or event—as a **symbol** of some abstract quality or idea.

1.  In this story Memorial Day and the family traditions Stephen associates with it represent something special for him. What is it that Memorial Day symbolizes?
2.  What does the missing diamond mean to Stephen? What is the significance of the fact that the diamond is found "glittering in a mess of leaves and bloated inchworms at the bottom of the pool"?

## Writer's Workshop

Write a story in which at least one event and one object symbolize something more than themselves.

## Alternate Media Response

Adapt this story into a short television script. The plot is simple, and you really only need one setting. You will have to make crucial choices. What in the story needs to stay in your script? What—if anything—can be excluded?

## Richard Wilbur

Richard Wilbur, who was born in 1921, has won two Pulitzer Prizes for his poetry as well as a National Medal of Arts. He has also served as United States poet laureate. His translations of several plays by the French writer Molière show his ability for working within traditional poetic forms, a talent he also demonstrates in "Boy at the Window."

*Which one understands the other better, the boy inside or the snowman outside?*

# Boy at the Window

Seeing the snowman standing all alone
In dusk and cold is more than he can bear.
The small boy weeps to hear the wind prepare
A night of gnashings and enormous moan.
5    His tearful sight can hardly reach to where
The pale-faced figure with bitumen[1] eyes
Returns him such a god-forsaken stare
As outcast Adam gave to Paradise.
The man of snow is, nonetheless, content,
10   Having no wish to go inside and die.
Still, he is moved to see the youngster cry.

---

1. **bitumen:** soft coal.

Though frozen water is his element,

He melts enough to drop from one soft eye

A trickle of the purest rain, tear

15  For the child at the bright pane surrounded by

Such warmth, such light, such love, and so much fear.

---

## Responding to the Poem

1.  What exactly is it that the boy at the window responds to in the snowman? Explain as precisely as you can the various feelings of the boy.
2.  What does the snowman sense in the boy? Why does the snowman shed a tear for the boy?

## Exploring the Author's Craft

Many poets put tight constraints on the construction of their works. They may, for example, use **rhyme schemes**, patterns in which certain lines rhyme with certain other lines. They may also use precise numbers of syllables in each line.

1.  Each of the lines of this poem has ten syllables. Therefore, we know that the writer has composed carefully. Analyze exactly where the rhymes come. What rhyme scheme do you see?
2.  In terms of sound and meaning, explain the contributions of the words *alone* and *moan* in this poem.

## Writer's Workshop

Compose a poem of six or eight lines. Make each line exactly ten syllables. Create a rhyme scheme with the first and third lines rhyming, then the second and fourth. If your poem is only six lines, have the last two rhyme; if it is eight lines, repeat the pattern of lines 1–4 in lines 5–8.

Of course, your poem must not only rhyme and have the correct number of syllables; it must make sense, too. The topic of your poem should be *something seen and commented upon*, as in "Boy at the Window."

## Alternate Media Response

If you are good at drawing, you may want to illustrate the two faces in this poem, that of the boy and that of the snowman. Refer carefully to the text to know what emotions to show in each face.

## Scott Margolin

When Scott Margolin was in fifth grade, his teacher wrote home, "Scott's poetry, especially concerning nature, is sensitive and beautiful. He should be encouraged to submit for publication; his writing is worthy of it." Years later, during Scott's freshman year at Middlebury College in Vermont, Professor John Elder taught Scott in a course called Visions of Nature. Professor Elder says of Scott Margolin, "Scott had a festive sense of life in this world and of belonging to something that was much bigger than himself." That same spring Scott wrote the following journal entries as part of his freshman English class.

*Searching for meanings in life doesn't necessarily stop after high school.*

# Journal: My Freshman Year in College

**February 20**

I had a strange dream last night. I was lying there on my friend's floor quietly, and everything kind of turned into a dream and I was not there anymore. I was watching my life from the outside and I was not an active player in it. Everything seemed very strange and unfamiliar, like I didn't know myself. I couldn't believe that I was in college and that I was in this room with these people who[m] it seemed I didn't even know. There they were, my friends, sitting there having their normal conversation. And I remember thinking, who are these people? I have known them only for five months, maybe less, and they seem to know each other so well. How can that be? I looked at the door and pictured myself leaving the room and walking down the hall and down the stairs to my own room and I couldn't believe that I live here. This is actually very hard for me to describe for some reason and I don't know if I can do it effectively,.

I thought to myself, what am I doing here? Not just at college but living at all and where is my life going and all that stuff. Of course, I didn't come to any conclusions. But I remember thinking that I can't really call it home here just because I haven't been here long enough and I don't know people well enough. On the other hand, my former life doesn't exist anymore either. Not as I know it anyway. Sure, I have my family and my best friends who[m] I talk to all the time and my house to go home to. But life as I knew it a year ago, five years ago, is over forever. When I go home I feel like I am on vacation, but at school I don't really feel like I'm at home, so where is home now? I'm not really sure and that makes me sad in a way. In a way it is also exciting, though. I have never before had opportunities like I do now. I have always complained of living in a boring place with nothing to do and the same stuff going on all the time. It is not like that anymore and for that I am grateful, I suppose.

Back to my dream. I pictured myself walking down to my room, and I couldn't believe that I knew the way (not that it's that complicated or anything). I felt like I was in someone else's life or watching a movie or something and I couldn't imagine stepping back into reality. Reality seemed so pointless for that short time during my dream. I observed the people in the room and came to the conclusion that under any normal circumstances I would be doing exactly what they were doing and would be participating in the same conversation as they were and would be passing time just as they were. I could distinctly tell the difference between the two worlds. It was very interesting and I wish I could make myself think that way whenever I want to because it gave me a unique perspective that I have never really had before. I was able to look at my life completely objectively, almost from the point of view of another person. It was very interesting. I wonder what this dream means.

Okay, I hope I haven't scared you. Yes, I am sane. Kind of.

## March 1
This past weekend I went skiing at Sugarbush with my family and one of my best friends from home. We both had reading to do over the weekend and last night we finally sat down to do it. She opened a large

history book and began to read. This made me wonder, why do we study history, anyway? What is the point? Some of it I can understand, like the formation and development of certain ideas and concepts over time, but why all the pointless memorization of dates and events? Can the title and date of the treaty that ended WWI really make any difference today? And who cares if it was Eli Whitney or someone else who invented the cotton gin? Does any of that really affect our lives now? History . . . why are we so concerned with specific details from the past? And it is only the recent past. We don't have the ability to specifically date events that occurred long ago in geologic time and we are no worse off for that.

## March 31

Since I've been here at college I have noticed that I seem to be living two separate lives, and I have written about it before. But it was so apparent today as I was sitting at a picnic table eating my lunch. I stopped at a New York Thruway rest stop and took a break to eat my lunch. I finished my sandwich and I sat facing traffic and just relaxed and thought for a while. It occurred to me that the cars headed south were going toward my home in New Jersey and my friends and my family and my relatives there and all the other familiar things that I have known all my life. And the cars going north were headed in the direction of my other, newer life at Middlebury College. The road served as the medium by which I make the transition from one life to the other—the time machine, if you will. However, it's not like traveling through time, which is the most amazing part; both worlds are in existence simultaneously. But it does not seem like the two have anything in common. No one here knows my family or knows anything about my background aside from what I chose to tell them. No one at home really knows my friends here or what I do from day to day. Sure, I tell them what goes on but they can't really comprehend life at Middlebury. It's very strange and I can't integrate the two. When I am at home and I think about going back to school it doesn't seem real and it is so far away—like another world that I know from a movie or something—not from experience. But when I am here and I am on the phone with people from home, Middlebury is the main world and the other is the fuzzy one—I can't imagine myself there. The ultimate strange experience was when a friend from home came here to visit. He just looked so out of place here with these people that have only known me for a few months. Something seemed wrong. I wonder if it will be like this throughout my four years here or if the worlds will somehow merge or at least become less rigidly defined.

## April 4

Tonight I watched the sunset. It was amazing as usual—I have yet to be disappointed by a sunset and I don't think I ever will be. Actually, sunsets and sunrises—anything having to do with the sun, come to think of it—are somewhat of a religious experience for me. I think the importance and meaning lies in the fact that the sun is always there and it is so dependable. The sun will never fail to show up one day. Imagine what would happen if it did, though—there would be chaos on Earth. Not just because of the darkness—that I think we could handle—but because the dependable sun didn't show up. Wouldn't that be a funny prank for Mother Nature to pull on us? I can't even compare it to an eclipse because we can predict those and they are no surprise. I sat there in the woods watching the sun set and I thought to myself how I might react if it just began to rise again. I pictured it dipping just below the horizon and popping back up. Man, what news stories that would make. But not to the animals—just to us.

I had some more thoughts as I made my way into the woods. The woods I speak of are Ridgeline Woods behind the tennis courts and Proctor Hall. To get there I have to walk through the cemetery. Usually I follow the road around the perimeter and avoid walking on the grass between the tombstones, out of respect or something, I suppose. But today I decided to walk right through; I didn't think they would mind. I looked at the stones as I passed. The oldest I could find marked the grave of a man born in 1854. Wow, that's BEFORE THE CIVIL WAR, I thought. That amazed me for some reason. As I looked at the other stones, it occurred to me that there were people underneath. People who once had lives and knew other people and had feelings and emotions and stuff. And they also had secrets. Not like classified military secrets or anything, just personal little things that they never bothered to tell anyone. It amazed me that these people were buried with secrets that no one will ever know, no matter what. It made me think about my own secrets and the little things I have never told anybody. If I died tomorrow, no one would ever know no matter what.

## April 7

A month of college left. Unbelievable. The year definitely flew by but the beginning seems so long ago. I remember the first day so clearly: I packed the car with my family and one of my friends the day before and then we were off for Vermont, in two separate cars. My mom rode with me for the first half of the journey and then my brother for the second half. They both wanted to get their last words in and spend their final moments with me. It was like I was going to the chair[1] or something. We arrived here and had to ask for directions to security where I picked up my key and was bombarded with more numbers than I thought I could ever remember (now I know them like my birthday) and we were off to the dorm. I was on the verge of tears when I walked into my room. Having arrived first I had the pleasure of seeing the bare walls and cold, empty floor. My mom said something like, "Maybe it will look better when you get used to it," and my dad and my brother were speechless. I pushed on bravely and directed the unloading of all my stuff from the cars. We worked all day on setting up my room, and I felt an eerie sense of foreboding—like I knew that no matter what I did, the next twenty-four hours would go by just as fast and I would be on my own. I spent the night in the hotel with my family and again it felt like I was waiting to be executed: I knew my time with them was limited. The next was a blur: met my roommate, went shopping for supplies, attended the president's lunch, said goodbye to my family, and met with my MOO[2] group. The actual goodbye was pretty hard—we were in my room alone and I hugged my mom, dad, and brother individually and then they walked out. I could see that my dad had tears in his eyes but my mom was playing it tough. I have never felt more empty or alone than that moment when they walked out of the room.

I recently found out that I am going to lead a MOO trip next year. I have chosen a major, and have my hopes set on getting a block with four of my friends. Not to mention four thousand other memories and experiences that have taken place in my time here. Hmm . . . retrospect is a weird thing.

---

1. **the chair:** the electric chair, the means of executing criminals in some states.
2. **MOO:** Middlebury Outdoor Orientation.

**April 10**

I can't believe I haven't written about this yet because it's something I've been thinking so much about recently. This summer, actually two or three days after I get home from Middlebury, I am going on a roadtrip with my two best friends. We are going out west without any significant plan (actually without any plan at all). We have some idea that we want to go to Wyoming, Colorado, Utah, Arizona, etc., but nothing definite. Just going to drive until we feel like stopping and hang out and explore and stay until we feel like moving on (or until June 15th anyway). This idea was originated last summer, about a week before we left for college. Chris and Dara, my best friends (who also happen to be together), were at my boat for the weekend. We had a great time as usual and we bonded probably more than ever but we were depressed at the same time. It's not that we thought our friendships would not last because I certainly didn't think that, but it felt like something was coming to an end. I guess something did come to an end—that whole high school-small town-small perspective era of my life in which the only things I knew, for the most part, were right there under my nose. Anyway, we fantasized about this abstract idea of a roadtrip kind of as a way to combat our depression. We imagined how great it would be to finish a year of college and emerge, still best friends, and travel across the country for a month. It was very idyllic but, to all of us, I think, seemed more than just far away—it seemed almost like wishful thinking. There must have been doubts in our minds not only about this grand idea but also about the state of our friendship after a year of college. Well, we never let the idea die. We talked and fantasized about it from then on and it eventually, somehow, became a reality. We now have a date set and summer plans based around a month away. But more than that, I am now convinced, more than ever, that we will be friends for a long, long time. This makes me happy.

**April 14**

I never thought I would say this, but I am sick of the snow and the cold and winter and basically everything. In years past, while I have always enjoyed the onset of spring, I was never bothered if it arrived late, if the groundhog saw his little shadow and scampered right back into his proverbial hole. But this year is different. I really enjoyed my first full

Vermont winter but now it's not time for winter anymore. The snow last weekend and the cold and gloom over the weekend were very depressing. All I could think of was relaxing in the sun and swimming and hanging out outside comfortably for extended periods of time. That made me think about being home—I guess because that is where my images of warmth and summer come from for the most part. I got the sensation that I really wanted to go home. I felt sick of my dorm and everyone's quirky personality traits that I have had to live with for the past seven months—my roommate's incessant messiness and disregard for my CDs that he just leaves haphazardly strewn about the room, my next door neighbor's constant blasting of bass-loaded rap that permeates through the cell-like bland and cold brick walls (bitter? maybe a little). I'm kinda sick of doing the work, too, and I don't feel like doing the rest of what has to be done. I guess I just have to tell myself that it will all be over in less than a month. Sorry . . . this has been nothing but a bitching session. Well, too bad!

**April 22**
"It was a warm, sunny morning just like this one 19 years ago . . ." I hear those words, or a variation of them, every year on April 22, my birthday. This time it was via e-mail, but my mom didn't fail to remind me that I was born on a morning "just like this one' and that made me feel very good. Not that it was a warm spring morning, but that my mom always remembers to keep that in mind and make it known to me. I love my mom—I know, all kids love their mothers, but I think she is a lot like me and we have much in common. Even though we don't talk bout everything in my life or have daily deep conversations, I feel that we really connect and know each other very well. We share the philosophy that a little kindness goes a long way and sometimes just smiling makes other people smile. So I try to smile whenever I can. Back to my birthday . . . Even though I don't feel older in any way, I feel important today for some reason. I feel like people are looking at me, whether they know me or not, and are thinking, "Wow, it's his birthday." I am aware, of course, that this is ridiculous and is not true, but nevertheless, I feel like this is my special day. And that makes me smile.

**April 24**

I got a birthday present in the mail today from my best friend. It was addressed to "sven margenhosen." In the box were many random items: a big blue piggy bank with "pig" painted on the back, corn skewers, small plastic instruments, a looping crazy straw, sugar cubes, rubber wrestling characters, and a bunch of other stuff. All was wrapped in toilet paper and lots of tape so that it was hard to unwrap. I got to one round object and continued to pull away paper until there was nothing left—and nothing inside. Heehee. There was another similarly shaped object and I figured he did the same thing so I groped and prodded and it felt like nothing. I figured I'd unwrap it quickly so I set it out on my bed and pulled the end of the toilet paper and whipped off the layers. A cranberry muffin was instantly scattered bout my bed (at least I think it was cranberry—it was badly squashed from the prodding). I laughed and then cleaned it up.

**April 25**

It was very strange to wake up this morning to snow. It's amazing how different weather can change your whole outlook on life. Just last night, even though it was raining, I was wearing shorts and frolicking in the rain, sure that spring had finally arrived. I had a feeling that school is almost over for the year, summer is fast approaching, days of long light are here. The smell of spring was in the humid and wet air and that made me feel sort of carefree and made me see the light at the end of the tunnel of my first year of college. This morning that all changed. Not only the obvious changes—I didn't wear shorts and it certainly didn't smell like spring, but more far-reaching ones. I don't feel as carefree, happy, excited, energized, or ready for the end of the school year. It seems like we have months left and it has not even begun to change from winter to spring yet. It seems like it should be getting dark at 4 or 5 o'clock and I should be drinking hot cider or hot chocolate. It makes me forget that it is Earth Week and that there is an all-campus sleepout scheduled for this weekend, and that bands will be playing outside all day today. I suppose it is all related to the mind/image thing. We are used to feeling a certain way in the winter when the weather is a certain way and we do certain things. This feeling is very different from that of spring for many reasons. I also suppose that this one of the things I love so much about Vermont—the unpredictability.

**April 28**

Okay, so this is the last week of journal entries. That's pretty cool in itself (while I enjoyed the process, I'm kinda sick of it) but it's indicative of much greater things to come . . . summer and all it brings. I know that I will especially appreciate summer this year after my first year of college because I miss my friends and just being at home, which I didn't really think would happen. I have found my niche here, I think, but I'm definitely ready for a break. I am amazed that some of my friends here are spending the summer here because they don't want to go home or they really have nothing to go home to. I feel sorry for them, even though I know they don't necessarily feel sorry for themselves and there's no need to. I can't imagine not wanting to go home and spend time with my friends and family and just be in that familiar setting that I have longed for off and on over the past year. I guess that's just me. Anyhow, I'm glad this is the last week of journal entries for many reasons.

**April 30**

All humans dream during sleep. Whether we are aware of our dreams or remember them in the morning is questionable, but it is a proven fact that all humans dream. It also cannot be argued that when we dream, at least sometimes, the dream seems real and indistinguishable from reality. During such a dream, we do not feel detached or out of place with our "usual" world because, for the time being, the dream world *becomes* reality and we know no other existence. Furthermore, it is possible to doze off for five minutes and have a dream that seems to span a much longer time period, maybe a day or a month. In other words, a dream that seems to incorporate a week certainly does not require a week of time as we know it. Since dreams are not restricted by traditional "time," would it not be possible for a dream to take up no time at all? Having established dreams as indistinguishable from reality and independent of time, I propose the possibility that life as we know it is a dream and that time does not exist at all. If this be the case, the dream must be taking place in one single mind, for an integrated totality would not be possible otherwise.

*Note: Scott, Dara, and Chris did go on their road trip when their respective freshman years ended. Tragically, Scott and Dara were killed in a car accident in New Mexico—Chris survived—while they were on the trip that the three had talked about and planned for a year.*

## Responding to the Journal

1. As you were reading, which entry spoke the most to you? What feelings and thoughts that Scott expressed did you identify with? Explain the connection for you.
2. How did you feel about Scott's journal after you learned what happened to him? Were there any entries that, looking back, seemed to carry a deeper message?

## Exploring the Author's Craft

When Scott Margolin wrote these entries, he wasn't thinking of any craft. He simply communicated his thoughts and feelings as frankly and sincerely as possible. When keeping a **journal**, this is a good formula for any writer to follow. Look back through Scott's journal entries and find at least three examples of different emotions he wrote about.

## Writer's Workshop

In the next four weeks, compose at least fifteen journal entries. In your own natural style, react to daily events, moods, and feelings as Scott Margolin did. Don't be hesitant to go back to a theme reported earlier; our lives are filled with repeated themes.

Make each entry lengthy enough for you to probe an idea in depth—at least three or four paragraphs long. By the end of the four weeks these journal entries should truly reflect what the time was like for you.

## Malcolm X

Malcolm X was born in 1925 as Malcolm Little. His father was murdered when Malcolm was only six, possibly by the Ku Klux Klan. As a young man Malcolm served time in prison for burglary, but during this period became an avid reader and thinker. Taking the name Malcolm X, he originally supported the Black Muslims, a group advocating racial separation. Later, after visiting the Islamic holy city of Mecca, he adopted the Arabic name El-Hajj Malik El-Shabazz and began speaking out in favor of racial solidarity. He was assassinated on February 21, 1965, by people allegedly associated with the Black Muslims.

*Sometimes a painful experience helps a person to grow up; sometimes it just causes humiliation.*

# from The Autobiography of Malcolm X

### My First Conk

Shorty soon decided that my hair was finally long enough to be conked.[1] He had promised to school me in how to beat the barbershops' three- and four-dollar price by making up congolene, and then conking ourselves.

I took the little list of ingredients he had printed out for me, and went to a grocery store, where I got a can of Red Devil lye, two eggs, and two medium-sized white potatoes. Then at a drugstore near the

---

1. **conked:** straightened.

poolroom, I asked for a large jar of vaseline, a large bar of soap, a large-toothed comb and a fine-tooth comb, one of those rubber hoses with a metal spray-head, a rubber apron and a pair of gloves.

"Going to lay on that first conk?" the drugstore man asked me. I proudly told him, grinning, "Right!"

Shorty paid six dollars a week for a room in his cousin's shabby apartment. His cousin wasn't at home. "It's like the pad's mine, he spends so much time with his woman," Shorty said. "Now, you watch me—"

He peeled the potatoes and thin-sliced them into a quart-sized Mason fruit jar, then started stirring them with a wooden spoon as he gradually poured in a little over half the can of lye. "Never use a metal spoon; the lye will turn it black," he told me.

A jelly-like, starchy-looking glop resulted from the lye and potatoes, and Shorty broke in the two eggs stirring real fast—his own conk and dark face bent down close. The congolene turned pale-yellowish. "Feel the jar," Shorty said. I cupped my had against the outside, and snatched it away. "Damn right, it's hot, that's the lye," he said. "So you know it's going to burn when I comb it in—it burns *bad*. But the longer you can stand it, the straighter the hair."

He made me sit down, and he tied the string of the new rubber apron tightly around my neck, and combed up my bush of hair. then, from the big vaseline jar, he took a handful and massaged it hard all through my hair and into the scalp. He also thickly vaselined my neck, ears and forehead. "When I get to washing out your head, be sure to tell me anywhere you feel any little stinging," Shorty warned me, washing his hands, then pulling on the rubber gloves, and tying on his own rubber apron. "You always got to remember that any congolene left in burns a sore into your head."

The congolene just felt warm when Shorty started combing it in. But then my head caught fire.

I gritted my teeth and tried to pull the sides of the kitchen table together. The comb felt as if it was raking my skin off.

My eyes watered, my nose was running. I couldn't stand it any longer; I bolted to the washbasin. I was cursing Shorty with every name I could think of when he got the spray going and started soap-lathering my head.

He lathered and spray-rinsed, lathered and spray-rinsed, maybe ten or twelve times, each time gradually closing the hot-water faucet, until the rinse was cold, and that helped some.

"You feel any stinging spots?"

"No," I managed to say. My knees were trembling.

"Sit back down, then. I think we got it all out okay."

The flame came back as Shorty, with a thick towel, started drying my head, rubbing hard. *"Easy, man, easy!"* I kept shouting.

"The first time's always worst. You get used to it better before long. You took it real good, homeboy. You got a good conk."

When Shorty let me stand up and see in the mirror, my hair hung down in limp, damp strings. My scalp still flamed, but not as badly; I could bear it. He draped the towel around my shoulders, over my rubber apron, and began again vaselining my hair.

I could feel him combing, straight back, first the big comb, then the fine-tooth one.

Then, he was using a razor, very delicately, on the back of my neck. then, finally, shaping the sideburns.

My first view in the mirror blotted out the hurting. I'd seen some pretty conks, but when it's the first time, on your *own* head, the transformation, after the lifetime of kinks, is staggering.

The mirror reflected Shorty behind me. We both were grinning and sweating. And on top of my head was this thick, smooth sheen of shining red hair—real red—as straight as any white man's.

How ridiculous I was! Stupid enough to stand there simply lost in admiration of my hair now looking "white," reflected in the mirror in Shorty's room. I vowed that I'd never again be without a conk, and I never was for many years.

This was my first really big step toward self-degradation: when I endured all of that pain, literally burning my flesh to have it look like a white man's hair. I had joined that multitude of Negro men and women in America who are brainwashed into believing that the black people are "inferior"–and white people "superior"—that they will even violate and mutilate their God-created bodies to try to look "pretty" by white standards.

## Responding to the Autobiography

1. Reduce this personal account to one sentence. What is the essential message here?
2. What experience have you had that is parallel to what Malcolm endured—not his physical ordeal but his action of trying to change who he was?

## Exploring the Author's Craft

Malcolm X used telling, **concrete details** to bring alive this vivid experience, an encounter he would never forget for both its literal and (as he reflected on it later) its emotional pain. Malcolm didn't editorialize until the end; by recapturing every moment and every reaction, he let the story tell itself. Find several examples of the kind of details that bring his story to life.

## Writer's Workshop

Bring alive for the reader a moment of your own that involved your sense of identity. Be as detailed as Malcolm X was, even if your experience didn't have the physical component that his had.

## Alternate Media Response

How would you go about filming the event described in this excerpt? What kinds of scenes would be most effective? Make a list of six to eight scenes that you would include, and indicate from which angle you would shoot them—close up, medium shot, or long shot. Remember that your goal is to convey how painful a process Malcolm was going through.

## Two Perspectives

### Stephen Spender

Stephen Spender, who lived from 1909 to 1995, was a British poet, prose writer, and literary critic. His most significant poetry, which was written during the 1930s and 1940s, dealt with large social concerns as well as small everyday issues and consistently showed him to be a self-critical, compassionate individual. In 1983 he was knighted by Queen Elizabeth II.

### Gwendolyn Brooks

Gwendolyn Brooks, born in Topeka , Kansas, in 1917, is one of the great American poets. The first African-American poet to win the Pulitzer Prize, she was also the first to write about ordinary events in the lives of black city-dwellers in such collections as *A Street in Bronzeville* and *The Bean Eaters.* She has worked selflessly to publish the works of young writers.

A joy at poetry festivals today is seeing middle school and high school students, young enough to be her grandchildren, crowd around Brooks and want to be near her. Her poem "We Real Cool" is one of the most famous in American literature.

*Are they always there—the rough kids, the cool kids?*

# My Parents Kept Me from Children Who Were Rough

Stephen Spender

My parents kept me from children who were rough
Who threw words like stones and who wore torn clothes.
Their thighs showed through rags. They ran in the street
And climbed cliffs and stripped by the country streams.

5   I feared more than tigers their muscles like iron
Their jerking hands and their knees tight on my arms.
I feared the salt coarse pointing of those boys
Who copied my lisp behind me on the road.

They were lithe,[1] they sprang out behind hedges
10  Like dogs to bark at my world. They threw mud
While I looked the other way, pretending to smile.
I longed to forgive them, but they never smiled.

---

1. **lithe:** moving easily; flexible; supple.

# We Real Cool

**Gwendolyn Brooks**

*The Pool Players.*
*Seven at the Golden Shovel.*

> We real cool. We
> Left school. We
>
> Lurk late. We
> Strike straight. We
>
> 5  Sing sin. We
> Thin gin. We
>
> Jazz June. We
> die soon.

---

## Responding to the Poems

1. What common elements do both groups of youths—the "children who were rough" and the pool players in "We Real Cool"—share? How are they alike? Explain.
2. At the end of "My Parents Kept Me from Children Who Were Rough" the speaker "pretend[s] to smile." Why?

3. Does it make sense that after all that the "rough" children had done to him, the speaker would "[long] to forgive them"? Explain the psychology here.
4. What is the effect of the last line in "We Real Cool"? How does the line contribute to the poem's overall meaning?

## Exploring the Authors' Craft

1. Stephen Spender's poem is filled with **similes**—comparisons between dissimilar objects using connecting words such as *like* or *as*. Identify three similes in "My Parents Kept Me from Children Who Were Rough" and state whether you think the comparisons are valid.
2. Gwendolyn Brooks doesn't use similes but instead composes succinct sentences that suggest many associations. Some of these sentences use **alliteration,** the repetition of consonant sounds at the beginning of words. What is evoked in your mind by the following alliterative sentences?
   a. "We/Lurk late."
   b. "We/Sing sin."
   c. "We/Jazz June."

## Writer's Workshop

Create a word portrait of a group of children or adolescents engaging in behavior that individually the people in the group might not participate in. Show the behavior of these people rather than simply telling about it. One way to do this is to create a setting, put the characters there, and then give them words—dialogue—to speak.

## Alternate Media Response

Draw the people in either poem. Let their faces reveal their characters.

## Cynthia Rylant

Born in 1954, Cynthia Rylant spent most of her childhood in Beaver, West Virginia, and claims this Appalachian Mountain upbringing as the inspiration for most of her writing. Her works include novels, children's books, and poetry and short story collections; one novel, *Missing May*, won the 1993 John Newbery Medal. About her approach to writing, Rylant says, "I found that the way I work best is that if I just daydream and relax and write only when I get that feeling that it's the right time to do it, then the words—they just kind of gush out of me on the paper."

*Just how far can an infatuation with someone you've never met take you?*

# Checkouts

**H**er parents had moved her to Cincinnati, to a large house with beveled glass windows and several porches and the *history* her mother liked to emphasize. You'll love the house, they said. You'll be lonely at first, they admitted, but you're so nice you'll make friends fast. And as an impulse tore at her to lie on the floor, to hold to their ankles and tell them she felt she was dying, to offer anything, anything at all, so they might allow her to finish growing up in the town of her childhood, they firmed their mouths and spoke from their chests and they said, It's decided.

They moved her to Cincinnati, where for a month she spent the greater part of every day in a room full of beveled glass windows, sifting through photographs of the life she'd lived and left behind. But it is difficult work, suffering, and in its own way a kind of art, and finally she didn't have the energy for it anymore, so she emerged from the beautiful house and fell in love with a bag boy at the supermarket.

Of course, this didn't happen all at once, just like that, but in the sequence of things that's exactly the way it happened.

She liked to grocery shop. She loved it in the way some people love to drive long country roads, because doing it she could think and relax and wander. Her parents wrote up the list and handed it to her and off she went without complaint to perform what they regarded as a great sacrifice of her time and a sign that she was indeed a very nice girl. She had never told how much she loved grocery shopping, only that she was "willing" to do it. She had an intuition which told her that her parents were not safe for sharing such strong, important facts about herself. Let them think they knew her.

Once inside the supermarket, her hands firmly around the handle of the cart, she would lapse into a kind of reverie and wheel toward the produce. Like a Tibetan monk in solitary meditation, she calmed to a point of deep, deep happiness; this feeling came to her, reliably, if strangely, only in the supermarket.

Then one day the bag boy dropped her jar of mayonnaise and that is how she fell in love.

He was nervous—first day on the job—and along had come this fascinating girl, standing in the checkout line with the unfocused stare one often sees in young children, her faced turned enough away that he might take several full looks at her as he packed sturdy bags full of food and the goods of modern life. She interested him because her hair was red and thick, and in it she had placed a huge orange bow, nearly the size of a small hat. That was enough to distract him, and when finally it was her groceries he was packing, she looked at him and smiled and he could respond only by busting her jar of mayonnaise on the floor, shards of glass and oozing cream decorating the area around his feet.

She loved him at exactly that moment, and if he'd known this perhaps he wouldn't have fallen into the brown depression he fell into, which lasted the rest of his shift. He believed he must have looked the jackass in her eyes, and he envied the sureness of everyone around him: the cocky cashier at the register, the grim and harried store manager, the bland butcher, and the brazen bag boys who smoked in the warehouse on their breaks. He wanted a second chance. Another chance to be confident and say witty things to her as he threw tin cans into her bags, persuading her to allow him to help her to her car so he might learn just a little about her, check out the floor of the car for signs of hobbies or fetishes and the bumpers for clues as to beliefs and loyalties.

But he busted her jar of mayonnaise and nothing else worked out for the rest of the day.

Strange, how attractive clumsiness can be. She left the supermarket with stars in her eyes, for she had loved the way his long nervous fingers moved from the conveyor belt to the bags, how deftly (until the mayonnaise) they had picked up her items and placed them into her bags. She had loved the way the hair kept falling into his eyes as he leaned over to grab a box or a tin. And the tattered brown shoes he wore with no socks. And the left side of his collar turned in rather than out.

The bag boy seemed a wonderful contrast to the perfectly beautiful house she had been forced to accept as her home, to the *history* she hated, to the loneliness she had become used to, and she couldn't wait to come back for more of his awkwardness and dishevelment.[1]

Incredibly, it was another four weeks before they saw each other again. As fate would have it, her visits to the supermarket never coincided with his schedule to bag. Each time she went to the store, her eyes scanned the checkouts at once, her heart in her mouth. And each hour he worked, the bag boy kept one eye on the door, watching for the red-haired girl with the big orange bow.

Yet in their disappointment these weeks there was a kind of ecstasy. It is reason enough to be alive, the hope you may see again some face which has meant something to you. The anticipation of meeting the bag boy eased the girl's painful transition into her new and jarring life in Cincinnati. It provided for her an anchor amid all that was impersonal and unfamiliar, and she spent less time on thoughts of what she had left behind as she concentrated on what might lie ahead. And for the boy, the long and often tedious hours at the supermarket which provided no challenge other than that of showing up the following workday . . . these house became possibilities of mystery and romance for him as he watched the electric doors for the girl in the orange bow.

And when finally they did meet up again, neither offered a clue to the other that he, or she, had been the object of obsessive thought for weeks. She spotted him as soon as she came into the store, but she kept

---

1. **dishevelment:** condition of being rumpled or disordered.

her eyes strictly in front of her as she pulled out a cart and wheeled it toward the produce. And he, to, knew the instant she came through the door—though the orange bow was gone, replaced by a small but bright yellow flower instead—and he never once turned his head in her direction but watched her from the corner of his vision as he tried to swallow back the fear in his throat.

It is odd how we sometimes deny ourselves the very pleasure we have longed for and which is finally within our reach. For some perverse[2] reason she would not have been able to articulate, the girl did not bring her cart up to the bag boy's checkout when her shopping was done. And the bag boy let her leave the store, pretending no notice of her.

This is often the way of children, when they truly want a thing, to pretend that they don't. And then they grow angry when no one tries harder to give them this thing they so casually rejected, and they soon find themselves in a rage simply because they cannot say yes when they mean yes. Humans are very complicated. (And perhaps cats, who have been known to react in the same way, though the resulting rage can only be guessed at.)

The girl hated herself for not checking out at the boy's line, and the boy hated himself for not catching her eye and saying hello, and they most sincerely hated each other without having ever exchanged even two minutes of conversation.

Eventually—in fact, within the week—a kind and intelligent boy who lived very near her beautiful house asked the girl to a movie and she gave up her fancy for the bag boy at the supermarket. And the bag boy himself grew so bored with his job that he made a desperate search for something better and ended up in a bookstore where scores of fascinating girls lingered like honeybees about a hive. Some months later the bag boy and the girl with the orange bow again crossed paths, standing in line with their dates at a movie theater, and, glancing toward the other, each smiled slightly, then looked away, as strangers on public buses often do, when one is moving off the bus and the other is moving on.

---

2. **perverse:** difficult in a wrongheaded sort of way.

## Responding to the Story

1.  What do you think is meant by "It is difficult work, suffering, and in its own way a kind of art"? Have you ever experienced what the writer is capturing here? If so, tell the story.
2.  What is ironic about the boy's insecurity after he breaks the jar of mayonnaise?
3.  Paraphrase this sentence: "It is reason enough to be alive, the hope you may see again some face which has meant something to you." How was it true for the characters in the story?
4.  When the two people do see each other again after a very long four weeks, "Neither offered a clue to the other that he, or she, had been the object of obsessive thought for weeks." Do you find this behavior realistic? Why or why not?

## Exploring the Author's Craft

The author's **style** in this story is to every so often enlarge her narration by inserting her own observations about human behavior and human nature.

1.  Find some examples of the author commenting in the story. Do you feel that her observations add to the story's overall effect or do they detract? Explain your view.
2.  Explain how the observation in the following sentence ties in with the story: "[They] looked away, as strangers on public buses often do, when one is moving off the bus and the other is moving on."

## Writer's Workshop

One nice thing about this story is its simplicity. There really are only two characters, and the story zeroes in on them very precisely. Try to follow this model as you write a short story about two people who look at each other from a distance and hardly interact, yet who still are important to each other.

## Reynolds Price

Reynolds Price, who was born in 1933, is an American writer who places most of his stories in his home state of North Carolina. His first novel, *A Long and Happy Life*, was published in 1962 and won the William Faulkner Award for a notable first novel. That book has never been out of print. Price has also written short stories, plays, poems, essays, and the autobiographical work *A Whole New Life* as well as scripts for movies and television.

*"How do you like having two fathers?"*

# Michael Egerton

**H**e was the first boy I met at camp. He had got there before me, and he and a man were taking things out of a suitcase when I walked into the cabin. He came over and started talking right away without even knowing me. He even shook hands. I don't think I had ever shaken hands with anyone my own age before. Not that I minded. I was just surprised and had to find a place to put my duffel bag before I could give him my hand. His name was Michael, Michael Egerton. He was taller than I was, and although it was only June, he already had the sort of suntan that would leave his hair white all summer. I knew he couldn't be more than twelve. I wouldn't be twelve until February. If you were twelve you usually had to go to one of the senior cabins across the hill. But his face was old because of the bones under his eyes that showed through the skin.

   He introduced me to the man. It was his father but they didn't look alike. His father was a newspaperman and the suitcase they were unpacking had stickers on it that said Rome and Paris, London and Bombay. His father said he would be going back to Europe soon to report about the Army and that Michael would be settled here in camp for a while. I was to keep an eye on Mike, he said, and if he got to France in time, he would try to send us something. He said he could tell that Mike and I were going to be great friends and that I might want to go with Mike to his aunt's when camp was over. I might like to see where Old Mike would be living from now on. It was a beautiful place, he said. I could tell he was getting ready to leave. He had seen Michael make up his bed and fill the locker with clothes, and he was beginning to talk the way everybody does when they are leaving somewhere— loud and with a lot of laughing.

He took Michael over to a corner, and I started unpacking my bag. I could see them though and he gave Michael some money, and they talked about how much Michael was going to enjoy the summer and how much bigger he would be when his father got back and how he was to think of his aunt just like a mother. Then Michael reached up and kissed his father. He didn't seem at all embarrassed to do it. They walked back towards me and in a voice louder than before, Mr. Egerton told me again to keep an eye on Old Mike—not that he would need it but it wouldn't hurt. That was a little funny since Michael was so much bigger than I was, but anyway I said I would because that was what I was supposed to say. And then he left. He said there wouldn't be any need for Mike to walk with him to the car, but Michael wanted to so I watched them walk down the hill together. They stood by the car for a minute, and then Michael kissed him again right in front of all those boys and parents and counselors. Michael stood there until his father's car had passed through the camp gate. He waved once. Then he came on back up the hill.

All eight of the boys in our cabin went to the dining hall together that night, but afterward at campfire Michael and I sat a little way off from the others and talked softly while they sang. He talked some about his father and how he was one of the best war correspondents in the business. It wasn't like bragging because he asked me about my father and what my mother was like. I started to ask him about his mother, but I remembered that he hadn't said anything about her, and I thought she might be dead. But in a while he said very matter-of-factly that his mother didn't live with him and his father, hadn't lived with them for almost a year. That was all. He hadn't seen his mother for a year. He didn't say whether she was sick or what, and I wasn't going to ask.

For a long time after that we didn't say anything. We were sitting on a mound at the foot of a tree just high enough to look down on the other boys around the fire. They were all red in the light, and those furthest from the blaze huddled together and drew their heads down because the nights in the mountains were cold, even in June. They had started singing a song that I didn't know. It was called "Green Grow the Rushes." But Michael knew it and sang and I listened to him. It was almost like church with one person singing against a large soft choir. At the end the camp director stood up and made a speech about this was going to be the best season in the history of Redwood which was the finest camp in the land as it was bound to be with as fine a group of boys and counselors as he had sitting right here in front of him. He said it would be a perfect summer if everybody would practice the Golden Rule twenty-four hours a day and treat everybody like we wanted to be treated—like real men.

When we got back to the cabin, the other boys were already running around in the lantern light naked and slapping each other's behinds with wet towels. But soon the counselor blew the light out, and we got in bed in the dark. Michael was in the bunk over me. We had sentence prayers. Michael asked God to bless his father when he got to France. One boy named Robin Mickle who was a Catholic said a Hail Mary. It surprised most of the others. Some of them even laughed as if he was telling a joke. Everything quieted down though and we were half asleep when somebody started blowing Taps on a bugle. It woke us all up and we waited in the dark for it to stop so we could sleep.

Michael turned out to be my best friend. Every morning after breakfast everybody was supposed to lie on their beds quietly for Thought Time and think about the Bible, but Michael and I would sit on my bed and talk. I told Michael a lot of things I had never told anyone else. I don't know why I told him. I just wanted him to know everything there was to know about me. It was a long time before I realized that I didn't know much about Michael except what I could see—that he didn't live with his mother and his father was a great war correspondent who was probably back in France now. He just wasn't the kind to tell you a lot. He would listen to everything you had to say as if he wanted to hear it and was glad you wanted to tell him. But then he would change the subject and start talking about baseball or something. He was a very good baseball player, the best on the junior cabin team. Every boy in our cabin was on the team, and it looked as if with Michael pitching we might take the junior title for the Colossians. That was the name of our team. All the athletic teams in camp were named for one of the letters that St. Paul[1] wrote. We practiced every afternoon after rest period, but first we went to the Main Lodge for mail. I got a letter almost every day, and Michael had got two or three from his aunt, but it wasn't until almost three weeks passed that he got the airmail letter from France. There weren't any pictures or souvenirs in it, but I don't suppose Mr. Egerton had too much time for that. He did mention me though I could tell by the way he wrote that he didn't remember my name. Still it was very nice to be thought of by a famous war correspondent. Michael said we could write him a letter together soon and that he would ask his father for a picture.

We wrote him twice but four weeks passed and nothing else came, not from France. I had any number of letters myself and the legal limit of boxes (which was one a week) that I wanted to share with just Michael but had to share with everybody, Robin Mickle included. Worse than the sharing, I dreaded my boxes because I kept thinking they would make me homesick, but with Michael and all the things to do, they never bothered me, and before I expected it, there was only a week of camp left and we would go home. That was why were playing the semifinals that day—so the winners could be recognized at the Farewell Banquet on the last night of camp. The Colossians were going to play the Ephesians after rest period. We were all in the cabin trying to rest, but everybody was too excited, everybody except Michael who was almost asleep when the camp director walked in and said that Michael Egerton was to go down to the Lodge porch right away as he had visitors. Michael got up and combed his hair, and just before he left he told everybody he would see them at the game and that we were going to win.

   The Lodge wasn't too far from our cabin, and I could see him walking down there. A car was parked by the porch. Michael got pretty close to

---

1. **Colossians . . . St. Paul:** In the New Testament, St. Paul wrote instructional letters to various groups who had converted to Christianity, including the Colossians and the Ephesians.

it. Then he stopped. I thought he had forgotten something and was coming back to the cabin, but the car doors opened and a man and a woman got out. I knew it was his mother. He couldn't have looked any more like her. She bent over and kissed him. Then she must have introduced him to the man. She said something and the man stepped up and shook Michael's hand. They started talking. I couldn't hear them and since they weren't doing anything I lay back down and read for a while. Rest period was almost over when I looked again. The car was gone and there was no one in front of the Lodge. It was time for the semifinals, and Michael hadn't showed up. Robin, who was in charge of the Colossians, told me to get Michael wherever he was, and I looked all over camp. He just wasn't there. I didn't have time to go up in the woods behind the cabins, but I yelled and there was no answer. So I had to give up because the game was waiting. Michael never came. A little fat boy named Billy Joe Moffitt took his place and we lost. Everybody wondered what had happened to Michael. I was sure he hadn't left camp with his mother because he would have told somebody first so after the game I ran back ahead of the others. Michael wasn't on his bed. I walked through the hall and opened the bathroom door. He was standing at the window with his back to me. "Mike, why in the world didn't you play?"

He didn't even turn around.

"We lost, Mike."

He just stood there tying little knots in the shade cord. When the others came in from the game, I met them at the door. I told them Michael was sick.

But he went to the campfire with me that night. He didn't say much and I didn't know what to ask him. "Was that your mother this afternoon?"

"Yes."

"What was she doing up here?"

"On a vacation or something."

I don't guess I should have asked him but I did. "Who was that with her?"

"Some man. I don't know. Just some man."

It was like every night. We were sitting in our place by the tree. The others were singing and we were listening. Then he started talking very fast.

"My mother said, 'Michael, this is your new father. How do you like having two fathers?'"

Before I could think what to say, he said he was cold and got up and walked back to the cabin. I didn't follow him. I didn't even ask him if he was feeling all right. When I got to the cabin, he was in bed pretending to be asleep, but long after Taps I could hear him turning. I tried to stay awake until he went to sleep. Once I sat up and started to reach out and touch him but I didn't. I was very tired.

All that was a week before the end of camp. The boys in our cabin started talking about him. He had stopped playing ball. He wouldn't swim in the camp meet. He didn't even go on the Sunday hike up to Johnson's Knob. He sat on his bed with his clothes on most of the time. They never did anything nice for him. They were always doing things like tying his shoelaces together. It was no use trying to stop them. All they knew was that Michael Egerton had screwed their chance to be camp baseball champions. They didn't want to know the reason, not even the counselor. And I wasn't going to tell them. They even poured water on his mattress one night and laughed the whole next day about Michael wetting the bed.

The day before we left camp, the counselors voted on a Camp Spirit Cabin. They had kept some sort of record of our activities and athletic events. The cabin with the most Good Camper points usually won. We didn't win. Robin and the others told Michael that he made us lose because he never did anything. They told everybody that Michael Egerton made our cabin lose.

That night we were bathing and getting dressed for the Farewell Banquet. Nobody had expected Michael to go, but without saying anything he started getting dressed. Someone noticed him and said something about Mr. Michael honoring us with his presence at dinner. He had finished dressing when four of the boys took him and tied him between two bunks with his arms stretched out. He didn't fight. He let them treat him like some animal, and he looked as if he was crucified. Then they went to the banquet and left him tied there. I went with them but while they were laughing about hamstringing that damned Michael, I slipped away and went back to untie him. When I got there he had already got loose. I knew he was in the bathroom. I could hear him. I walked to the door and whispered "Mike, it's me." I don't think he heard me. I started to open the door but I didn't. I walked back out and down the hill to the dining hall. They even had the porch lights on, and they had already started singing.

---

## Responding to the Story

1. Are Michael Egerton's changes of behavior and personality understandable? Explain.
2. From the way he deals with them, Michael seems to have different feelings about his mother and his father. How would you describe the way he relates to each one?
3. Why do you think the boys in the cabin, other than the narrator, react to Michael as they do? Is it because of the changes they see in him, a belief that he has let them down, or something else?

## Exploring the Author's Craft

Writers use various techniques to make their characters come to life. In this story the **characterization** of Michael comes largely through the narrator's description of the things he says or does.

1. How do these descriptions of Michael's activities help to form a picture of his character?
   a. "He came over and started talking right away without even knowing me. He even shook hands."
   b. "In a while he said very matter-of-factly that his mother didn't live with him and his father, hadn't lived with them for almost a year. That was all."
   c. "The Colossians were going to play the Ephesians . . . . We were all in the cabin trying to rest, but everybody was too excited, everybody except Michael who was almost asleep . . . ."

2. What symbol do you see in the following description? What kind of parallel is being made? "[Michael] had finished dressing when four of the boys took him and tied him between two bunks with his arms stretched out. He didn't fight. He let them treat him like some animal, and he looked as if he was crucified."

## Writer's Workshop

The narrator of "Michael Egerton" tells what happens to his friend, but never really explains how he feels about what is going on. Assume that you are the narrator and explain your reactions to the events in the story. Do this in a letter to one of Michael's parents.

## Lawrence Otis Graham

Lawrence Otis Graham, a lawyer in New York City, wrote this essay for the Op-Ed page of *The New York Times.*

*Sometimes the things we most hope will change never really do.*

# The "Black Table" Is Still There

During a recent visit to my old junior high school in Westchester County, I came upon something that I never expected to see again, something that was a source of fear and dread for three hours each school morning of my early adolescence: the all-black lunch table in the cafeteria of my predominantly white suburban junior high school.

As I look back on 27 years of often being the first and only black person integrating such activities and institutions as the college newspaper, the high school tennis team, summer music, camps, our all-white suburban neighborhood, my eating club at Princeton or my private social club at Harvard Law School, the one scenario that puzzled me the most then and now is the all-black lunch table.

Why was it there? Why did the black kids separate themselves? What did the table say about the integration that was supposedly going on in home rooms and gym classes? What did it say about the black kids? The white kids? What did it say about me when I refused to sit there, day after day, for three years?

Each afternoon, at 12:03 P.M., after the fourth period ended, I found myself among 600 12-, 13- and 14-year-olds who marched into the brightly-lit cafeteria and dashed for a seat at one of the 27 blue formica lunch tables.

No matter who I walked in with—usually a white friend—no matter what mood I was in, there was one thing that was certain: I would not sit at the black table.

I would never consider sitting at the black table.

What was wrong with me? What was I afraid of?

I would like to think that my decision was a heroic one, made in order to express my solidarity with the theories of integration that my community was espousing. But I was just 12 at the time, and there was nothing heroic in my actions.

I avoided the black table for a very simple reason: I was afraid that by sitting at the black table I'd lose all my white friends. I thought that by sitting there I'd be making a racist, anti-white statement.

Is that what the all-black table means? Is it a rejection of white people? I no longer think so.

At the time, I was angry that there was a black lunch table. I believed that the black kids were the reason why other kids didn't mix more: I was ready to believe that their self-segregation was the cause of white bigotry.

Ironically, I even believed this after my best friend (who was white) told me I probably shouldn't come to his bar mitzvah[1] because I'd be the only black and some people would feel uncomfortable. I even believed this after my Saturday afternoon visit, at age 10, to a private country club pool prompted incensed white parents to pull their kids from the pool in terror.

In the face of this blatantly racist (anti-black) behavior, I still somehow managed to blame only the black kids for being the barrier to integration in my school and my little world. What was I thinking?

I realize now how wrong I was. During that same time, there were at least two tables of athletes, an Italian table, a Jewish girls' table, a Jewish boys' table (where I usually sat), a table of kids who were into heavy metal music and smoking pot, a table of middle class Irish kids. Weren't these tables just as segregationist as the black table? At the time, no one thought so. At the time, no one even acknowledged the segregated nature of these other tables.

Maybe it's the color difference that makes all-black tables or all-black groups attract the scrutiny and wrath of so many people. It scares and angers people; it exasperates. It did those things to me, and I'm black.

---

1. **bar mitzvah:** religious ceremony, often followed by a celebration, in which a 13-year-old Jewish boy is recognized as having reached the age of religious responsibility.

As an integrating black person, I know that my decision *not* to join the black lunch table attracted its own kind of scrutiny and wrath from my classmates. At the same time that I heard angry words like "Oreo"[2] and "white boy" being hurled at me from the black table, I was also dodging impatient questions from white classmates: "Why do all those black kids sit together?" or "Why don't you ever sit with the other blacks?"

The black lunch table, like those other segregated tables, is a comment on the superficial inroads that integration has made in society. Perhaps I should be happy that even this is a long way from where we started. Yet, I can't get over the fact that the 27th table in my junior high school cafeteria is still known as the "black table"—14 years after my adolescence.

---

2. **Oreo:** derogatory term suggesting that a black person is white on the inside—that is, thinks and acts like a white person.

---

## Responding to the Essay

1. Why did Lawrence Otis Graham avoid sitting at the "black table" when he was in junior high school?
2. Looking back as he writes this essay years later, does Graham now see his cafeteria experience the same way? Explain.
3. In your own school, are there separate tables for separate ethnic or special-interest groups? If so, do you consider this phenomenon to be good or bad?

## Analyzing the Author's Craft

One standard **essay** format has the writer raising a question or espousing a certain position, responding or elaborating with specific examples, and then reaching a conclusion. Evaluate how well Lawrence Otis Graham follows that classic model.

## Writer's Workshop

"The black lunch table, like those other segregated tables, is a comment on the superficial inroads that integration has made in society." Based on your own observations and experiences, do you believe that we have made only "superficial inroads" on integration? Write a short essay backing up your views with specific examples and anecdotes from your own experience.

## Two Perspectives

### Gail Hosking Gilberg

Gail Hosking Gilberg was 47 when *Snake's Daughter*, her first book, was published in 1997. To the readers of this book she says, "When I was your age I never imagined I would one day be a writer, and the mother of two sons, and a wife. Nor did I have any plans for the two master's degrees I finally received. I had no idea that what I carried around as my personal history was really a part of my country's larger history. I could no more have imagined finding my place in that history than I could have spoken up about my mother's alcoholism or my soldier-father's absence. What I did instead was what many of us do in life: I drew my attention to the moment—these friends, this school, this football game, this Friday night. And moment by moment I moved along life's timeline, making decisions here and there that twirled me into the next moment. I met people along the way who knew more than I—many of them my teachers—and I listened and tucked their ideas away. When I was your age I didn't realize that the pieces of our lives add up to something; slowly we become who it is we need to be. If we are paying attention, we do what it is that needs to be done. So it was years after I was your age that I finally opened the door on a piece of history I thought I could bury. *Snake's Daughter* was a result of that effort."

## Seamus Heaney

Irish poet Seamus Heaney won the Nobel Prize for Literature in 1995—the highest award the world can offer a writer for a lifetime of achievement. Heaney divides his time between Dublin, Ireland, his legal residence; Oxford University in England, where he is Professor of Poetry; and Harvard University in Cambridge, Massachusetts, where he also teaches. Heaney's publisher says that Heaney's "concern is with what endures, whether in memory or in actuality." Much of his poetry is rooted in the rural life of Northern Ireland, where he was born in 1939.

*The influence of a parent can persist long after childhood.*

# from Snake's Daughter

### Gail Hosking Gilberg

It's difficult to know where to begin the story of my father's life. Should I start with the man whose name is carved on panel 17E, line 5, of the Vietnam Memorial Wall and work backward, or should I begin with his running away from home at age sixteen to join the Canadian army and go forward from there? Perhaps it doesn't matter. Either way I end up looking at his death—a death that either has been or will be.

Survivors who knew him tell me my father had an invincible quality about him. He survived the Second World War in the 509th Paratrooper Infantry Battalion: only forty-seven out of its six hundred men were left on their feet after the Battle of the Bulge. While stationed in Europe with the Special Forces in the 1950s, he was hand-picked for secret missions into Africa. It was said he trained hard, kept the morale of the others up, and had a "resourceful knowledge of foreign weapons." During the Vietnam War, when he went back for the third time to rejoin the "Mike Force," others volunteered when they heard "the Snake" had returned. He was so legendary with the Chinese Nung and Cambodian soldiers[1] after his first tour of duty there that when he came back to Vietnam, several came out of retirement to fight with him.

My father was a man of many opposites. His high IQ gave him opportunities to become an officer, but he enjoyed being "at the bottom with the best," as he repeatedly said. He was a private person and yet a team player. He joined a subculture that stressed order and precision, and within it he found his personal way of doing things—he was an "outlaw," as a fellow soldier described him. My father was not a religious person, and yet he spent his R&R[2] free time doing what was unusual for American soldiers in Vietnam to do—visiting Buddhist monks. When I was a child, he made my sisters and me go to Sunday school every Sunday; we weren't allowed to play outside the rest of the day if we didn't. But he never went to church himself. I could come home and find him washing his car—something I was taught in Sunday school one wasn't supposed to do on the Sabbath.

He was intensely patriotic but felt most at home on foreign soil and speaking other languages—among them Vietnamese, an accomplishment for any Westerner. Friends describe my father as a sensitive man, capable of deep feelings, yet he spent his whole adult life in a society that taught him to compartmentalize his feelings. He loved his family, but at important moments he was always someplace else.

As I look back, I know I lived constantly with my father's greatest paradox.[3] By nature his work was contradictory, full of puzzles. He was a professional soldier, a job he got paid for and which paid the family bills. Like other fathers, he went to work Monday through Friday from nine to five, and most of the time nothing happened. But the false proposition of his seemingly secure work was that sometimes, even on routine training exercises, some things did happen. Once a bazooka weapon exploded by accident at Fort Campbell and killed all the men in front of my father, but not him. Such was the unspoken side of his

---

1. **Chinese Nung and Cambodian soldiers:** groups who fought against the North Vietnamese during the Vietnam War. The Nung were mercenary soldiers hired by the United States.
2. **R&R:** "rest and recreation"—that is, time off from the war.
3. **paradox:** statement or situation that seems to say two opposite, but true, things.

life. He lived with death, which he buried with duty, determination, and drink. This part he never shared.

Sometimes in the middle of the night, my father would silently pack his gear and leave. In the morning he wouldn't be home. The army called it "maneuvers," as if it were only a game. But it was really a rehearsal for conflict. When called on alert, my father wouldn't know if it was a real war or not—or even where his parachute might land. He knew only that he was to have his gear prepared and be ready to follow orders.

Our household changed when he left. His need for order went with him, creating a more relaxed mood at home. At the same time, his leaving made us feel left without direction, and we struggled to carry on without him. We never knew where he was or how long he'd be gone. Even in the quiet of home there was a lingering sense of our own readiness, as if we too were waiting for a disaster, some military crisis that would inevitably change our lives at a moment's notice. The unspoken potential for loss hung in the air.

Whole chunks of our father's life were off-limits to us. When he returned, we never heard about where he went or what he saw. I don't recall anyone ever saying out loud that we weren't to ask questions, but we children knew that anyway. As I grew up, the gap between my father and me widened, and I knew less and less about him. The army asked a great deal of its dependents, without ever verbalizing it. We were to support my father's comings and goings, not distract him in any way, and go along with any regulations or change in orders. We were the silent, unpaid staff in the background, growing accustomed to the military's way of life with every year my father remained a soldier. We knew no other life. Orders were orders.

In our time together, my father stressed manners and discipline with us. To him it was important how we sat at the table, how we sipped our soup, how we greeted those who spoke to us. He insisted I follow through on projects I began, like the scrapbook of my life he helped me start. I remember his carefully gluing in n aerial view of our base in Germany with an arrow pointing to our apartment, building 106, C-2. Under it he placed my third-grade class photograph into the four photograph corners and showed me where to glue a birthday card from my grandmother across the ocean in New Jersey.

In doing so, I see now how he instilled a structure and a self-reliance within me that was the gift he left behind. It was a form to live with and provided in the years since his death a link to all other worlds I've entered and a method of working with the materials of my life. He wanted for my sisters, brother, and me what he wanted for himself: not to be "just an ordinary GI on the streets," as he repeatedly counseled other soldiers and his family. He wanted us to have the discipline and manners that could carry us in and out of anywhere we wanted to go.

My father taught me to ski and encouraged me when I didn't think I could learn. He read fairy tales out loud from the orange Childcraft books he bought from a traveling salesman. He insisted I make good grades in school and often helped me with my homework. I don't remember what we talked about at the table as I did my math problems and he shined his black army boots, waxing them in small strokes with a stained rag until they shone, or took apart his guns piece by piece and put them back together in blind memory. In those days, I thought all fathers did this, as I though all fathers were born with tattoos on their arms.

My father loved to travel, and he took us on many trips. In the summer of my eleventh year, we camped along the beach in Barcelona, Spain. He took us to a bullfight on a hot afternoon, and while he described everything that was happening—jumping from his seat with cries of victory when the matador was successful—my sisters and I were more interested in buying cold drinks. We fanned ourselves with our paper fans, and he teased us about covering our eyes. That night, my mother found my father in a bar with my youngest sister, Betty Ann, on his lap. He was drinking and laughing with a group of local Spaniards. Other summers we picnicked along a Bavarian lake called the Tegernsee, hiked in the German Alps, or visited King Ludwig's castles.[4] In France, he insisted we visit cemeteries of Second World War soldiers. The white crosses, interrupted by a Star of David now and then, lined up across the field at an angle more perfect than I have ever seen since.

When I was twelve—still singing songs with my Girl Scout troop about "making new friends, but keeping the old, one is silver and the other gold"—my parents thought of separating. On a cold, winter day we children and my mother boarded the USNS *General William O. Darby* at

---

4. **King Ludwig's castles:** series of extravagant castles built in the Bavarian Alps during the 1860s-1880s by King Ludwig II, later declared insane.

the port of Bremerhaven, Germany, and headed for the United States. A cold breeze blew that day, creating white-capped waves that surrounded the ship even before it left the harbor. My mother stood on deck with her black jacket trimmed with white fur around the hood. We left my father as the ship blew its loud horn. I remember carrying my pet white mouse, Nancy, in a covered basket, my rock collection in a trunk, and my heart in a steel box. We waved good-bye to my soldier-father, who remained on shore, and it is only today as I write this that I wonder how he let us all go in one swoop. It was 1963, one of the most painful years of my life, branded by the awareness of a family's unraveling.

Within six months, my parents changed their minds about their separation, and they pulled up together at my grandmother's house in a brand new white Ford Falcon station wagon. They came to pick up my sisters and me, and we drove to North Carolina. Even as we settled into new schools, his orders came for Vietnam. He never lived with us for more than a few months at a time after that, and it never seemed the same with my parents again. It was as if I was already witnessing their love fading like the sun disappearing below the horizon. Though he would come home after a long tour of duty, he never seemed to find his bearings. While many fathers went to Vietnam once, my father kept going back until he died there.

Once on one of his return trips home, he sat on the floor of our apartment wearing black Vietnamese pajamalike clothes, eating rice with chopsticks. While we ate meat loaf and mashed potatoes at the table, we listened to him speak about the men he left behind. I see now that the magical country of Vietnam had taken over his life, just like the war and the men at his side who became the reasons for fighting the war. Vietnam had a curious hold on my father I couldn't begin to understand then.

On another visit home, he went with me to a high school football game dressed in his full military dress uniform. I had spent my life seeing him in uniform, and I knew he took it seriously. His pants were tucked into his polished black boots and all his insignia were aligned in their proper places. But that night as he stood on the bleachers dressed differently from anyone else, surrounded by civilians, I began to feel uncomfortable. It confused me. Had I known the right words then, I would have asked what it was all about: the war, the uniform, his always going away. I don't remember one person in that small midwestern town ever once speaking about the war. And if they did, I don't ever remember listening. The loneliness of living within two worlds that never touched often brought me to tears, alone in my bedroom. I would lie on my bed and cry for hours curled up like a baby, never once knowing at the time what the tears were about.

In the weeks before my seventeenth birthday, my father sent me a string of Mikimoto pearls[5] he had bought in either Saigon or Hong Kong. It arrived inside a green velvet box lined with white satin. On the outside yellow cardboard box he wrote with a red pen that he hoped I received the pearls in time for the prom and that he could hardly believe I was seventeen years old. At first I felt they must have been for my mother because I understood myself to be too young for pearls. I imagine, in his sense of formality, he saw these perfectly shaped white pearls as something every young woman should have.

On the first day of spring that same year, only a week after my seventeenth birthday, my father was killed at the age of forty-two. After crossing the Song Be River under sniper fire on a single span of a blown-up bridge lying about a foot under the surface of the water, my father captured a sniper and prepared to link up with his command group. Realizing the prisoner would need his arms to get across the river, my father began to untie the rope. The prisoner suddenly grabbed a hand grenade from my father's belt and began running toward the company command group, which consisted of two American and two Vietnamese soldiers. Realizing the prisoner intended to kill the men, my father leaped on the prisoner's back and grasped him in a bear hug, forcing the grenade against the prisoner's chest. With my father's background of precision and experience, he had to have known that what he did in that instance would surely mean his own death. My father wrestled the prisoner to the ground and covered his body until the grenade detonated. The blast killed both the prisoner and my father instantly. . . .

Early in the war, yellow cabs delivered the death notices. People speak now of having lived in fear of seeing a yellow cab in their neighborhood, of having heart attacks when a yellow cab pulled into their driveway. By the time my father was killed, the army sent soldiers

---

5. **Mikimoto pearls:** Japanese pearls of the highest quality.

as messengers—young soldiers whose duty it was to knock on the doors
of strangers and speak the terrifyingly intimate words of death. Our
messenger stood in his pressed uniform and polished black boots in the
cold March air, telling us words he had memorized. My father, he said,
had been killed in the line of duty near the Song Be River. The other
details became a blur to me, and I only heard him ask where the army
should send the body. After he left, my sisters and my mother and I sat
in our apartment with the shades pulled down. My sisters cried, and my
mother sat quietly in shock. My six-year-old brother, wearing the
Special Forces jungle hat my father had sent him, looked at us in
confusion, then continued to play with his toys. I couldn't cry then. I
was afraid the whole world might cave in if I did. I remember to this
day how I got dressed and left for a date with my boyfriend. From that
moment, I erected walls around my heart.

Two years later, in the spring of 1969, when my sisters, brother, and I
were living with my Uncle Bob and Aunt Val in New Jersey, we were
invited to the White House to receive my father's Congressional Medal
of Honor, posthumously awarded. It was like anyone can imagine: a
basket of fruit in our fancy hotel room, dinners out with military staff, a
trip around Washington, D.C., a private tour of the White House, and
then the formal presentation by President Nixon and Melvin Laird,
secretary of defense. The ceremony was well planned, and we were all
told where to stand and what to do. I remember looking down at the
president's shiny black shoes, my face mirrored in them, and feeling as if
I were watching a movie of someone else's life. . . . The next day I flew
back to college in upstate New York and blended into the crowd with
my lips held shut.

Years of rationalizing about my father's death followed: I felt like my
path was gone, dropped off the edge. I told a friend his death had been
"all for the best," as if I readily believed it. I said public opinion about
the military was turning negative and that my father wouldn't be happy
in uniform or in civilian life. Out of the corner of my eye, I noticed my
friend with a curious, confused look on his face, but he didn't say
anything. Even so, I tried to show that I could bear my father's death.
After all, hadn't my life with the military taught me to "carry on"?
Wasn't I the "real trooper" my father had taught me to be?

But as the years went on, a terrible vague sadness would erupt at
unexpected moments. At a stop sign once while in my car, I turned to

see a Memorial Day army exhibition taking place in the park. An older soldier in the distance directed a helicopter where to land. As a country-western tune—the kind of music I had heard in every snack bar on every base I had ever lived—played on my radio, I burst into tears. The naive phrase "for the best" flashed across my mind, and I felt a sudden loneliness. I wondered how it would be to have a father.

Another time, when I was carrying my second child, I stood alongside my curly-haired husband and three-year-old blond son before the Vietnam Memorial Wall, looking at my pregnant reflection in the shiny black granite. My husband, Bruce, wasn't sure what to say as he held my hand and tried to keep an eye on our son as well. I had come for the first time, wanting to show them my father's name and to see why it was that so many people talked about this wall. A mother had left a letter, now framed, to her son and had placed his teddy bear next to it. I thought my heart would break as I fell to my knees. I felt, for the first time, the immensity of this war and all those lives that never returned home. . . .

At the wall I saw that I was a mixture of the Asian and American way. I had identified with the Asian way of making my way around something wrong rather than confronting it. And yet there I was facing this wall head on, confronting it in my quiet but American way. In the years to come, I was to learn more of this Asian concept of standing still through pain instead of moving away from it, and I was to become more bold in my American acknowledgment of this wall that had been built to heal our Vietnam War wounds.

Going through my desk drawers years after seeing the wall, I found a photograph of my father eating with chopsticks in Vietnam. He was the only American in the picture. Everything about him was familiar: his olive-drab uniform, his dog tags peering out from under his collar, and his blond hair combed back from his receding hairline. The place, with sandbags piled up behind him and Vietnamese soldiers standing next to him, suddenly seemed odd to me. I realized how little I knew about my father, that even all the photographs I *did* have of him still couldn't tell his story. . . .

At this juncture I began experiencing a burden and a desire I had carried around since my teenage years without ever being aware of them. I needed suddenly to know my father, to talk about war, to understand the life I had come from and how it had affected who I was. . . .

As I studied the first photograph of my father that I found, I realized that my father was my age. Suddenly I had caught up to him. The distance between us shifted, and I was no longer the child. I looked at him as if looking at myself, wanting to know more. His age exposed his humanness, and I felt ready to explore that. I searched for other photographs and found several albums and boxes of slides: pictures of my father, his friends, the places he saw, and his family. They were neither unique nor sensational but had been collected by my father over time as if he knew early on he'd need to document his life for the next generation. He wasn't an artist, nor did he propose to be a photographer, but he did fiddle with film and camera when others might not have. I had known about the photographs but had never before given them more than a quick look. He organized the pictures by month and year—all neatly labeled by a man constantly on the move. Suddenly I wondered why. Why did he make this effort? Did he know I wouldn't have him around when I grew older? Did he want me to remember him and understand him, even though he could no longer speak? Did he know that his images would someday spark my own lost words?

My writing mentor and friend, Finvola Drury, suggested that the photograph collection was a gift. That perhaps my father had come back into my life now as a guide, and that through the photographs he would lead me to address all the questions and feelings I had allowed to surface. He had come and gone as he had done all my childhood, and now he was back. In this way, she said, he had stayed around longer than most fathers. The photographs were all I had left of him, and I felt he wanted me to look at them carefully. It occurs to me now that that same old sense of my father's formal precision and discipline was helping me recreate my own life. At times, as I spoke to his buddies on the phone, listened to Finvola's compelling interest and insightful connections, or sat at my desk late at night, pen in hand and tears in my eyes, I felt that we were all working together. I felt beckoned on this journey to find my father.

At first, entering many of his photographs was like getting through a guarded gate. Behind the entrance sat the world a daughter can't know intimately—men and the military. I asked questions for the first time about a society in which I had learned never to ask questions. In searching the photographs I listened to their silence, waiting for details to rise on their own. I stared, sometimes though a magnifying glass, looking at moments that stopped when his camera clicked.

Over time, as the details of the photographs enlarged, I began seeing life in the flat images. I could swear, after a reverent look, that I saw a knee move or a puff of smoke actually come out of someone's cigarette. I felt his sun's heat, and I heard a helicopter buzzing in the distant sky. A leaf ruffled with the breeze, and I walked into the photographs. The photographs' places seized me, and I could no longer remember not being there.

What I found even more difficult in my search was something I had not been aware of before, something the photographs could not show. I realized I would have to struggle to move among and overcome the clichés of the Vietnam era—both those of the military and those opposed to the war. The loss of my father was an obvious pain, but not so the other wounds made by the war. Many in this country, peers and soldiers included, wanted to draw a line between those who fought and those who opposed. Some wanted to believe that men who went to Vietnam were fools or bloodthirsty types, and that nothing good ever happens in war. They believed that the strong were absolutely strong and the weak were absolutely weak. What was and remains is the gray area in between—the most difficult to look at. Just as with my father's photograph collection, no part can stand for the whole, no whole can stand for its parts. . . .

During the project I spoke to many people who had known my father. I advertised in a Special Forces magazine, the *Drop*, and a paratrooper newspaper called the *Static Line*—both titles refer to parachute jumping. My phone began ringing after that. Men from all over the United States called me to tell me about my father—men who had known him as a nineteen-year-old paratrooper in the Second World War, men who had been stationed with him in Europe with the original Special Forces group, and men who fought with him in Vietnam. The stories poured in from letters and phone calls. They were full of names, connections, and memories. "One hell of a soldier," they all said. "A character, sharp, hard-nosed, great sense of humor," "Your dad was a hero," said Charles Petty, who fought at the Battle of the Bulge with my father. "You don't receive the Medal of Honor for nothing. I still think of your father often, and I have his photograph right here on my wall."

The first phone call came from a soldier who knew my father from their early days together in Germany. Sgt. Harry McGloughlin called one night after seeing my request for information. As I sat with my cordless phone on my deck under a night's sky of stars, I felt strangely like a daughter again and that this was my father on the other end. With a nervousness I had not anticipated, I ran for a pen and paper, not knowing where to begin with my questions. I also felt like the child who believed it was sacrilege to call a military man by his first name. I wasn't sure what to call him—Harry? Sergeant McGloughlin? Mr. McGloughlin?

His voice was the voice of a long-lost friend I didn't even know I knew or had missed until this moment. He was like family talking about the "old country." The strangeness of years melted as we spoke that night.

At the same time I recognized a defense I had carried around since childhood in the fortress: that kind of muscle-tightening defense I've always had when there's drink in the voice, stories on the edge. It's as if I've always been afraid of something exploding or the seams of life coming unraveled, knowing that the melting edges of lust and adventure and lightheartedness would never be able to put back together the lives of the men who surrounded my childhood. These men, like my father, lived as if perched on top of a mountain with one foot reaching for death across the way and the same grin my father wore on his face, as if he knew the dilemma of his life and chose to laugh.

To talk to Harry McGloughlin that night was to enter that world of the fortress again. I knew even as his voice came through the wires that there were no roads back from this journey, that from this night forward I risked opening up all that I had sealed up tightly. I risked knowing the men whom I had last seen at my father's funeral some twenty-three years before, and therefore I risked knowing my father. Little did I know then that the months ahead would roll into years and I would be adrift in time, extending my father's story into mine, photograph by photograph. Little did I know that the images he left behind would spark my own words and bring my past into my present.

But now I know that first phone call from Sgt. McGloughlin to the girl my father left behind to "carry on" was a chance happening between two strangers speaking in the night about a man they each once loved dearly. In discovering the loss of others who loved my father, I was to discover my own loss in ways I had buried. His call was a gift from the gods, one of many I would receive along my way.

He told me that he had seen my sister's request for information several years back but had felt at the time that we would be too young to her what he had to say. But this time, he felt in his heart that it was indeed the time. He died a few months after that first phone call, neither of us knowing the seriousness of his illness at the time. The last time we spoke, I could tell from his fading voice that he was suffering greatly from his diabetes and heart trouble. I got off the phone and cried, and I wasn't sure why. I knew this soldier friend would someday take all the stories he had of my father to his grave. When he did die very soon afterward, I couldn't erase his address for the longest time from my address book, as if to do so was to erase the threads of my connection to my father. I had so wanted to tell this Harry, this sergeant, this Mr. McGloughlin that he helped push me on the path I needed to take.

And so began my steps into the unknown, my journey of a generation. It is two journeys actually: the journey to find myself and the one to find my father. To understand him through the pictures he left behind, I had to come to the photographs as a little girl and as a daughter of a soldier, but also as a mother and a wife. Though the photographs, I hoped to find the place where all those pieces of myself came together.

Finding our fathers, like finding ourselves, is a journey we all take at one time or another—sometimes while our fathers are alive, and sometimes long after they have died. Sometimes during war, and sometimes during peace. The courage to reach back through time, to cautiously probe into the dark loam, mysteriously comes at some given moment as if dropped from the angels above.

# Follower

**Seamus Heaney**

My father worked with a horse-plough,
His shoulders globed like a full sail strung
Between the shafts[1] and the furrow.
The horses strained at his clicking tongue.

5   An expert. He would set the wing
And fit the bright steel-pointed sock.[2]
The sod rolled over without breaking.
At the headrig, with a single pluck

Of reins, the sweating team turned round
10 And back into the land. His eye
Narrowed and angled at the ground,
Mapping the furrow exactly.

I stumbled in his hob-nailed wake,
Fell sometimes on the polished sod;
15 Sometimes he rode me on his back
Dipping and rising to his plod.

---

1. **shafts:** pair of long bars between which a horse is hitched to a plow.
2. **sock:** the large pointed blade of a plow.

I wanted to grow up and plough,

To close one eye, stiffen my arm.

All I ever did was follow

20  In his broad shadow round the farm.


I was a nuisance, tripping, falling,

Yapping always. But today

It is my father who keeps stumbling

Behind me, and will not go away.

---

## Responding to the Selections

1. What conflicting feelings does Gail Hosking Gilberg have about her father after his death? In what sense are her feelings similar to those of the narrator in Seamus Heaney's poem?
2. What are some of the contradictory behaviors that Gilberg remembers in her father?
3. Gilberg is not sure why her father so carefully assembled the photo albums and boxes of slides that she later found. What do you think his purpose was?
4. If the narrator of "Follower" could have one photo of his father, what do you think he would want that photo to show?


## Exploring the Authors' Craft

A **metaphor,** like a simile, compares two unlike things; unlike a simile, however, a metaphor is an implied comparison and doesn't use the words *like* or *as*. For example, when Gilberg says she "erected walls around [her] heart," *walls* is used as a metaphor: she created wall-like mental barriers to hold in her feelings. Writers often use metaphors to compress their meaning and heighten the impact of what they say.

1.  Do you think the sentiment expressed in the metaphor of erecting walls is believable? Why or why not?
2.  Explain the meaning of the metaphor in this line from *Snake's Daughter:* "I've always been afraid of . . . the seams of life coming unraveled."
3.  What mental image do you form from the metaphor "His shoulders globed" in line 2 of "Follower"?

## Writer's Workshop

In any written form you choose—poem, memoir, short fiction—create a piece of writing dealing with the influence upon you of a parent or other caregiver. Include specific examples of interaction between you and the other individual. If possible, try to create a metaphor within your piece.

## Alternate Media Response

Gail Hosking Gilberg tells us that photographs played a big role in evoking her father for her. Create a collection of between 10 and 15 photographs—some from years earlier and some taken by you just for this assignment—as a photographic portrait of a parent or caregiver. You can have text, too, but try to have the pictures speak for themselves.

## Making Connections in
# PART ONE

As the first section of this book ends, you should see a number of connections among the pieces. Here you will try to pull some of these connections together. Complete one or more of the following assignments as your teacher directs.

1.  Choose three pieces of writing from Part One that cover different aspects of the idea of searching. Explain precisely the nature of each search in a five-paragraph essay. Use the first paragraph to state your main idea, or thesis. Use the second, third, and fourth paragraphs to discuss each selection. Present your conclusion or summary in the fifth paragraph.

2.  Think of any three pieces of writing in Part One that have to do with parents and children. List similarities and differences in the pieces as far as relationships between the parents and children are concerned.

3.  Part One already contains two pairings of selections: "My Parents Kept Me from Children Who Were Rough" and "We Real Cool"; and the excerpt from *Snake's Daughter* and "Follower." Think of two other selections that you think could be paired because of some strong similarity—or contrast—between them. Write an essay explaining your choices.

4.  Speaking about herself as a high school student, Gail Hosking Gilberg recalls, "What I did . . . was . . . I drew my attention to the moment—these friends, this school, this football game, this Friday night. And moment by moment I moved along life's timeline, making decisions here and there that twirled me into the next moment."
    a.  Reflect on two or three decisions in your life that "twirled [you] into the next moment." In other words, have there been some events that definitely were caused by decisions you had made earlier? If so, explain the connections.
    b.  In the midst of being "twirled," have you had the kind of awareness about your life that Gilberg came to after high school, when she understood how she had protected herself emotionally after her father's death in Vietnam? If you have, tell about what you came to realize.

# Competing

One way or another, we spend many hours of our lives competing.

Some competition, of course, takes place on the athletic field. In Part Two writer Bob Greene explores the pain of not measuring up to a coach's standards in the sports arena. And we share in some of the rewards of competition as we go on the road for a girls' championship basketball game.

Competition also occurs off the playing field. For example, how do we measure up to our friends? How do we fit in with others' concepts of us and their expectations for us? And how might we deal with those who have bullied us? You might get a laugh from Richard Peck's view of that universal problem.

All in all, in this section you will see people your age facing situations no different from those you may encounter as you compete every day in your life.

## Bob Greene

Born in 1947, Bob Greene is best known for the regular column he writes for the *Chicago Tribune*, a column syndicated in over 200 newspapers. Referring to the breadth of Greene's topics, one writer said, "Water covers two-thirds of the earth, and Bob Greene covers the rest." Greene has written two biographies of basketball player Michael Jordan as well as the novel *All Summer Long*; his columns have also been collected into several books. The following piece tells a lot about Greene and a significant moment in his own coming of age.

*Have you ever been cut from a team? If so, you know how Bob Greene felt.*

# Cut

**I** remember vividly the last time I cried. I was twelve years old, in the seventh grade, and I had tried out for the junior high school basketball team. I walked into the gymnasium; there was a piece of paper tacked to the bulletin board.

It was a cut list. The seventh-grade coach had put it up on the board. The boys whose names were on the list were still on the team; they were welcome to keep coming to practices. The boys whose names were not on the list had been cut; their presence was no longer desired. My name was not on the list.

I had not known the cut was coming that day. I stood and I stared at the list. The coach had not composed it with a great deal of subtlety; the names of the very best athletes were at the top of the sheet of paper, and the other members of the squad were listed in what appeared to be a descending order of talent. I kept looking at the bottom of the list, hoping against hope that my name would miraculously appear there if I looked hard enough.

I held myself together as I walked out of the gym and out of the school, but when I got home I began to sob. I couldn't stop. For the first time in my life, I had been told officially that I wasn't good enough. Athletics meant everything to boys that age; if you were on the team, even as a substitute, it put you in the desirable group. If you weren't on the team, you might as well not be alive.

I had tried desperately in practice, but the coach never seemed to notice. It didn't matter how hard I was willing to work; he didn't want me there. I knew that when I went to school the next morning I would have to face the boys who had not been cut—the boys whose names were on the list, who were still on the team, who had been judged worthy while I had been judged unworthy.

All these years later, I remember it as if I were still standing right there in the gym. And a curious thing has happened: in traveling around the country, I have found that an inordinately large proportion of successful men share that same memory—the memory of being cut from a sports team as a boy.

I don't know how the mind works in matters like this; I don't know what went on in my head following that day when I was cut. But I know that my ambition has been enormous ever since then; I know that for all of my life since that day, I have done more work than I had to be doing, taken more assignments than I had to be taking, put in more hours than I had to be spending. I don't know if all of that came from a determination never to allow myself to be cut again—never to allow someone to tell me that I'm not good enough again—but I know it's there. And apparently it's there in a lot of other men, too.

Bob Graham, thirty-six (at the time this essay was published), is a partner with the Jenner & Block law firm in Chicago. "When I was sixteen, baseball was my whole life," he said. "I had gone to a relatively small high school, and I had been on the team. But then my family moved, and I was going to a much bigger high school. All during the winter months I told everyone that I was a ballplayer. When spring came, of course I went out for the team.

"The cut list went up. I did not make the team. Reading that cut list is one of the clearest things I have in my memory. I wanted not to believe it, but there it was.

"I went home and told my father about it. He suggested that maybe I should talk to the coach. So I did. I pleaded to be put back on the team. He said there was nothing he could do; he said he didn't have enough room.

"I know for a fact that it altered my perception of myself. My view of myself was knocked down; my self-esteem was lowered. I felt so embarrassed; my whole life up to that point had revolved around sports, and particularly around playing baseball. That was the group I wanted to be in—the guys on the baseball team. And I was told that I wasn't good enough to be one of them.

"I know now that it changed me. I found out, even though I couldn't articulate it at the time, that there would be times in my life when certain people would be in a position to say 'You're not good enough' to me. I did not want that to happen ever again.

"It seems obvious to me now that being cut was what started me in determining that my success would always be based on my own abilities, and not on someone else's perceptions. Since then I've always been something of an overachiever; when I came to the law firm I was very aggressive in trying to run my own cases right away, to be the lead lawyer in the cases with which I was involved. I made partner at thirty-one; I never wanted to be left behind.

"Looking back, maybe it shouldn't have been that important. It was only baseball. You pass that by. Here I am. That coach is probably still there, still a high school baseball coach, still cutting boys off the baseball team every year. I wonder how many hundreds of boys he's cut in his life?"

Maurice McGrath is senior vice-president of Genstar Mortgage Corporation, a mortgage banking firm in Glendale, California. "I'm forty-seven years old, and I was fourteen when it happened to me, and I still feel something when I think about it," he said.

"I was in the eighth grade. I went to St. Philip's School in Pasadena. I went out for the baseball team, and one day at practice the coach came over to me. He was an Occidental College student who had been hired as the eighth-grade coach.

"He said, 'You're no good.' Those were his words. I asked him why he was saying that. He said, 'You can't hit the ball. I don't want you here.' I didn't know what to do, so I went over and sat off to the side, watching the others practice. The coach said I should leave the practice field. He said that I wasn't on the team, and that I didn't belong there anymore.

"I was outwardly stoic about it. I didn't want anyone to see how I felt. I didn't want to show that it hurt. But oh, did it hurt. All my friends played baseball after school every day. My best friend was the pitcher on the team. After I got whittled down by the coach, I would hear the other boys talking in class about what they were going to do at practice after school. I knew that I'd just have to go home.

"I guess you make your mind up never to allow yourself to be hurt like that again. In some way I must have been saying to myself, 'I'll play the game better.' Not the sports game, but anything I tried. I must have been saying, 'If I have to, I'll sit on the bench, but I'll be part of the team.'

"I try to make my own kids believe that, too. I try to tell them that they should show that they're a little bit better than the rest. I tell them to think of themselves as better. Who cares what anyone else thinks? You know, I can almost hear that coach saying the words, 'You're no good.'"

Author Malcolm MacPherson *(The Blood of His Servants)*, forty, lives in New York. "It happened to me in the ninth grade, at the Yalesville School in Yalesville, Connecticut," he said. "Both of my parents had just been killed in a car crash, and as you can imagine, it was a very difficult time in my life. I went out for the baseball team, and I did pretty well in practice.

"But in the first game I clutched. I was playing second base; the batter hit a popup, and I moved back to catch it. I can see it now. I felt dizzy as I looked up at the ball. It was like I was moving in slow motion, but the ball was going at regular speed. I couldn't get out of the way of my own feet. The ball dropped to the ground. I didn't catch it.

"The next day at practice, the coach read off the lineup. I wasn't on it. I was off the squad.

"I remember what I did: I walked. It was a cold spring afternoon, and the ground was wet, and I just walked. I was living with an aunt and uncle, and I didn't want to go home. I just wanted to walk forever.

"It drove my opinion of myself right into a tunnel. Right into a cave. And when I came out of that cave, something inside of me wanted to make sure in one manner or another that I would never again be told I wasn't good enough.

"I will confess that my ambition, to this day, is out of control. It's like a fire. I think the fire would have pretty much stayed in control if I hadn't been cut from that team. But that got it going. You don't slice ambition two ways; it's either there or it isn't. Those of us who went through something like that always know that we have to catch the ball. We'd rather die than have the ball fall at our feet.

"Once that fire is started in us, it never gets extinguished, until we die or have heart attacks or something. Sometimes I wonder about the home-run hitters; the guys who never even had to worry about being cut. They may have gotten the applause and the attention back then, but I wonder if they ever got the fire. I doubt it. I think maybe you have to get kicked in the teeth to get the fire started.

"You can tell the effect of something like that by examining the trail you've left in your life, and tracing it backward. It's almost like being a junkie with a need for success. You get attention and applause and you like it, but you never quite trust it. Because you know that back then you were good enough if only they would have given you a chance. You don't trust what you achieve, because you're afraid that someone will take it away from you. You know that it can happen; it already did.

"So you try to show people how good you are. Maybe you don't go out and become Dan Rather; maybe you just end up owning the Pontiac dealership in your town. But it's your dealership, and you're the top man, and every day you're showing people that you're good enough."

Dan Rather, fifty-two, is anchor of the "CBS Evening News." "When I was thirteen, I had rheumatic fever," he said. "I became extremely skinny and extremely weak, but I still went out for the seventh-grade baseball team at Alexander Hamilton Junior High School in Houston.

"The school was small enough that there was no cut as such; you were supposed to figure out that you weren't good enough, and quit. Game after game I sat at the end of the bench, hoping that maybe this was the time I would get in. The coach never even looked at me; I might as well have been invisible.

"I told my mother about it. Her advice was not to quit. So I went to practice every day, and I tried to do well so that the coach would be impressed. He never even knew I was there. At home in my room I would fantasize that there was a big game, and the three guys in front of me would all get hurt, and the coach would turn to me and put me in, and I would make the winning hit. But then there'd be another game, and the late innings would come, and if we were way ahead I'd keep hoping that this was the game when the coach would put me in. He never did.

"When you're that age, you're looking for someone to tell you you're okay. Your sense of self-esteem is just being formed. And what that experience that baseball season did was make me think that perhaps I wasn't okay.

"In the last game of the season something terrible happened. It was the last of the ninth inning, there were two outs, and there were two strikes on the batter. And the coach turned to me and told me to go out to right field.

"It was a totally humiliating thing for him to do. For him to put me in for one pitch, the last pitch of the season, in front of all the other guys on the team . . . I stood out there for that one pitch, and I just wanted to sink into the ground and disappear. Looking back on it, it was an extremely unkind thing for him to have done. That was nearly forty years ago, and I don't know why the memory should be so vivid now; I've never known if the coach was purposely making fun of me—and if he was, why a grown man would do that to a thirteen-year-old boy.

"I'm not a psychologist. I don't know if a man can point to one event in his life and say that that's the thing that made him the way he is. But when you're that age, and you're searching for your own identity, and all you want is to be told that you're all right . . . I wish I understood it better, but I know the feeling is still there."

---

## Responding to the Essay

1. "For the first time in my life, I had been told officially that I wasn't good enough." Explain exactly what these words would mean to a 12-year-old like Bob Greene or to someone your own age.
2. Did it surprise you how callously most of the "cut" individuals were treated by their coaches? Is there any nice way to drop players from a team? Discuss.

3.  How did being told they were not good enough actually have a positive influence on most of the people Greene interviewed?
4.  Newsman Dan Rather says, "When you're that age, you're looking for someone to tell you you're okay. Your sense of self-esteem is just being formed." Think of a personal encounter that helped you see you are "okay." The message may have been communicated in either spoken or unspoken form. Explain how what happened helped to build your self-esteem.

## Exploring the Author's Craft

An **exemplification essay** uses concrete examples to make its points. Briefly state Bob Greene's main idea in "Cut"; then explain how each of his examples contributes to the overall effectiveness of the essay. What natural connection is there between the last two examples—those of Malcolm MacPherson and Dan Rather?

## Writer's Workshop

Think of an issue or behavior pattern affecting people your age. It could be anything from the ramifications of a new school rule to opinions on body piercing. Once you have an issue, interview at least three different students in your school and record their experiences and thoughts about it. Follow Bob Greene's structure: first write a paragraph about *your* reactions to the issue, then give your parallel examples. Be sure to quote people's exact words.

## Alternate Media Response

Do the same task as listed above in Writer's Workshop, but do it as a video segment, complete with the interviews. If you have a television broadcast facility in your school, try to get your segment on the air.

## Doris Lessing

British writer Doris Lessing, born in 1919, spent much of her childhood and early adult years in Zimbabwe (known then as Rhodesia), in southern Africa. She has written novels, short stories, and poems, many dealing with life in Africa. The book for which she is best known, however, and which most critics consider her major achievement is the novel *The Golden Notebook*. The following story, "Through the Tunnel," displays among other things her ability to create a vivid setting.

*Sometimes what begins as a competition with others ends up being a struggle with yourself.*

# Through the Tunnel

Going to the shore on the first morning of the vacation, the young English boy stopped at a turning of the path and looked down at a wild and rocky bay, and then over to the crowded beach he knew so well from other years. His mother walked on in front of him, carrying a bright striped bag in one hand. Her other arm, swinging loose, was very white in the sun. The boy watched that white, naked arm, and turned his eyes, which had a frown behind them, toward the bay and back again to his mother. When she felt he was not with her, she swung around. "Oh, there you are, Jerry!" she said. She looked impatient, then smiled. "Why, darling, would you rather not come with me? Would you rather—" She frowned, conscientiously worrying over what amusements he might secretly be longing for, which she had been too busy or too careless to imagine. He was very familiar with that anxious, apologetic smile. Contrition sent him running after her. And yet, as he ran, he looked back over his shoulder at the wild bay; and all morning, as he played on the safe beach, he was thinking of it.

Next morning, when it was time for the routine of swimming and sunbathing, his mother said, "Are you tired of the usual beach, Jerry? Would you like to go somewhere else?"

"Oh, no!" he said quickly, smiling at her out of that unfailing impulse of contrition—a sort of chivalry. Yet, walking down the path with her, he blurted out, "I'd like to go and have a look at those rocks down there."

She gave the idea her attention. It was a wild-looking place, and there was no one there; but she said, "Of course, Jerry. When you've had enough, come to the big beach. Or just go straight back to the villa, if you like." She walked away, that bare arm, now slightly reddened from yesterday's sun, swinging. And he almost ran after her again, feeling it unbearable that she should go by herself, but he did not.

She was thinking, Of course he's old enough to be safe without me. Have I been keeping him too close? He mustn't feel he ought to be with me. I must be careful.

He was an only child, eleven years old. She was a widow. She was determined to be neither possessive nor lacking in devotion. She went worrying off to her beach.

As for Jerry, once he saw that his mother had gained her beach, he began the steep descent to the bay. From where he was, high up among red-brown rocks, it was a scoop of moving bluish green fringed with white. As he went lower, he saw that it spread among small promontories[1] and inlets of rough, sharp rock, and the crisping, lapping surface showed stains of purple and darker blue. Finally, as he ran sliding and scraping down the last few yards, he saw an edge of white surf and the shallow, luminous movement of water over white sand, and, beyond that, a solid, heavy blue.

He ran straight into the water and began swimming. He was a good swimmer. He went out fast over the gleaming sand, over a middle region where rocks lay like discolored monsters under the surface, and then he was in the real sea—a warm sea where irregular cold currents from the deep water shocked his limbs.

When he was so far out that he could look back not only on the little bay but past the promontory that was between it and the big beach, he floated on the buoyant surface and looked for his mother. There she

------

1. **promontories:** high cliffs along a shore extending out over the water.

was, a speck of yellow under an umbrella that looked like a slice of orange peel. He swam back to shore, relieved at being sure she was there, but all at once very lonely.

On the edge of a small cape that marked the side of the bay away from the promontory was a loose scatter of rocks. Above them, some boys were stripping off their clothes. They came running, naked, down to the rocks. The English boy swam toward them, but kept his distance at a stone's throw. They were of that coast; all of them were burned smooth dark brown and speaking a language that he did not understand. To be with them, of them, was a craving that filled his whole body. He swam a little closer; they turned and watched him with narrowed, alert dark eyes. Then one smiled and waved. It was enough. In a minute, he had swum in and was on the rocks beside them, smiling with a desperate, nervous supplication. They shouted cheerful greetings at him; and then, as he preserved his nervous, uncomprehending smile, they understood that he was a foreigner strayed from his own beach, and they proceeded to forget him. But he was happy. He was with them.

They began diving again and again from a high point into a well of blue sea between rough, pointed rocks. After they had dived and come up, they swam around, hauled themselves up, and waited their turn to dive again. They were big boys—men, to Jerry. He dived, and they watched him; and when he swam around to take his place, they made way for him. He felt he was accepted and he dived again, carefully, proud of himself.

Soon the biggest of the boys poised himself, shot down into the water, and did not come up. The others stood about, watching. Jerry, after waiting for the sleek brown head to appear, let out a yell of warning. They looked at him idly and turned their eyes back toward the water. After a long time, the boy came up on the other side of a big dark rock, letting the air out of his lungs in a sputtering gasp and a shout of triumph. Immediately the rest of them dived in. One moment, the morning seemed full of chattering boys; the next, the air and the surface of the water were empty. But through the heavy blue, dark shapes could be seen moving and groping.

Jerry dived, shot past the school of underwater swimmers, saw a black wall of rock looming at him, touched it, and bobbed up at once to the surface, where the wall was a low barrier he could see across. There was no one visible; under him, in the water, the dim shapes of the swimmers had disappeared. Then one, and then another of the boys came up on the far side of the barrier of rock, and he understood that they had swum through some gap or hole in it. He plunged down again. He could see nothing through the stinging salt water but the blank rock. When he came up the boys were all on the diving rock, preparing to attempt the feat again. And now, in a panic of failure, he yelled up, in English, "Look at me! Look!" and he began splashing and kicking in the water like a foolish dog.

They looked down gravely, frowning. He knew the frown. At moments of failure, when he clowned to claim his mother's attention, it was with just this grave, embarrassed inspection that she rewarded him. Through his hot shame, feeling the pleading grin on his face like a scar that he could never remove, he looked up at the group of big brown boys on the rock and shouted, *"Bonjour! Merci! Au revoir! Monsieur, monsieur!"*[2] while he hooked his fingers round his ears and waggled them.

Water surged into his mouth; he choked, sank, came up. The rock, lately weighted with boys, seemed to rear up out of the water as their weight was removed. They were flying down past him, now, into the water; the air was full of falling bodies. Then the rock was empty in the hot sunlight. He counted one, two, three. . . .

At fifty, he was terrified. They must all be drowning beneath him, in the watery caves of the rock! At a hundred, he stared around him at the empty hillside, wondering if he should yell for help. He counted faster, faster, to hurry them up, to bring them to the surface quickly, to drown them quickly—anything rather than the terror of counting on and on into the blue emptiness of the morning. And then, at a hundred and sixty, the water beyond the rock was full of boys blowing like brown whales. They swam back to the shore without a look at him.

He climbed back to the diving rock and sat down, feeling the hot roughness of it under his thighs. The boys were gathering up their bits of clothing and running off along the shore to another promontory. They were leaving to get away from him. He cried openly, fists in his eyes. There was no one to see him, and he cried himself out.

---

2. *Bonjour! Merci! Au revoir! Monsier, monsieur:* Good day! Thank you! Good-bye! Sir, sir! [French]

It seemed to him that a long time had passed, and he swam out to where he could see his mother. Yes, she was still there, a yellow spot under an orange umbrella. He swam back to the big rock, climbed up, and dived into the blue pool among the fanged and angry boulders. Down he went, until he touched the wall of rock again. But the salt was so painful in his eyes that he could not see.

He came to the surface, swam to shore and went back to the villa to wait for his mother. Soon she walked slowly up the path, swinging her striped bag, the flushed, naked arm dangling beside her. "I want some swimming goggles," he panted, defiant and beseeching.

She gave him a patient, inquisitive look as she said casually, "Well, of course, darling."

But now, now, now! He must have them this minute, and no other time. He nagged and pestered until she went with him to a shop. As soon as she had bought the goggles, he grabbed them from her hand as if she were going to claim them for herself, and was off, running down the steep path to the bay.

Jerry swam out to the big barrier rock, adjusted the goggles, and dived. The impact of the water broke the rubber-enclosed vacuum, and the goggles came loose. He understood that he must swim down to the base of the rock from the surface of the water. He fixed the goggles tight and firm, filled his lungs, and floated, face down, on the water. Now, he could see. It was as if he had eyes of a different kind—fish eyes that showed everything clear and delicate and wavering in the bright water.

Under him, six or seven feet down, was a floor of perfectly clean, shining white sand, rippled firm and hard by the tides. Two grayish shapes steered there, like long, rounded pieces of wood or slate. They were fish. He saw them nose toward each other, poise motionless, make a dart forward, swerve off, and come around again. It was like a water dance. A few inches above them the water sparkled as if sequins were dropping through it. Fish again—myriads[3] of minute fish, the length of his fingernail, were drifting through the water, and in a moment he could feel the innumerable tiny touches of them against his limbs. It was like swimming in flaked silver. The great rock the big boys had

---

3. **myriads:** extremely large numbers.

swum through rose sheer out of the white sand—black, tufted lightly with greenish weed. He could see no gap in it. He swam down to its base.

Again and again he rose, took a big chestful of air, and went down. Again and again he groped over the surface of the rock, feeling it, almost hugging it in the desperate need to find the entrance. And then, once, while he was clinging to the black wall, his knees came up and he shot his feet out forward and they met no obstacle. He had found the hole.

He gained the surface, clambered about the stones that littered the barrier rock until he found a big one, and, with this in his arms, let himself down over the side of the rock. He dropped, with the weight, straight to the sandy floor. Clinging tight to the anchor of stone, he lay on his side and looked in under the dark shelf at the place where his feet had gone. He could see the hole. It was an irregular, dark gap; but he could not see deep into it. He let go of his anchor, clung with his hands to the edges of the hole and tried to push himself in.

He got his head in, found his shoulders jammed, moved them in sidewise, and was inside as far as his waist. He could see nothing ahead. Something soft and clammy touched his mouth; he saw a dark front moving against the grayish rock, and panic filled him. He thought of octopuses, of clinging weed. He pushed himself out backward and caught a glimpse, as he retreated, of a harmless tentacle of seaweed drifting in the mouth of the tunnel. But it was enough. He reached the sunlight, swam to shore, and lay on the diving rock. He looked down into the blue well of water. He knew he must find his way through that cave, or hole, or tunnel, and out the other side.

First, he thought, he must learn to control his breathing. He let himself down into the water with another big stone in his arms, so that he could lie effortlessly on the bottom of the sea. He counted. One, two, three. He counted steadily. He could hear the movement of blood in his chest. Fifty-one, fifty-two. . . . His chest was hurting. He let go of the rock and went up into the air. He saw that the sun was low. He rushed to the villa and found his mother at her supper. She said only "Did you enjoy yourself?" and he said "Yes."

All night the boy dreamed of the water-filled cave in the rock, and as soon as breakfast was over he went to the bay.

That night, his nose bled badly. For hours he had been underwater, learning to hold his breath, and now he felt weak and dizzy. His mother said, "I shouldn't overdo things, darling, if I were you."

That day and the next, Jerry exercised his lungs as if everything, the whole of his life, all that he would become, depended upon it. Again his nose bled at night, and his mother insisted on his coming with her the next day. It was a torment to him to waste a day of his careful self-training, but he stayed with her on that other beach, which now seemed a place for small children, a place where his mother might lie safe in the sun. It was not his beach.

He did not ask for permission, on the following day, to go to his beach. He went, before his mother could consider the complicated rights and wrongs of the matter. A day's rest, he discovered, had improved his count by ten. The big boys had made the passage while he counted a hundred and sixty. He had been counting fast, in his fright. Probably now, if he tried, he could get through that long tunnel, but he was not going to try yet. A curious, most unchildlike persistence, a controlled impatience, made him wait. In the meantime, he lay underwater on the white sand, littered now by stones he had brought down from the upper air, and studied the entrance to the tunnel. He knew every jut and corner of it, as far as it was possible to see. It was as if he already felt its sharpness about his shoulders.

He sat by the clock in the villa, when his mother was not near, and checked his time. He was incredulous and then proud to find he could hold his breath without strain for two minutes. The words "two minutes," authorized by the clock, brought close the adventure that was so necessary to him.

In another four days, his mother said casually one morning, they must go home. On the day before they left, he would do it. He would do it if it killed him, he said defiantly to himself. But two days before they were to leave—a day of triumph when he increased his count by fifteen—his nose bled so badly that he turned dizzy and had to lie limply over the big rock like a bit of seaweed, watching the thick red blood flow on to the rock and trickle slowly down to the sea. He was frightened. Supposing he turned dizzy in the tunnel? Supposing he died there, trapped? Supposing—his head went around, in the hot sun, and he almost gave up. He thought he would return to the house and lie down, and next summer, perhaps, when he had another year's growth in him— *then* he would go through the hole.

But even after he had made the decision, or thought he had, he found himself sitting up on the rock and looking down into the water; and he knew that now, this moment, when his nose had only just stopped bleeding, when his head was still sore and throbbing—this was the moment when he would try. If he did not do it now, he never would. He was trembling with fear that he would not go; and he was trembling with horror at that long, long tunnel under the rock, under the sea. Even in the open sunlight, the barrier rock seemed very wide and very heavy; tons of rock pressed down on where he would go. If he died there, he would lie until one day—perhaps not before next year—those big boys would swim into it and find it blocked.

He put on his goggles, fitted them tight, tested the vacuum. His hands were shaking. Then he chose the biggest stone he could carry and slipped over the edge of the rock until half of him was in the cool, enclosing water and half in the hot sun. He looked up once at the empty sky, filled his lungs once, twice, and then sank fast to the bottom with the stone. He let it go and began to count. He took the edges of the hole in his hands and drew himself into it, wriggling his shoulders in sidewise as he remembered he must, kicking himself along with his feet.

Soon he was clear inside. He was in a small rockbound hole filled with yellowish-gray water. The water was pushing him up against the roof. The roof was sharp and pained his back. He pulled himself along with his hands—fast, fast—and used his legs as levers. His head knocked against something; a sharp pain dizzied him. Fifty, fifty-one, fifty-two. . . . He was without light, and the water seemed to press upon him with the weight of rock. Seventy-one, seventy-two. . . . There was no strain on his lungs. He felt like an inflated balloon, his lungs were so light and easy, but his head was pulsing.

He was being continually pressed against the sharp roof, which felt slimy as well as sharp. Again he thought of octopuses, and wondered if the tunnel might be filled with weed that could tangle him. He gave himself a panicky, convulsive kick forward, ducked his head, and swam. His feet and hands moved freely, as if in open water. The hole must have widened out. He thought he must be swimming fast, and he was frightened of banging his head if the tunnel narrowed.

A hundred, a hundred and one. . . . The water paled. Victory filled him. His lungs were beginning to hurt. A few more strokes and he would be out. He was counting wildly; he said a hundred and fifteen, and then, a long time later, a hundred and fifteen again. The water was a clear jewel-green all around him. Then he saw, above his head, a crack running up through the rock. Sunlight was falling through it, showing the clean, dark rock of the tunnel, a single mussel shell, and darkness ahead.

He was at the end of what he could do. He looked up at the crack as if it were filled with air and not water, and if he could put his mouth to it to draw in air. A hundred and fifteen, he heard himself say inside his head—but he had said that long ago. He must go on into the blackness ahead, or he would drown. His head was swelling, his lungs cracking. A hundred and fifteen, a hundred and fifteen pounded through his head, and he feebly clutched at rocks in the dark, pulling himself forward, leaving the brief space of sunlit water behind. He felt he was dying. He was no longer quite conscious. He struggled on in the darkness between lapses into unconsciousness. An immense, swelling pain filled his head, and then the darkness cracked with an explosion of green light. His hands, groping forward, met nothing; and his feet, kicking back, propelled him out into the open sea.

He drifted to the surface, his face turned up to the air. He was gasping like a fish. He felt he would sink now and drown; he could not swim the few feet back to the rock. Then he was clutching it and pulling himself up on to it. He lay face down, gasping. He could see nothing but a red-veined, clotted dark. His eyes must have burst, he thought; they were full of blood. He tore off his goggles and a gout[4] of blood went into the sea. His nose was bleeding, and the blood had filled the goggles.

He scooped up handfuls of water from the cool, salty sea, to splash on his face, and did not know whether it was blood or salt water he tasted. After a time, his heart quieted, his eyes cleared, and he sat up. He could see the local boys diving and playing half a mile away. He did not want them. He wanted nothing but to get back home and lie down.

In a short while, Jerry swam to shore and climbed slowly up the path to the villa. He flung himself on his bed and slept, waking at the sound of feet on the path outside. His mother was coming back. He rushed to the bathroom, thinking she must not see his face with bloodstains, or tearstains, on it. He came out of the bathroom and met her as she walked into the villa, smiling, her eyes lighting up.

---

4. **gout:** spurt.

"Have a nice morning?" she asked, laying her hand on his warm brown shoulder a moment.

"Oh, yes, thank you," he said.

"You look a bit pale." And then, sharp and anxious, "How did you bang your head?"

"Oh, just banged it," he told her.

She looked at him closely. He was strained; his eyes were glazed-looking. She was worried. And then she said to herself, Oh, don't fuss! Nothing can happen. He can swim like a fish.

They sat down to lunch together.

"Mummy," he said, "I can stay under water for two minutes—three minutes, at least." It came bursting out of him.

"Can you, darling?" she said. "Well, I shouldn't overdo it. I don't think you ought to swim any more today."

She was ready for a battle of wills, but he gave in at once. It was no longer of the least importance to go to the bay.

---

## Responding to the Story

1. Name some of Jerry's motivations for swimming through the tunnel. How do these change during the course of the story?
2. Why is it so important to Jerry that he have the swimming goggles "this minute, and no other time"? What does this reaction suggest about Jerry?
3. How does Jerry change as he makes his preparations for the swim?
4. How do you explain Jerry's thought at the end of the story: "It was no longer of the least importance to go to the bay"?

## Exploring the Author's Craft

An **allegory** is a story in which people, things, and events have a larger meaning beyond the story. "Through the Tunnel" may be considered a coming-of-age allegory—an allegory of growth into adulthood. Looking at the story in this way, what do each of the following elements represent?
a. the older boys
b. the tunnel
c. the swim

## Writer's Workshop

This story has two extraordinary features: its lyrical capturing of nature and its clearcut symbolism of the young man's coming of age. Here are two activities to help you emulate Doris Lessing's accomplishments in this story.

1. Think of any nature location that you know especially well. In at least three paragraphs try to place us there by telling us of every key detail that makes the place so vivid to you. When you mention a specific aspect of the place, develop that aspect with description; don't just move on to another detail. Look back to Lessing's beach and underwater descriptions to see how she brought them alive.
2. Outline a story you could write that would be an allegory. Be sure that your story, like "Through the Tunnel," works both on a literal and a symbolic level.

## Bill Zavatsky

Bill Zavatsky grew up in Bridgeport, Connecticut. Of his sports experiences Zavatsky says, "To tell the truth, I was an erratic athlete at best, and baseball (not to mention other sports) plunged me into moments of the deepest shame and grief that I experienced as a child. Some days I could hit anything anywhere; my glove was foolproof, immense. Then during one game I charged a little infield dribbler and, instead of scooping it up, I kicked it across the diamond into the opposing team's dugout.

"The end-of-season 'grudge match' in the poem took place pretty much as described. And even though I felt a tremendous sense of relief when I was old enough to bury my hat and glove in my closet forever, the sport did give me the gift of a poem that I'm proud of." Zavatsky, who was born in 1943, has published a book, *Theories of Rain and Other Poems*.

*Imagine a fly ball dropping right toward you. Do you catch it—or do you miss it?*

# Baseball

We were only farm team
not "good enough" to
make big Little League
with its classic uniforms
5    deep lettered hats.
But our coach said

we *were* just as good
maybe better
so we played
10  the Little League champs
in our stenciled tee shirts
and soft purple caps
when the season was over.

What happened that afternoon
15  I can't remember—
whether we won or tied.
But in my mind I lean back
to a pop-up hanging
in sunny sky
20  stopped
nailed to the blue
losing itself in a cloud
over second base
where I stood waiting.

25  Ray Michaud who knew
my up-and-down career
as a local player
my moments of graceful genius
my unpredictable ineptness
30  screamed arrows at me
from the dugout

where he waited to bat:
"He's gonna drop it! He
don't know how to catch,
35   you watch it drop!"

The ball kept climbing
higher, a black dot
no rules of gravity, no
brakes, a period searching
40   for a sentence, and the sentence read:
"You're no good, Bill
you won't catch this one now
you know you never will."

I watched myself looking up
45   and felt my body rust, falling
in pieces to the ground
a baby trying to stand up
an ant in the shadow of a house

I wasn't there
50   had never been born
would stand there forever
a statue squinting upward
pointed out laughed at
for a thousand years
55   teammates dead, forgotten

bones of anyone who played baseball
forgotten
baseball forgotten, played no more
played by robots on electric fields
60  who never missed
or cried in their own sweat

I'm thirty-four years old.
The game was over twenty years ago.
All I remember of that afternoon
65  when the ball came down

is that
I caught it.

---

## Responding to the Poem

As this poem was progressing and you heard the taunts of his opponent,
did you think the speaker would catch or drop the ball? Why do you
think you had that expectation?

## Exploring the Author's Craft

"Baseball" is a **narrative poem**; it tells a story. Like any narrative, it contains action, characters, a setting.

1. How long does the main action in the poem actually take? How does the writer make it seem longer than it is?
2. One of the pleasures of the poem is the suspense the writer builds up over one seemingly insignificant pop-up. Explain where and how Zavatsky keeps the reader in suspense. Are the "delaying words" he uses meaningless or significant?

## Writer's Workshop

Write a narrative poem but keep us in suspense; make the reader wonder what is going to happen by the time the poem ends. This poem should be **free verse**; that is, have no regular rhythm (accented syllables or "beats" per line) or rhyme.

## Budge Wilson

Budge Wilson, who was born in 1927, has published a novel and two collections of short stories, *The Leaving*, which won the Canadian Library Association's Young Adult Book Award in 1991, and *The Dandelion Garden*. Many of her stories are set in the Canadian province of Nova Scotia, but they deal with issues young people everywhere can relate to. One critic gives Wilson the ultimate compliment by saying her stories are "universal in theme." This, of course, is what every author wants to achieve, universality.

*What is sibling rivalry? Is it alive and well in all families?*

# Waiting

**Y**ou must realize, of course, that Juliette is a very complex child." My mother was talking on the telephone. Shouting, to be more exact. She always spoke on the phone as though the wires had been disconnected, as though she were trying to be heard across the street through an open window. "She's so many-*sided*," she continued. "Being cute, of course, is not enough, although heaven knows she could charm the legs off a table. But you have to have something more than personality."

I was not embarrassed by any of this. Lying on the living room floor on my stomach, I was pretending to read *The Bobbsey Twins at the Seashore*. But after a while I closed the book. Letting her words drop around me, I lay there like a plant enjoying the benefit of a drenching and beneficial rain. My sister sat nearby in the huge wingback chair, legs tucked up under her, reading the funnies.

"I hope you don't regard this as *boasting*, but she really is so very, *very* talented. Bright as a button in school—three prizes, can you believe it, at the last school closing—and an outstanding athlete, even at eight years old."

Resting my head on my folded arms, I smiled quietly. I could see myself eight years from now, receiving my gold medal, while our country's flag rose in front of the Olympic flame. The applause thundered as the flag reached its peak, standing straight out from the pole, firm and strong. As the band broke into a moving rendition of "O Canada,"[1] I wept softly. I stood wet and waterlogged from my last race, my tears melding with the chlorine and coursing slowly down my face. People were murmuring, "So young, so small, and so attractive."

"And such a leader!" My mother's voice hammered on. "Even at her age, she seems forever to be president of this and director of that. I feel very blessed indeed to be the mother of such a child." My sister stirred in her chair and coughed slightly, carefully turning a page.

It was true. I was president of grade 4, and manager of the Lower Slocum Elementary School Drama Club. I had already starred in two productions, one of them a musical. In an ornate crêpe paper costume composed of giant overlapping yellow petals, I had played Lead Buttercup to a full house. Even Miss Prescott's aggressive piano playing had failed to drown me out, had not prevented me from stealing the show from the Flower Queen. My mother kept the clipping from *The Shelburne Coast Guard* up on the kitchen notice board. It included a blurred newspaper picture of me with extended arms and open mouth. Below it, the caption read, "Juliette Westhaver was the surprise star of the production, with three solos and a most sprightly little dance, performed skillfully and with gusto. Broadway, look out!"

Mama was still talking. "Mm? Oh. Henrietta. Yes, well, she's fine, I guess, just fine. Such a serious, responsible little girl, and so fond of her sister." I looked up at Henrietta, who was surveying me over the top of her comics. There was no expression on her face at all.

But then Henrietta was not often given to expression of any kind. She was my twin, but apart from the accident of our birth, or the coincidence, we had almost nothing in common. It was incredible to me that we had been born to the same parents at almost the same moment, and that we had been reared in the same house.

---

1. "O Canada": the Canadian national anthem.

But Henrietta was my friend and I hers. We were, in fact, best friends, as is so often the case with twins. And as with most close childhood friendships, there was one dominant member, one submissive. There was no doubt in this case as to who played the leading role.

Henrietta even looked submissive. She was thin and pale. She had enormous sky-blue eyes surrounded by a long fringe of totally colorless eyelashes. Her hair was a dim beige color without gradations of light or dark, and it hung straight and lifeless from two barrettes. Her fingers were long and bony, and she kept them folded in her lap, motionless, like a tired old lady. She had a straight little nose, and a mouth that seldom smiled—it was serious and still and oddly serene. She often looked as though she were waiting for something.

Untidy and flamboyant, my personality and my person flamed hotly beside her cool apathy.[2] My temper flared, my joys exploded. With fiery red cheeks and a broad snub nose, I grinned and hooted my way through childhood, dragging and pushing Henrietta along as I raced from one adventure to the next. I had a mop of wild black curls that no comb could tame. I was small, compact, sturdy, well-coordinated and extremely healthy. Henrietta had a lot of colds.

When I start talking about Henrietta and me, I always feel like I'm right back there, a kid again. Sometimes, you know, I got fed up with her. If you have a lot of energy, for instance, it's no fun to go skiing with someone who's got lead in her boots. And for heaven's sake, she kept falling all the time. Scared to death to try the hills, and likely as not going down them on the seat of her pants. "Fraidy-cat! Fraidy-cat!" I'd yell at her from the bottom of the hill where I had landed right side up, and she would start down the first part of the slope with straight and trembling knees, landing in a snowbank before the hill even got started. There were lots of fields and woods around our town, and good high hills if you were looking for thrills. You could see the sea from the top of some of them, and the wild wind up there made me feel like an explorer, a brave Micmac hunter, the queen of the Maritime Provinces.[3] Sometimes I would let out a yell just for the joy of it all—and there,

---

2. **apathy:** unconcern; indifference.

3. **Micmac . . . Maritime Provinces:** The Micmac are an Algonquian Indian tribe that originally inhabited eastern Canada, the present-day location of the Maritime Provinces.

panting and gasping and falling up the hill would be old Henrietta, complaining, forever complaining, about how tired she was, how cold.

But I guess I really loved Henrietta anyway, slowpoke though she was. I had lots and lots of other friends who were more interesting than she was. But it's a funny thing—she was nearly always my first choice for someone to play with.

There was a small woodlot to the east of the village, on land owned by my father. We called it The Grove. It had little natural paths in it, and there were open spaces under the trees like rooms or houses or castles, or whatever you wanted them to be that day. The grove of trees was on the edge of a cliff overhanging some big rocks, and at high tide the sea down there was never still, even when it was flat oil calm. So it could be a spooky kind of place to play in, too. I loved to go there when it was foggy, and play spy. It was 1940 and wartime, and by then we were ten, going on eleven. From The Grove we could sometimes see destroyers, and once even a big aircraft carrier. In the fog, it wasn't hard to believe that the Nazis were coming, and that we were going to be blown to bits any minute.

We never told Mama or Papa about going to the cliff when the mist was thick. Henrietta hardly ever wanted to go on those foggy days. She was afraid of falling off the cliff onto the rocks, sure she would drown in the churned-up water, nervous about the ghostly shapes in the thick gray-white air. But she always went. I used to blackmail her. "If you don't go, I'll tell Mama about the time you pretended to be sick and stayed home from school because you didn't have your homework done and were scared of Miss Garrison." Or I would just plain order her around. "I'm *going*, Henrietta, so get a move on and *hurry*!" She'd come padding out of the house in her stupid yellow raincoat, so that she wouldn't get a cold in the wet wind, and off we'd go—me fast and complaining about her slowness, and her slow and complaining about my speed. But she'd be there and we'd be together and we'd have fun. I'd be the spy, and she'd be the poor agonized prisoner of war, tied up to a tree by a bunch of Nazis. Sometimes I'd leave her tethered good and long, so she'd look *really* scared instead of pretend scared, while I prowled around and killed Nazis and searched for hidden weapons. Or we'd play Ghost, and I'd be the ghost—floating along the edge of the cliff, and shrieking in my special death shriek that I saved for·ghost games. It started out low like a groan, and then rose to a wail, ending in a scream so thin and high that it almost scared *me*. Sometimes, if she was especially wet and tired, Henrietta would start to cry, and that *really* made me mad. Even now, I can't stand cry babies. But you had to have a victim, and this was something she was extra good at. No point in wasting my death shriek on a person who wasn't afraid of ghosts. No fun to have the Nazis tying up someone who was big and strong and brave, particularly when the Nazis weren't actually there and you had to think them up and pretend the whole thing.

One time when we went there with a bunch of kids instead of just us two, I forgot all about her being tied to the tree, and got nearly home before I raced back the whole half mile to untie her. She never said a word. It was snowing, and there were big fat snowflakes on those long white lashes of hers, and her eyes looked like they were going to pop right out of her head. I said I was real sorry, and next week I even bought her a couple of comic books out of my own allowance money, when she was home sick with bronchitis. Mama said she should have had the sense to wear a scarf and a warm hat, being as she was so prone to colds, and that's certainly true. She never told on me, and I don't know why. She sat up against the pillows and colored in her coloring book or read her funnies, or more often she just lay there on the bed, her hands lying limp on the quilt, with that patient, quiet, waiting look of hers.

When the spring came a gang of us would always start going out to The Grove on weekends to start practicing for our summer play. Year after year we did this, and it had nothing to do with those school plays in which I made such a hit. We'd all talk about what stories we liked, and then we'd pick one of them and make a play out of it. I would usually select the play because I was always the one who directed it, so it was only fair that I'd get to do the choosing. If there was a king or a queen, I'd usually be the queen. If you're the director, you can't be something like a page or a minor fairy, because then you don't seem important enough to be giving out instructions and bossing people around, and the kids maybe won't pay attention to all the orders. Besides, as my mother pointed out, I was smart and could learn my lines fast, and you couldn't expect some slow dummy to memorize all that stuff.

Henrietta's voice was so soft and quiet that no one could ever hear her unless they were almost sitting on her lap; so of course it would have been stupid to give her a part. She couldn't even be the king's horse or the queen's milk-white mule because she was so darn scrawny. You can't have the lead animal looking as though it should be picked up by the Humane Society and put in quarantine. But she was really useful to the production, and it must have been very satisfying for her. She got to find all the costume parts, and rigged up the stage in the biggest cleared space among the trees, making it look like a ballroom or a throne room or whatever else we needed. She did a truly good job, and if it weren't for the fact that I can't stand conceited people, I probably would even have told her so. I liked Henrietta the way she was. I didn't want her strutting around looking proud of herself and putting on airs. One time one of the kids said, "Hey, Henrietta, that's a really great royal bedroom you made," and right away she started standing and moving around in a way that showed she thought she was a pretty smart stage manager.

I hate that kind of thing, and I knew the others wouldn't like it either. So I said, "Oh, sure! And the king must have just lost his kingdom in the wars. Who ever heard of a king sleeping on a pile of branches or having an old torn dishtowel at the window? Some king!" And everyone laughed. I always think that laughter is very important. It makes everyone happy right away, and is a good way to ease tensions.

We had a lot of fun practicing for those plays. No one went away for the summer. No one needed to. The sea was right there alongside the village, with a big sandy beach only a quarter mile away. Some of the fishermen let us use their smaller flats for jigging,[4] and we could always swim or dig for clams or collect mussels. Besides, the war was on; people weren't spending money on cottages or trips. Seems to me that everyone just stuck around home and saved paper and counted their ration stamps[5] and listened to the news on the radio. There was a navy base nearby, and sometimes sailors came to dinner. They'd tell us about life on the base, and all the dangers they were expecting and hoping to experience when they started sailing to Europe. I envied them like anything, and couldn't for the life of me see why you had to be eighteen

---

4. **jigging:** pulling a fishing lure through the water to catch fish.
5. **ration stamps:** stamps issued during World War II to obtain gasoline, food, and other items in short supply.

before you joined the navy, or why they wouldn't let girls run the ships or use the guns. Henrietta said she didn't want to be a sailor anyway, because she'd be too scared, which of course is only what you'd expect. Apart from that, there wasn't much excitement. So the play practices were our main entertainment during those years. In the summer, we practiced on most fine days, and in August we put on the play in front of all our mothers and fathers and uncles and aunts, and for the sisters and brothers too young to take part.

The play we put on in 1942 was about a rich nobleman called Alphonse who falls in love with an exquisitely beautiful but humble country girl called Genevieve. I played the part of Genevieve, and it was the nicest part I had ever played. In the last scene, Genevieve and the nobleman become engaged, and she gets to dress up in a very gorgeous gown for a big court ball. I had a real dress for this scene, instead of the usual pieced-together scraps of material dug out of old trunks from our attics. My mother let me use one of her long dance dresses from when she was young. It was covered with sequins and even had some sort of fluffy feather stuff around the hem; and it was pale sapphire blue and very romantic looking. I had trouble getting into it because I was almost thirteen now and sort of big through the middle. But my mother put in a new zipper instead of the buttons, and I was able to wear it after all. I had to move a little carefully and not take very deep breaths, but I was as tall as Mama now, and I felt like a real woman, a true beauty. The neck was kind of low, but I was pretty flat, so I didn't need to worry about being indecent in front of Harold Boutilier, who played the part of Alphonse. Mama put a whole lot of makeup on me, covering up the pimples I was starting to get, and I thought I looked like a movie star, a genuine leading lady. The zipper wasn't put into the dress in time for the dress rehearsal, but Harold wore a big bow at his neck and his mother's velvet shorty coat, with a galvanized chain around his waist that shone like real silver. He had on his sister's black stockings and a pair of high rubber boots, and he looked very handsome. Up until this year he had just seemed like an okay boy to me, as boys go, but this summer I'd spent a lot of time watching him and thinking about him when I went to bed at night. I guess I had a big crush on him. And I was pretty sure that when he saw me in that blue dress, he'd have a crush on me right away, too.

On the day of the play, all our families started arriving at The Grove theater a full hour before we got started. It didn't rain, and there wasn't even one of those noisy Nova Scotian winds that shake the trees and keep you from hearing the lines. My mother was hustling around backstage helping with clothes and makeup. Mostly she was fussing with my face and my first costume and telling me how pretty I looked. We had rigged up eight bedspreads, some torn and holey, some beautiful, depending on the fear or the pride of the mothers who lent them, and behind this strung-out curtain, we prepared ourselves for the two o'clock production. Henrietta was moving quietly about on the stage, straightening furniture, moving props, standing back to look at the effect. Later on, just before the curtain went up, or rather was drawn aside, she went off and sat down against a tree, where she'd have a good view of the performance, but where she'd be out of sight. If any of us needed anything, she could get it for us without the audience seeing what she was doing.

In the first part of the play, the nobleman ignores the beautiful peasant girl, who comes on dressed in rags but heavily made up and therefore beautiful. He is of course looking for a wife, but no one even thinks of her as a possible candidate. She does a lot of sighing and weeping, and Alphonse rides around on his horse (George Cruikshank) looking handsome and tragic. Harold did this very well. Still, I could hardly wait for the last scene in which I could get out of those rags and emerge as the radiant court butterfly. But I put all I had into this first scene, because when Alphonse turns down all the eligible and less beautiful women of the land and retires to a corner of the stage to brood (with George Cruikshank standing nearby, munching grass), Genevieve arrives on the scene to a roll of drums (our wooden spoon on Mrs. Eisner's pickling kettle). As Alphonse turns to look at her dazzling beauty, he recognizes her for what she is—not just a poor commoner, but a young woman of great charm and loveliness, worthy of his hand. At this point, she places her hand on her breast and does a deep and graceful curtsy. He stands up, bends to help her rise, and in a tender and significant gesture kisses her outstretched hand.

And that's exactly how we did it, right there on the foxberry patch, which looked like a rich green carpet with a red pattern, if you happened to have the kind of imagination to see it that way. I thought I would faint with the beauty of it all. Then the string of bedspreads was drawn across the scene, curtain hoops squeaking, and the applauding audience awaited the final scene.

I didn't waste any time getting into my other costume. Dressed in my blue gown, I peeked through the hole in Mrs. Powell's bedspread to assess the audience. I had not had the time to look until now, but Mama had dressed me first, and she had six other girls to get ready for the ball scene. The crowd outside was large. There must have been forty-five or fifty people of various sizes and ages, sitting on the cushions placed on top of the pine needles. The little kids were crawling and squirming around like they always do, and mothers were passing out pacifiers and bags of chips and jelly beans and suckers to keep them quiet during intermission. One little boy—Janet Morash's brother—was crying his head off, and I sure as fire hoped he'd stop all that racket before the curtain went up. While I watched all this, I looked over to the left, and saw three sailors coming through the woods. I knew them. They'd been to our house for supper a couple of times, but I never dreamt we'd be lucky enough to have the navy at our play. My big scene was going to be witnessed by more than just a bunch of parents and kids. There was even a little group of grade 12 boys in the back row.

We were almost ready to begin. Backstage, most of the makeup was done, and Mrs. Elliot was standing by the tree, making up Henrietta just for the heck of it. Henrietta had set up the stage and handed out the costumes, and she was putting in time like some of the rest of us. She just had on that old blue sweatshirt of hers and her dungarees, and it seemed to me that all that makeup was going to look pretty silly on someone who didn't have a costume on; but I didn't really care. If Henrietta wanted to make a fool of herself, it wasn't going to bother *me*.

In the last scene, all the courtiers and aristocrats are milling around in the ballroom, waiting for the nobleman to arrive with his betrothed.[6] The orchestra is playing Strauss waltzes (on Mrs. Corkum's portable wind-up gramophone) and you can see that everyone is itchy footed and dying to dance, but they have to wait around until Alphonse arrives with Genevieve. It is a moment full of suspense, and I had to do a lot of smart and fierce directing to get that bunch of kids to look happy and

---

6. **betrothed:** person engaged to be married.

excited and impatient all at the same time. But they did a really good
job that afternoon. You could see that they thought they actually were
lords and ladies and that it was a real live ball they had come to.

Suddenly there is a sound of trumpets (little Horace Miller's
Halloween horn) and Alphonse comes in, very slow and stately, with
Genevieve on his arm. She is shy, and enters with downcast eyes; but he
turns around, bows to her, and she raises her head with new pride and
confidence, lifting her arms to join him in the dance. We did all this
beautifully, if I do say so myself, and as I started to raise my arms, I
thought I would burst with joy and splendor of that moment.

As it turned out, burst is just about exactly what I did. The waltz
record was turned off during this intense scene, and there was total
silence on the stage and in the audience. As my arms reached shoulder
level, a sudden sound of ripping taffeta reached clear to the back of the
audience. (Joannie Sherman was sitting in the last row, and she told me
about it later.) I knew in one awful stupefying moment that my dress
had ripped up the back, the full length of that long zipper. I can
remember standing there on the stage with my arms half raised, unable
to think or feel anything beyond a paralyzed horror. After that day,
whenever I heard that someone was in a state of shock, I never had to
ask the meaning of that term. I knew. Joannie told me later that the
whole stageful of people looked like they had been turned to stone, and
that it really had been a scream to see.

Suddenly, as quiet and quick as a cat, Henrietta glided onstage. She
was draped in one of the classier bedspreads from the curtain, and no
one would have known that she wasn't supposed to be there. I don't
know how anyone as slow-moving as Henrietta could have done so
much fast thinking. But she did. She was carrying the very best
bedspread—a lovely blue woven one that exactly matched my dress.
She stopped in front of me, and lifting the spread with what I have to
admit was a lot of ceremony and grace, she placed it gravely over my
shoulders. Fastening it carefully with one of the large safety pins that
she always kept attached to her sweatshirt during performances, she
then moved backward two paces, and bowed first to me and then to
Harold, before moving slowly and with great dignity toward the exit.

Emerging from my shock with the kind of presence of mind for which I
was noted, I raised my arms and prepared to start the dance with

Alphonse. But Harold, eyes full of amazement, was staring at Henrietta as she floated off the stage. From the back of the audience, I could hear two long low whistles, followed by a deep male voice exclaiming, "Hubba, *hubba*!" to which I turned and bowed in graceful acknowledgment of what I felt to be a vulgar but nonetheless sincere tribute. The low voice, not familiar to me, spoke again. "Not *you*, pie-face!" he called, and then I saw three or four of the big boys from grade 12 leave the audience and run into the woods.

Somehow or other I got through that scene. Harold pulled his enchanted eyes back onstage, and the gramophone started the first few bars of "The Blue Danube" as we began to dance. Mercifully, the scene was short, and before long we were taking our curtain calls. "Stage manager! Stage manager!" shouted one of the sailors, and after a brief pause, old Henrietta came shyly forward, bedspread gone, dressed once more in her familiar blue sweatshirt and dungarees. The applause from the audience went on and on, and as we all bowed and curtsied, I stole a look at Henrietta. Slender, I thought, throat tight. Slender, not skinny anymore. All in an instant I saw everything, right in the midst of all that clapping and bowing. It was like one of those long complicated dreams that start and finish within the space of five minutes, just before you wake up in the morning. Henrietta was standing serenely, quietly. As the clapping continued, while the actors and actresses feverishly bobbed up and down to acknowledge the applause, she just once, ever so slightly, inclined her head, gazing at the audience out of her astonishing eyes— enormous, arresting, fringed now with long dark lashes. Mrs. Elliot's makeup job had made us all see what must have been there all the time—a strikingly beautiful face. But there was something else there now that was new. As I continued to bow and smile, the word came to me to describe that strange new thing. *Power*. Henrietta had power. And what's more, she had it without having to *do* a single thing. All she needs to do, I thought, is *be*. The terrible injustice of it all stabbed me. There I was, the lead role, the director, the brains and vigor of our twinship, and suddenly, after all my years in first place, it was she who had the power. Afterwards I looked at them—the boys, the sailors, *Harold*—as they gazed at her. All she was doing was sauntering round the stage picking up props. But they were watching, and I knew, with a stunning accuracy, that there would always be watchers now, wherever she might be, whatever she wore, regardless of what she would be doing. And I also knew in that moment, with the same sureness, that I would never have that kind of power, not ever.

The next day, Mama stationed herself at the telephone, receiving all the tributes that came pouring in. A few moments per call were given over to a brief recognition of my acting talents and to an uneasy amusement over the split dress. The rest of the time was spent in shouted discussion of Henrietta's startling and surprising beauty. I lay face downward on my bed and let the words hail down upon me. "Yes, indeed. *Yes.* I quite agree. Simply beautiful. And a real bolt from the blue. She quite astonished all of us. Although of course I recognized this quality in her all along. I've often sat and contemplated her lovely eyes, her milky skin, her delicate hands, and thought, 'Your time will come, my dear! Your time will come!'"

"Delicate hands!" I whispered fiercely into the mattress. "Bony! Bony!"

I suppose, in a way, that nothing changed too drastically for me after that play. I continued to lead groups, direct shows, spark activities with my ideas, my zeal. In school I did well in all my subjects, and was good at sports, too. Henrietta's grades were mediocre, and she never even tried out for teams or anything, while I was on the swim team, the baseball team, the basketball team. She still moved slowly, languidly,[7] as though her energy was in short supply, but there was a subtle difference in her that was hard to put your finger on. It wasn't as though she went around covered with all that highly flattering greasepaint that Mrs. Elliot had supplied. In fact, she didn't really start wearing makeup until she was fifteen or sixteen. Apparently she didn't need to. That one dramatic walk-on part with the blanket and the safety pin had done it all, although I'm sure I harbored a hope that we might return to the old Henrietta as soon as she washed her face. Even the sailors started coming to the house more often. They couldn't take her out, of course, or *do* anything with her. But they seemed to enjoy just looking at her, contemplating her. They would sit there on our big brown plush chesterfield[8] under the stern picture of Great-great-grandmother Logan

---

7. **languidly:** in a manner lacking force or vitality.
8. **chesterfield:** sofa.

in the big gold frame, smoking cigarette after cigarette, and watching Henrietta as she moved about with her infuriatingly slow, lazy grace, her grave confidence. Her serenity soothed and excited them, all at the same time. Boys from grades 9 and 10 hung around our backyard, our verandah, the nearest street corner. They weren't mean to me. They simply didn't know I was there, not really.

I didn't spend much time with Henrietta anymore, or boss her, or make her go to The Grove in the fog or try to scare her. I just wasn't all that crazy about having her around the entire time, with those eyes looking out at me from under those long lashes, quiet, mysterious, full of power. And of course you had to trip over boys if you so much as wanted to ask her what time it was. Every once in a while I'd try to figure out what the thing was that made her so different now; and then, one day, all of a sudden, I understood. We were down at the beach, and she was just sitting on a rock or something, arms slack and resting on her knees, in a position I had often seen over the years. And in that moment I knew. Everything else was the same—the drab white skin, the bony, yes, bony hands, the limp hair. But she had lost her waiting look. Henrietta didn't look as though she were waiting for anything at all anymore.

## Responding to the Story

1.  As you read the story, how did you react to the narrator, Juliette? Did you like her? Explain what things that she says and does contributed to your feelings about her. Be very specific.
2.  Juliette claims through most of the story to be her sister's "best friend." Did you believe her? Why or why not?
3.  How did you respond to these words late in the story: *"Power. Henrietta had power. And what's more, she had it without having to do a single thing. All she needs to do, I thought, is be. The terrible injustice of it all stabbed me."*
4.  Explain the story's title.

## Exploring the Author's Craft

"Waiting" is told from the **first-person point of view.** It uses a first person narrator, an "I" who in this case is a major character in the story. Such narrators often have a distinctive voice—that is, they clearly reveal their motivations and personalities through the things they say.

Sometimes, as in the case of Juliette, a first person narrator may reveal more of herself than she intends or even realizes. What do you learn about Juliette from each of the following?

a. Regarding her twin's value to the theatrical production, Juliette says, "She did a truly good job, and if it weren't for the fact that I can't stand conceited people, I probably would have told her so."

b. Describing her costume for the production, she remarks, "I had trouble getting into it because I was almost thirteen now and sort of big through the middle."

c. After ridiculing Henrietta's set design, which another player had just complimented, Juliette reports, "[E]veryone laughed. I always think that laughter is very important. It makes everyone happy right away, and is a good way to ease tensions."

## Writer's Workshop

1.  Write the first page or two of the story from Henrietta's point of view.

2.  Create your own first-person voice. Make it different from your own; in other words, this is not to be your "sincere, essay-writing voice" from school. You might decide to be conceited and arrogant, or unsure and reserved, or something else entirely. Then write five paragraphs introducing yourself. Be sure to maintain a consistent voice throughout.

## Alternate Media Response

Take any scene from this story that you think is particularly vivid, and draw both Juliette and Henrietta in it. Be sure that we can see their faces.

## Two Perspectives

### Michael T. Kaufman

Michael T. Kaufman is a former writer for *The New York Times*. Among other jobs there, he wrote the "About New York" column; he also was a correspondent in Poland. Presently, Kaufman is the editor of *Transition* magazine.

### Rita Dove

Rita Dove, one of our nation's finest poets, was born in 1952 in Akron, Ohio. She won the Pulitzer Prize in 1987 for *Thomas and Beulah*, a cycle of poems about her grandparents. Dove served as poet laureate of the United States and consultant in poetry at the Library of Congress from 1993 to 1995; she has also taught at various universities. Among her many poetry collections is *Grace Notes*, in which "Flash Cards" appears.

*There are times when our expectations of people get in the way of reality.*

# Of My Friend Hector and My Achilles Heel

Michael T. Kaufman

This story is about prejudice and stupidity. My own.

It begins in 1945 when I was a 7-year-old living on the fifth floor of a tenement walkup on 107th Street between Columbus and Manhattan Avenues in New York City. The block was almost entirely Irish and Italian, and I believe my family was the only Jewish one around.

One day a Spanish-speaking family moved into one of the four apartments on our landing. They were the first Puerto Ricans I had met. They had a son who was about my age named Hector, and the two of us became friends. We played with toy soldiers and I particularly remember how, using rubber bands and wood from orange crates, we made toy pistols that shot off little squares we cut from old linoleum.

We visited each other's home and I know at the time I liked Hector and I think he liked me. I may even have eaten my first avocado at his house.

About a year after we met, my family moved to another part of Manhattan's West Side and I did not see Hector again until I entered Booker T. Washington Junior High School as an 11-year-old.

The class I was in was called 7SP–1; the SP was for special. Earlier, I recall I had been in the IGC class, for "intellectually gifted children." The SP class was to complete the seventh, eighth and ninth grades in two years and almost all of us would then go to schools like Bronx Science, Stuyvesant or Music and Art, where admission was based on competitive exams. I knew I was in the SP class and the IGC class. I guess I also knew that other people were not.

Hector was not. He was in some other class, maybe even 7–2, the class that was held to be the next-brightest, or maybe 7–8. I remember I was happy to see him whenever we would meet, and sometimes we played punchball during lunch period. Mostly, of course, I stayed with my own classmates, with other Intellectually Gifted Children.

Sometimes children from other classes, those presumably not so intellectually gifted, would tease and taunt us. At such times I was particularly proud to have Hector as a friend. I assumed that he was tougher than I and my classmates and I guess I thought that if necessary he would come to my defense.

For high school, I went uptown to Bronx Science. Hector, I think, went downtown to Commerce. Sometimes I would see him in Riverside Park, where I played basketball and he worked out on the parallel bars. We would acknowledge each other, but by this time the conversations we held were perfunctory[1]—sports, families, weather.

After I finished college, I would see him around the neighborhood pushing a baby carriage. He was the first of my contemporaries to marry and to have a child.

A few years later, in the 60s, married and with children of my own, I was once more living on the West Side, working until late at night as a reporter. Some nights as I took the train home I would see Hector in the car. A few times we exchanged nods, but more often I would pretend that I didn't see him, and maybe he also pretended he didn't see me. Usually he would be wearing a knitted watch cap, and from that I deduced that he was probably working on the docks as a longshoreman.[2]

I remember quite distinctly how I would sit on the train and think about how strange and unfair fate had been with regard to the two of us who had once been playmates. Just because I had become an intellectually gifted adult or whatever and he had become a longshoreman or whatever, was that any reason for us to have been left with nothing to say to each other? I thought it was wrong and unfair, but I also thought that conversation would be a chore or a burden. That is pretty much what I thought about Hector, if I thought about him at all, until one Sunday in the mid-70s, when I read in the drama section of this newspaper that my childhood friend, Hector Elizondo, was replacing Peter Falk in the leading role in "The Prisoner of Second Avenue."

Since then, every time I have seen this versatile and acclaimed actor in movies or on television I have blushed for my assumptions. I have

1. **perfunctory:** done from force of habit; meaningless.
2. **longshoreman:** person who loads and unloads ships.

replayed the subway rides in my head and tried to fathom why my thoughts had led me where they did.

In retrospect it seems far more logical that the man I saw on the train, the man who had been my friend as a boy, was coming home from an Off Broadway theater or perhaps from a job as a waiter while taking acting classes. So why did I think he was a longshoreman? Was it just the cap? Could it be that his being Puerto Rican had something to do with it? Maybe that reinforced the stereotype I concocted, but it wasn't the root of it.

No, the foundation was laid when I was 11, when I was in SP–1 and he was not, when I was in the IGC class and he was not.

I have not seen him since I recognized how I had idiotically kept tracking him for years and decades after the school system had tracked both of us. I wonder now if my experience was that unusual, whether social categories conveyed and absorbed before puberty do not generally tend to linger beyond middle age. And I wonder, too, that if they affected the behavior of someone like myself who had been placed on the upper track, how much more damaging it must have been for someone consigned to the lower.

I have at times thought of calling him, but kept from doing it because how exactly does one apologize for thoughts that were never expressed? And there was still the problem of what to say. "What have you been up to for the last 40 years?" Or "Wow, was I wrong about you!" Or maybe just, "Want to come over and help me make a linoleum gun?"

# Flash Cards

**Rita Dove**

In math I was the whiz kid, keeper
of oranges and apples. *What you don't understand,*
*master,* my father said; the faster
I answered, the faster they came.

5   I could see one bud on the teacher's geranium,
one clear bee sputtering at the wet pane.
The tulip trees always dragged after heavy rain
so I tucked my head as my boots slapped home.

My father put up his feet after work
10   and relaxed with a highball and *The Life of Lincoln.*
After supper we drilled and I climbed the dark

before sleep, before a thin voice hissed
numbers as I spun on a wheel. I had to guess.
*Ten,* I kept saying, *I'm only ten.*

## Responding to the Selections

1. What kind of competition is going on in "Of My Friend Hector and My Achilles Heel"? in "Flash Cards"?
2. At one point Kaufman says, "I have blushed for my assumptions." What were those assumptions? Has the father in "Flash Cards" made similar unwarranted assumptions? Explain your ideas.
3. Look in a mythology book to find out what "Achilles heel" means and who Hector was. What was Kaufman's Achilles heel? Could the expression be applied to anyone in "Flash Cards"?
4. What ideas about education are suggested by these two works?

## Exploring the Authors' Craft

**Tone** in a piece of writing is the author's or narrator's attitude toward the subject matter. Though not all writing has a clearly defined tone, in many selections, or parts of selections, we may find tones of happiness, anger, humor, and so on.

1. What tone comes through in Kaufman's essay from the point where he reveals who Hector really is?
2. Define the tone in the last line of "Flash Cards."

## Writer's Workshop

"Of My Friend Hector and My Achilles Heel" deals with lowered expectations about someone. "Flash Cards" deals with expectations that are perhaps too high. Write your own creative work exemplifying the theme of unrealistic expectations and the impact those expectations can have.

## Richard Peck

Richard Peck is a prolific writer of poems, short stories, and novels, often directed at adolescents. His novels include *Are You in the House Alone?* and *Father Figure*, both of which were chosen as Best Books for Young Adults by the American Library Association.

Peck, a former teacher, was born in 1934 and presently lives in New York City. He often sits in coffee shops near schools to listen in on teenage conversation to help him create the conversation in his fiction.

*Is there any way to compete with a bully?*

# Priscilla and the Wimps

**L**isten, there was a time when you couldn't even go to the *rest room* around this school without a pass. And I'm not talking about those little pink tickets made out by some teacher. I'm talking about a pass that could cost anywhere up to a buck, sold by Monk Klutter.

Not that Mighty Monk ever touched money, not in public. The gang he ran, which ran the school for him, was his collection agency. They were Klutter's Kobras, a name spelled out in nailheads on six well-known black plastic windbreakers.

Monk's threads were more . . . subtle. A pile-lined suede battle jacket with lizard-skin flaps over tailored Levis and a pair of ostrich-skin boots, brassed-toed and suitable for kicking people around. One of his Kobras did nothing all day but walk a half step behind Monk, carrying a fitted bag with monk's gym shoes, a roll of rest-room passes, a cashbox, and a switchblade that Monk gave himself manicures with at lunch over at the Kobras' table.

Speaking of lunch, there were a few cases of advanced malnutrition among the newer kids. The ones who were a little slow in handing over a cut of their lunch money and were therefore barred from the cafeteria. Monk ran a tight ship.

I admit it. I'm five foot five, and when the Kobras slithered by, with or without Monk, I shrank. And I admit this, too: I paid up on a regular basis. And I might add: so would you.

This school was old Monk's Garden of Eden. Unfortunately for him, there was a serpent in it. The reason Monk didn't recognize trouble when it was staring him in the face is that the serpent in the Kobras' Eden was a girl.

Practically every guy in school could show you his scars. Fang marks from Kobras, you might say. And they were all highly visible in the shower room: lumps, lacerations, blue bruises, you name it. But girls usually got off with a warning.

Except there was this one girl named Priscilla Roseberry. Picture a girl named Priscilla Roseberry, and you'll be light years off. Priscilla was, hands down, the largest student in our particular institution of learning. I'm not talking fat. I'm talking big. Even beautiful, in a bionic way. Priscilla wasn't inclined toward organized crime. Otherwise, she could have put together a gang that would turn Klutter's Kobras into garter snakes.

Priscilla was basically a loner except she had one friend. A little guy named Melvin Detweiler. You talk about The Odd Couple. Melvin's one of the smallest guys above midget status ever seen. A really nice guy, but, you know—little. They even had lockers next to each other, in the same bank as mine. I don't know what they had going. I'm not saying this was a romance. After all, people deserve their privacy.

Priscilla was sort of above everything, if you'll pardon a pun. And very calm, as only the very big can be. If there was anybody who didn't notice Klutter's Kobras, it was Priscilla.

Until one winter day after school when we were all grabbing our coats out of our lockers. And hurrying, since Klutter's Kobras made sweeps of the halls for after-school shakedowns.

Anyway, up to Melvin's locker swaggers one of the Kobras. Never mind his name. Gang members don't need names. They've got group identity. He reaches down and grabs little Melvin by the neck and slams his head against his locker door. The sound of skull against steel rippled all the way down the locker row, speeding the crowds on their way.

"Okay, let's see your pass," snarls the Kobra.

"A pass for what this time?" Melvin asks, probably still dazed.

"Let's call it a pass for very short people," says the Kobra, "a dwarf tax." He wheezes a little Kobra chuckle at his own wittiness. And already he's reaching for Melvin's wallet with the hand that isn't circling Melvin's windpipe. All this time, of course, Melvin and the Kobra are standing in Priscilla's big shadow.

She's taking her time shoving her books into her locker and pulling on a very large-size coat. Then, quicker than the eye, she brings the side of her enormous hand down in a chop that breaks the Kobra's hold on Melvin's throat. You could hear a pin drop in that hallway. Nobody's ever laid a finger on a Kobra, let alone a hand the size of Priscilla's.

Then Priscilla, who hardly ever says anything to anybody except to Melvin, says to the Kobra, "Who's your leader, wimp?"

This practically blows the Kobra away. First he's chopped by a girl, and now she's acting like she doesn't know Monk Klutter, the Head Honcho of the World. He's so amazed, he tells her. "Monk Klutter."

"Never heard of him," Priscilla mentions. "Send him to see me." The Kobra just backs away from her like the whole situation is too big for him, which it is.

Pretty soon Monk himself slides up. He jerks his head once, and his Kobras slither off down the hall. He's going to handle this interesting case personally. "Who is it around here doesn't know Monk Klutter?"

He's standing inches from Priscilla, but since he'd have to look up at her, he doesn't. "Never heard of him," says Priscilla.

Monk's not happy with this answer, but by now he's spotted Melvin, who's grown smaller in spite of himself. Monk breaks his own rule by reaching for Melvin with his own hands. "Kid," he says, "you're going to have to educate your girl friend."

His hands never quite make it to Melvin. In a move of pure poetry Priscilla has Monk in hammerlock. His neck's popping like gunfire, and his head's bowed under the immense weight of her forearm. His suede jacket's peeling back, showing pile.

Priscilla's behind him in another easy motion. And with a single mighty thrust forward, frog-marches Monk into her own locker. It's incredible. His ostrich-skin boots click once in the air. And suddenly he's gone, neatly wedged into the locker, a perfect fit. Priscilla bangs the door shut, twirls the lock, and strolls out of school. Melvin goes with her, of course, trotting along below her shoulder. The last stragglers leave quietly.

Well, this is where fate, an even bigger force than Priscilla, steps in. It snows all that night, a blizzard. The whole town ices up. And school closes for a week.

---

## Responding to the Story

1. Are the bullies in this story like the bullies you've known? Explain.
2. The opening paragraphs of the story suggest that a serious situation will be the focus. Where did you begin to realize that the story was going to be humorous?

## Exploring the Author's Craft

1. One of the key ingredients of all fiction is effective characterization. Ideally, each character in a work is distinct from all the other characters. Describe the uniqueness of each of the following characters. If you can, find sentences in the story that you think clearly define each one.
   a. Monk Klutter
   b. Priscilla Roseberry
   c. Melvin Detweiler
2. A **tall tale** takes a larger-than-life, almost superhuman character, puts him or her in a situation where impossible tasks must be performed, and creates a resolution that is unbelievable but a lot of fun. Is "Priscilla and the Wimps" a tall tale? Explain your answer.

## Writer's Workshop

Write your own tall tale based on a school setting and situation.

## Alternate Media Response

What would happen if the parts in this story were cast using well-known TV and movie actors? Who would play the part of each main character? Write a cast list for a production of "Priscilla and the Wimps." Explain why each actor you choose is appropriate for the role.

## Robin F. Brancato

Robin F. Brancato recalls that several moves during her childhood caused her to feel sorry for herself and to "try to bury that sorrow in writing and in reading books." Born in 1936, Brancato has been an English teacher as well as a writer. She notes, "My students have been the major influences on my writing, especially in such novels as *Winning, Come Alive at 505,* and *Uneasy Money.*"

Of "Fourth of July" Brancato says, "In real life, one of my sons had reason to feel revengeful when a so-called friend stole money from him. I wanted to create a fictional teenager, something like my son, and I wanted to put him in the position of having the opportunity to get revenge. As a high school teacher I see young people facing such dilemmas all the time. Is it possible to back off and still save face? Is violence ever the answer? What price may the avenger have to pay, and will it be worth it? The teacher in me compels me to ask questions, and these are the ones that interested me in 'Fourth of July.'"

*Given the opportunity, would you go for revenge?*

# Fourth of July

Chuck draws the squeegee carefully across the windshield and lets it sink back into the bucket of water at his feet. "Check the oil, sir?" he asks.

"No, thanks."

"That'll be fifteen dollars even, then."

The customer hands him the money and starts up the engine.

"Happy Fourth of July," Chuck calls, standing there for a moment, stretching the muscles of his arms, as the car pulls away from the pump. Nice night, he thinks. Crickets singing behind the station. Drum and bugle corps warming up in the distance. Kids setting off caps somewhere down the street. Seventy-four degrees, Chuck sees by the thermometer mounted on the side of the oilcan rack. Warm enough for a midnight dip in Kate's pool maybe, after the fireworks. If he gets out of here on time, that is.

"Chuck?"

"Coming." He turns toward the white tile building—the station where's he's worked for two summers now. Could be worse, he decides, glancing up at the TUNE UP HERE sign and at the red, white, and blue banners flapping over his head. He could be filing papers in an office, or have no job at all. Next summer, with high school behind him, he'll try for something else.

"Chuck?"

He can see Kate, sitting on the desk in the office part of the station, her profile so excellent in the neon glow. Freshly washed hair, pushed back behind her ears. Graceful, like a dancer, especially compared to Bobby-the-Hulk, who's tilting back on the station's one beat-up chair.

"Think we should go on, Chuck?" Kate is framed in the doorway now. "Should Bobby and I pick up Eileen and get a good place to sit, and you'll meet us later?"

Chuck pauses just outside the door, by the potted geraniums. "Yeah, you'd better, in a couple of minutes," he says reluctantly. "I can't get out of here until ten at the earliest." Squeezing Kate's arm as he passes, he opens the cash register and puts in the bills. "Vic *said* something, you know, the last time he came by and saw I had company."

"Said something?" Bobby rocks forward heavily. "You mean Big Boss Victor gave you flak because of us?"

Chuck closes the register. "Says he doesn't want the place to look like a hangout." He smiles. "Don't worry. All you have to do is get off your butt and buy a quart of oil if he comes around."

"I couldn't if I wanted to." Bobby sticks his hands in the pockets of his painter's pants. "Spent my last couple of bucks until payday on these." With a flourish he pulls out several little red cylinders and holds them up by their fuses. "M–80s. I got more in my car. Bottle rockets, too, and some other junk. I'm putting on my own show when the firemen finish theirs tonight."

"Oh, but the fireworks in the park are so nice," Kate says. "*Those* things . . ." She makes a face.

"Where'd you get' em?" Chuck asks.

Bobby's chair creaks. "My sister's boyfriend brought them up from down South. The best you can get. Each M–80 equals one-fifth stick of dynamite." He looks at Chuck. "Want to go halves with me?"

"Nope, I got better things to do with my money."

Bobby, rocking back and forth, balances the M-80s on his stomach. "You mean you're hurting as bad as I am?"

"Let's say she's making me watch the bucks." Straightening the pile of road maps by the register, Chuck nods toward Kate. "She's being a good influence, you know?"

"Sounds pretty boring to me. Did she get you to quit smoking yet?"

"Not yet. In the fall I'm going to quit."

Bobby, sighing, makes the firecrackers dance on his stomach. "What are you guys saving up for—*a down payment on a house?*"

Kate's laugh rings out.

"Hell, no, man." Chuck smiles. "I'm still thinking cars. *You* put a car first until you got one—you should know."

"How much more do you need?"

"A lot. What did I figure yesterday, Kate? Another five hundred?"

"About that."

Bobby, picking up the M–80s by their fuses, rotates them gently. "Five hundred's a lot." He glances up. "Think you'll ever get back what Sager took from you?"

Chuck turns abruptly. "Don't even bring that up, okay? I go crazy when I hear his name. *No.* I told you before, I'm not getting anything back. The judge invited Sager to court and slapped his hands, that's all."

"I don't get it." Bobby shifts in the chair. "Can't they make Sager's mother pay?"

"I don't know if they can, but the point is, they *didn't.*" Chuck glances out as a car takes a shortcut through the station. "I did all I could," he goes on. "Kate'll tell you how much time it took. When I heard Sager was finally going to court a couple of months ago, I wrote a letter to the judge."

"It was a really good letter," Kate says.

"What'd you say?" Bobby slips the M-80s under his T-shirt.

"Hell, I told him the whole story. 'Dear Judge.'" Chuck cracks his knuckles. "'This is about something that happened to me almost a year ago. How would *you* feel if a guy on your street that you never liked but always tried to be decent to, came over to your house one night when you were home alone, and you're rapping with him, and you mention you just got your last two weeks' pay, and while you're getting him a Coke he sneaks up to your bedroom and helps himself to your two hundred bucks?'"

A chair spoke pops as Bobby sits up. "The judge knew Sager did it, right? He knew the cops got his fingerprints off your bureau?"

"Everybody knows Sager did it," Chuck says. "They've had his prints on file for three years. They had him in court that day on five other charges besides mine!"

"What'd you want the judge to do with him?"

"Have him make restitution. 'The only way I'll be satisfied,' I told the judge, 'is if the court makes him pay me back—me and the other people he stole from.'"

"No dice, though, huh?" Bobby sniffs. "Some judge."

Chuck feels himself heating up. "Yeah, losing two hundred bucks is nothing to those guys."

"Wait a second." Kate's hand is on his arm. "That's probably not true. Maybe the judge thinks giving him one more chance will straighten him out. You know what they say about prisons, how awful they are."

"Oh, man, not *this* again!" Chucks snaps his eyes shut. "Poor Sager, his father died when he was a kid, so we got to let him get away with everything! Come off it, Kate." He walks away from her, toward the tire rack. "Lots of guys have no father, and they don't all become crooks— crooks who specialize in ripping off *friends*." Chuck bangs his elbow against the rack. "What the hell, what do *you* know? If you were a guy you'd understand."

Kate shakes her head wearily. "That has nothing to do with it. I can't stand Jack Sager, you know that. And I know how you worked for that money." She gathers her hair up in one hand. "It's just that—I don't think it's so dumb to think that people can change. *You've* changed since I met you. You're much saner. Isn't that true?"

Chuck yanks at his T-shirt. "Yes . . . *no*! Who's talking about me, anyway?"

"Oh, boy," Bobby snorts. "Better watch yourself, man. Stick with this chick and you'll get to be pope—Pope Chuck the First. Listen," he says, rising from the chair, "I got one thing to tell you, and then her and me'll get moving. I saw Sager today. He's back in town from wherever his mother shipped him off to."

Kate rolls her eyes.

"Where?" Chuck asks. "Where'd you see him?"

"Cruising the park this afternoon. In a practically new green Buick."

"*His?*"

"He said it was. Who knows?"

"You talked to him?"

"A little. Not about your money."

"He denies it," Chuck says angrily. "He swore to the cops that his fingerprints were in my room because I took him up there to smoke a joint."

Bobby slaps the cigarette machine. "Look, you want advice? Forget the judge. Even things up on your own, man. Punch him out if you see him, or slit his tires. Rip off two hundred bucks' worth of stuff from his old lady. She's not poor."

Kate groans.

Bobby, pulling car keys from his pocket, nudges her playfully. "Just kidding, Katie. Katie doesn't go for that stuff. Come on, let's pick up Eileen."

Kate pauses in the doorway as Bobby squeezes past her. "Chuck?"

"Yeah?" He loves her hair in the yellow neon light. He loves that serious expression of hers.

"You'll stay away from Jack, won't you?"

"Do I look like I'm about to get up a posse?"

Kate, inching closer, reaches for his hand. "I mean, if you see him at the park or somewhere, you won't get involved with him? Don't think about the money, Chuck. You're doing so well—"

"The money's only part of it."

"I know, but *avoid* him—promise?"

Pulling her toward him, he feels her softness and strength.

"You don't have to prove anything," Kate says.

"Don't *worry*." He lets his hands slide down her arms. "Where'll I see you—on the hill where we sat last time?"

She nods. "I brought a blanket. It's a long walk to the park from here. I hope you can get there before it's over."

"I'll make it as soon as I can." Hugging her again, he kisses her hard.

"Hey!" Bobby, by the pumps, pounds on a five-gallon can. "This isn't good-bye forever, you guys. Come on, Katie, time's up!"

Chuck watches them cross the lot and climb into Bobby's Chevy. "See you later," he calls as they drive away. Then, drifting back to the office, he lights a cigarette with his Bic. Slow night. Might as well start cleaning up the place. He stoops to pick up a paper cup, a gum wrapper—what's that thing? Stamping out his cigarette, he scoops up the red cylinder, one of Bobby's stray toys. Then, distracted by a customer driving up to the island, he drops the M–80 into his pocket. "Evening, sir," he says. "Would you like me to fill it up?"

Chuck glances at the clock. Two minutes to ten. He hears the far-off *boom* of drums now. There's a low whistling sound, too, and when he looks up he sees an orange burst. They've started the aerial fireworks. As soon as he closes up, he can take off for the park. First, haul down the green flag and lock up the oilcan rack. Don't trip over the water bucket. Bring in the credit card machine. Open the safe and put in the cash. Make sure the safe is closed tight. What else? Fix the spoke on the broken chair, so Vic won't take a fit.

Getting a pad and pencil from the desk drawer, Chuck goes out and records the final readings on the pumps. A long, low whistle sounds again. He watches with pleasure as a tiny orange ball rises and explodes into a flower in the sky. Snakelike things wriggle from its center, and Chuck is so caught up that he isn't aware of the green Buick until it comes to a stop on the near side of the pump.

The sound of rock radio pours through the car's open windows. Chuck feels his whole body clenching.

"Hey!" Jack Sager's long, narrow face is eerie in the fluorescent light.

Chuck, clearing his throat, doesn't move.

"Still on the job, huh?" Sager, a faint smile on his lips, turns off the engine and adjusts his handkerchief headband. "How's it going?"

The core of heat rising in Chuck lodges in his throat.

Sager dangles one sinewy arm out the window. A shock of straight dark hair, free of the headband, falls in his eyes. "You open for business or what?"

"*Closing*," Chuck says. He clears his throat again.

"But not actually *closed*, right? Give me eight bucks' worth." Sager digs into his pocket.

Chuck still doesn't move. A chain of memories set off by Sager's grin fixes him to the spot: Sager handing him a soapsuds milkshake; Sager forging his name on a dirty note to a girl; Sager looking over his shoulder in the biology exam . . . All of this he shrugged off because Sager was just kidding around, right? Or else—Chuck feels himself sweating—or else because of fear that the guy, when crossed, might do even worse. How come whenever his parents warned him about Sager he'd get mad, not at Sager but at *them*? No more letting things go by. "I'm closed," Chuck says. "I already wrote down the totals."

"Hey, have a heart." Sager's face bursts into a smile. "I'm running on empty," he says. "You know that song?"

"Yeah," Chuck answers. "Walk home and stick it up your tape deck."

Sager laughs. "I'm not kidding around, man. I glided in here on my last drop."

"Good. Sit here all night."

Sager, his smile fading, opens the car door and sets one foot on the ground. "What's the problem? You still think I took your money?"

"I know you did." Sweat is trickling down Chuck's armpits.

Sager shakes his head "You got a overactive imagination," he says, "you and the cops, both. You're lucky they didn't find your stash in your bureau that night."

Chuck clenches his hands. "Your crooked lawyer's the only one who'd believe that ridiculous story."

Sager's other foot drops to the ground. "Give me the gas, man, or I help myself. You don't want to be eight bucks short, do you?"

Chuck's eyes dart from Sager's face to the five-gallon can by the pump. Eight bucks' worth. He lifts the can—it's empty. Go ahead, why not? Steadying his voice, he says, "Cool it, Sager. I'll give it to you. Get in your car and fork over the money. See the sign? 'Exact change after nine P.M.' *Up front*, that means."

"What's the matter," Sager smirks, "you guys don't trust your customers?" Sitting back in the seat, he pulls out a five and three ones.

Chuck stuffs the money in his pocket. Then as Sager slams the car door and starts fiddling with the radio, Chuck lifts the hose off the pump. Heavy-metal rock drifts through the open windows of the Buick. Partly hidden by the pump, Chuck keeps both eyes on Sager. In his right hand is the hose. In his left, the empty can. Letting the gas flow, Chuck catches it in the can that is on the ground under the tank. Perfect.

Sager glances over his shoulder at the pump's spinning numbers, then turns up the radio and slouches in the seat, his head resting on the seatback. Numbers spin—two dollars, three dollars, four—

Sager is singing along with the radio now, tapping rhythms on the wheel. Chuck stares in fascination as the gas level rises in the can. When it reaches the top, he puts the hose on the ground and lets a little more run out. And when the meter reads $8.00, he cuts the flow and puts the hose back on the pump. "Okay, Sager, get going."

Sager doesn't hear him at first because the music is so loud. Chuck stands there with his hands in his pockets. "I'm in a hurry, get going!"

The *thump-thump* of the radio fades and Sager's head pops out the window. "Trying to get rid of me? What kind of a attitude is that?"

Chuck, glaring in the window, feels his fingers touch something in his pocket.

Sager grins. "Still holding a grudge, huh? How do you know one of your other friends didn't rip you off?"

Chuck's hand closes over the fuse, the cardboard shell.

"Maybe Bobby," Sager insists. "He needed money to buy his car then."

Chuck's other hand touches his lighter.

Sager turns up the radio again. "Why not let bygones be bygones, man? I'm going back to Texas tomorrow for good. Did you say you were in a hurry? How about if I drop you somewhere?"

"Okay," Chuck says hoarsely. His heart pounds along with the radio. "Wait'll I—shut these off."

Easing behind the pumps, he flicks his lighter and a bright flame leaps upward. He draws the cylinder toward it, but the fuse doesn't catch. His hands are shaking so bad that the M-80 wobbles. His ears are ringing, as if people are shouting at him. Try again! And make it quick, before Sager notices the gas gauge still on empty. He flicks again. This time the fuse catches and a red flame creeps down.

In a daze Chuck sweeps around the car, almost tripping over the water bucket. He measures the distance to the open back window of the Buick, knowing he'll never get another chance like this. Throw it!

"What's taking so long?"

Chuck juggles the thing in one hand. Gas fumes are floating up—get rid of it! Gas is trickling toward him from under the car. The fuse is almost gone. Get rid of it now!

He does. With a sudden whirling motion he tosses it into the bucket of water by the pump. Do they explode in water? Please, no.

"Y'almost ready?" Sager calls.

Chuck's eyes are shut. When he opens them, the bucket is still there. He stares at it to make sure. "Go on without me, Sager," he says hoarsely, stepping out from behind the pumps. "I just remembered my dad's picking me up."

"Yeah? When?"

"Any minute. This'll be him, probably." Shielding his eyes, he nods at a car stopping for the light on the corner.

"Your old man?"

"Yeah, it should be. See you around, Sager," Chuck says.

Sager, looking over his shoulder, revs the engine noisily. "Tell him hello from me." He smirks as the car bucks forward.

"I will," Chuck says, slapping the Buick as if to push it off.

Sager leans out the window. "Hope you catch the right guy one of these days!" Burning rubber, he digs out.

Chuck watches the Buick's taillights fade. As the car that has been waiting at the light starts up and goes on, Chuck quickly empties the water bucket in the bushes, puts the eight dollars in the safe, turns off the lights, and locks the station door. Then, with the rumble of fireworks in his ears, he jogs to meet Kate, taking surprisingly little satisfaction from the thought that very soon Sager may be stalled out on a dark, lonely road.

## Responding to the Story

1. Does Chuck do the right thing in taking the revenge he did? Why or why not?
2. Why do you think Chuck takes "surprisingly little satisfaction from the thought that very soon Sager may be stalled out on a dark, lonely road"?

## Exploring the Author's Craft

Every piece of fiction has a **plot**, a series of actions and events that move the story forward. In this story, the author had to think out a great many plot details—how to bring Chuck and Sager together again, for example, and what Chuck would do with the M-80.

1. Did you like the plot planning that the author did? What, if anything, would you have changed, and why?
2. List at least five key plot steps in this story.

## Writer's Workshop

This is a tough sort of story, involving stealing, fury, revenge, and the threat of violence. A gas station and a car play a big role. The story may hit a raw nerve with you if you look for "real things" in your reading.

Write a real-life story of your own using many of the same elements found in "Fourth of July." Clearly think out the steps in the plot that will move the story forward.

## Madeleine H. Blais

Madeleine H. Blais wrote a slightly longer version of this piece for *The New York Times Magazine*. It was later expanded into a book with the same title. Blais, who was born in 1947, has worked as an associate professor of journalism at the University of Massachusetts and has written other nonfiction works.

*How does it feel to be one step away from a championship?*

# In These Girls, Hope Is a Muscle: A Season in the Life of the Amherst Hurricanes

The voice of the coach rises above the din of shuffling footsteps, loud greetings, the slamming of metal, the thud of books. "Listen up. I want you to check right now. Do you have your uniforms? Your shoes and your socks? Do you have any other items of clothing that might be needed?"

Coach Ron Moyer believes it's possible to pack abstractions along with one's gear, intangibles[1] like "intensity" and "game face" and "consistency" and "defense." As the members of the Amherst Regional High School girls' basketball team prepare to board the Hoop Phi Express on their way to the Centrum in Worcester, more than an hour away from the Massachusetts state championship, he tells them, "Today, I want you to pack your courage."

The team is 23–1 going into this game, losing only to Agawam, which, like the Haverhill team they are facing this evening, has some real height. Haverhill, known for aggressive ball, nothing dirty but just

---

1. **intangibles:** things that can't actually be touched.

short of it, has two girls over six feet nicknamed Twin Towers. Moyer has prepped his team with a couple of specialized plays, the Murphy and the Shoelace, and he tells them: "Expect to play a little football." Amherst girls have a reputation for being afraid to throw their elbows, but this year they have learned to take the words "finesse team"[2] as an insult. Although Coach has been careful to avoid saying "state championship" to goad his team, last fall he did tell one aging gym rat in town, "I have the two best guards in the state and probably the nation, but it all depends on the girls up front. There's an old saying—'Guards win games, but forwards win championships.' We'll have to see."

At 6 foot 6, Moyer looms over his players. With a thick cap of graying brown hair and bangs that flop down over his forehead, he resembles a grizzly bear on spindly legs. The girls are more like colts. For Moyer, turning them into a team has nothing to do with breaking their spirit and everything to do with harnessing it.

As Jen Pariseau listens to Coach before leaving for Worcester, her legs can't stop twitching. One of the six seniors on the team playing high-school hoop together for the last time, she has thick, dark eyebrows and long, lanky limbs. For her, tonight's game is the perfect revenge, not just against Haverhill but also against some of the rebuffs she suffered as an athlete on the way up. For three years, she played on one of Amherst's Little League teams, the Red Sox. She was pitcher, shortstop and first baseman. When it was time to choose the all-star league, she was told her bunts were not up to par.

Jen's teammates are just as hyped up. Half of them are giving the other half piggybacks. There are lots of hand-slapping and nudges. They swirl around one another, everyone making a private point of touching Jamila Wideman, Jen's co-captain, as if one dark-haired, brown-eyed girl could transmit the power of her playing to all the others. Jamila is an all-America, recipient of more than 150 offers of athletic scholarships. On the court, the strong bones on her face are like a flag demanding to be heeded; she is a study in quickness and confidence, the ball becoming a part of her body. Her nickname is Predator.

Jen Pariseau is two-time all-Western Mass, and together the two guards delighted fans all season with the way they delivered the ball to

---

2. "finesse team": team that relies on quickness and skill rather than brute force.

each other, sometimes in a dipsy doo behind the back or between the legs, often in an open shot. JennyandJamila. In Amherst, it's one word.

Coach pauses. He looks as though he is about to rebuke the girls for all the squirming, but he shrugs and gives a big smile. "Let's go." Then, perhaps more to himself than to them: "While we're still young."

Shortly after 5 in the evening, the sky is thick and gray and hooded, the cloud cover a welcome hedge against what has been a bitter New England winter. The bus the girls board is different from the usual.

"Hooked up and smooth," says Jen Pariseau, admiring the special features, including upholstered seats, a toilet, four television sets and a VCR mounted on the ceiling—a definite step up from the yellow tin cans they have taken to every other game. There are some cheerleaders on the bus as well as Tricia Lea, an assistant coach with her own high-school memories about what it was like to go up against those Hillies from Haverhill in their brown and yellow uniforms with the short shorts. "Haverhill. I don't know what they eat up there, but they can be slightly ruthless. Sportsmanship does not run very deep in that town."

A few years back, Coach had trouble convincing players and their families of the seriousness of the commitment to girls' basketball. JennyandJamila remember playing in varsity games five and six years ago when the gym would be empty of spectators except for their parents and maybe a few lost souls who had missed the late bus. Coach remembers girls who would cut practice to go to their boyfriends' games, and once during the playoffs, a team captain left to go on a school-sponsored cultural exchange for three weeks in the former Soviet Union. As far as he's concerned, the current policy could not be clearer: You want cultural exchange? You can have it with Hamp [archrival Northampton].

Tonight, Amherst is sending three "pep" buses to the game, unprecedented support for an athletic event, boys' or girls'. Amherst is a place that tends to prize thought over action, tofu over toughness.[3] It prefers to honor the work of the individual dedicated to a life of monastic scholarship rather than some noisy group effort. But this

---

3. **tofu over toughness:** preferring things associated with the niceties of life rather than with the nitty-gritty.

season, there were sellout crowds. There was even that ultimate badge: a wary cop on the premises for the first time in the history of a girls' event.

To look at the six seniors on the team, who all appear to be lit from within, one would assume that their lives have been seamless journeys. In fact, as Jen Pariseau puts it, she does not come from a "Dan Quayle kind of family"—and neither do most of the others.

Whatever sadness or disruption they've been dealt, an opposite force follows them onto the court. JennyandJamila have not gone it alone; they have had Kathleen's strong right hand, an almost irresistible force heading toward the basket. She never wastes a motion: the ball is in her hands one second, then quietly dropping through the hoop the next, without dramatics, almost like an afterthought. There's Kristin. Her flushed cheeks are not a sign of exhaustion but of some private fury. When the ball comes curling out of the basket, more often that not it is Kristin who has pushed and shoved her way to the prize.

The only underclass starter, Emily Shore, is so serious about her chance to play with the famous JennyandJamila that she spent the bulk of her summer lifting weights and battling in pickup games on Amherst's cracked and weather-ravaged outdoor courts with a succession of skeptical and then grudgingly appreciative young men.

They have become what every opponent fears most: a team with a mission.

As good as it gets. That is, of course, the exact sentiment the girls feel toward their fancy bus.

"Fasten your seat belts," says Coach. "Beverage service will commence shortly after takeoff. There'll be turbulence coming to Haverhill when the Hurricanes hit Worcester." Then he announces the people to whom he would like them to dedicate the entire season. "And that's to the 140 girls who are now playing youth basketball in Amherst for the first time this year."

Jen Pariseau says she wants to read a letter from Diane Stanton, the mother of Chris Stanton, the star of the boys' basketball team.

"Jenny and Jamila," the letter began. Diane Stanton said she was addressing them because she knew them best, but the letter was for the whole team. "Your existence as a team represents a lot of things to a lot of women like me. . . . As a young girl I remember standing outside the Little League fence and watching the boys and knowing that I could hit and catch better than at least a third of them. When our high-school intramural field hockey team and softball team asked for leagues, we were told flatly—NO, because there was no money. . . . When this group of girl athletes got together to form an intramural basketball team, we were subjected to ridicule and anger from some of the student body. . . . I lost courage, I'm embarrassed to admit, in my junior year and would no longer play intramural sports. Part of it was a protest against the failure of my school . . . to recognize that we needed to play as much as boys. I know the struggle."

Coach gives the driver a signal and the vehicle starts to roll.

A police car just ahead suddenly activates its lights and in a slow ceremony leads the vehicle to the corner of Main and Triangle Streets, where another officer has been summoned to stop traffic. Coach is beaming and silently thanks his old pal, Capt. Charlie Sherpa, over in the Police Department for coming through. In addition to being a guidance counselor, Moyer has been the girls' coach off and on since 1961, a task he enjoys because unlike with boys, whose arrogance and confidence often have to be eroded before he can get the team to work, this is all constructive. The way to build a girls' team is to build their individual self-confidence.

The bus heads down Main (a street that is most famous for being the site of the house where Emily Dickinson was born, where she lived, died and wrote her poetry) to the corner of northeast, where they get to run a red light, turning in front of Fort River Elementary School, then heading out to Route 9, where the escort lasts all the way to the town line. In an instant, the sign that says "Entering Pelham" appears, and in another instant a new one looms ahead that says "Entering Belchertown."

The girls watch the film they had chosen unanimously to pump them for the game—"A League of Their Own."[4] The six seniors are lost in their own thoughts.

Kim Warner knows her mother, who works in personnel at the University of Massachusetts, will be at the game, plus her two sisters, plus her boyfriend's family. Her father lives in Florida, and although she sends him news accounts of all the games, he has never seen her play.

---

4. **A League of Their Own:** 1992 film about an all-woman baseball team and their efforts to succeed.

She hasn't seen him since the 10th grade. She plans to go to Westfield State and major in early childhood education. On the way to the game, Kim writes a fantasy letter in her head: "Dear Dad, At long last a lot of hard work paid off."

Patri Abad's mother, a bilingual teacher, has to be at work, and although Patri will miss her, she knows she can count on a large cheering section of friends. She almost didn't get to play this year. During her junior year, she had moved to Chicago with her mother and her new stepfather. Patri, who is Cuban on her father's side and Puerto Rican on her mother's, prayed incessantly to the Virgin. She received constant mail from teammates like Lucia Maraniss, back when Lucia was a gushing eighth grader; "Patri, I will always remember you as one of the wisest, most caring and compassionate people I've ever met. I'm going to miss you very, very, very, very, very, very, very, very, very, very, very, very, very, very much."

Whether it was divine intercession or that 14th "very " from Lucia, the resolve of Patri's mother to stay in Chicago eventually vanished. They returned to the Happy Valley, as Amherst is called, and Patri could finish her senior year as a member of the Hurricanes. She has been accepted at Drew, Clark and the University of Massachusetts, pre-med.

Kristin Marvin, also known as Jolly, Jolly Green and Grace (her teammates have misinterpreted her tenacity as clumsiness), is going to Holy Cross College, pre-med. She likes medicine because it has a strong element of knowability. Her parents were divorced when she was young and she lived with a lot of uncertainty. Her mother has since married a builder whose first wife married Kristin's father, who works in Connecticut and often rushes to the games after work in his business suit. The marital realignment has created a circumstance in which the daughter of her stepfather and stepmother is Kristin's double stepsister.

Coach calls Kathleen Poe his silent assassin—the girl with two distinct personalities. The demure senior with the high grades, with applications at Williams, Haverford, Duke and Dartmouth, is Kathleen; the girl on the court is her ferocious twin, Skippy. He concocted the dichotomy[5] because when Kathleen first started playing she said "Excuse me" all the time and would pause to pick her opponents up off the floor. She wants

---

**5. dichotomy:** division of a whole into two distinctly different or contradictory parts.

to be like Jamila: someone you don't want to meet on the court but who will be a good friend off it.

Jamila plans to study law and African-American studies at Stanford. Like her mother, Judy Wideman, who is in her second year of law school, she hopes to be a defense attorney. As a child of mixed races, she has told interviewers she identifies not with being black or white but with being herself. Still, her bedroom has pictures of Winnie Mandela, Jesse Jackson, and the children of Soweto.[6] After the riot in Los Angeles, she wrote several poems that reflected her feelings.

In "Black," she wrote:

*I walk the tightrope between the fires*
*Does anyone know where I fall through?*
*Their forked daggers of rage reflect my eye*
*Their physical destruction passes me by*
*Why does the fire call me?*

Jen is known locally as the best thing that ever happened to Pelham, which is that little twinge on the highway on Route 9. Since Jen was 2 and her brother, Chris, was 4, they have lived with their father, who is a manager of reservoirs and waste treatment in Amherst. She is planning to play ball for Dartmouth and to major in engineering. She turned down Princeton, especially after the recruiter, who made a home visit, would not let her father, who has a stutter, talk.

The door to her room is plastered with Nike inspirational ads. She calls the wall above her bed her "strong women wall," and it is filled with pictures of her favorite role models, including Ann Richards and Toni Morrison.[7] By her bedside, she keeps a clothbound book—given to her by her teammate Rita Powell—in which she writes her favorite quotes, a customized Bartlett's.

Marilyn Monroe: "If I'm going to be alone, I'd rather be by myself."
Colette: "You will do foolish things, but do them with enthusiasm."
Zora Neale Hurston: "The dream is the truth."

---

6. **Winnie Mandela . . . Soweto:** Winnie Mandela was the wife of South African leader Nelson Madela. Soweto is a group of townships near Johannesburg housing black South Africans.
7. **Ann Richards and Toni Morrison:** Richards was the first woman governor of Texas. Morrison was the first African-American woman to win the Nobel Prize for Literature.

The team bonding among these six seniors and the 10 younger girls is one reason they have played so well: the sisterhood-is-powerful quest for unity. They have a team song, "Real Love," and they have team trinkets (beaded necklaces with their names and plastic rings and scrunchies with basketballs), team teddy bears, team towels. At team dinners, Jamila's mother carbo-loads them with slivered chicken cooked in garlic and oil and lemon and served on a bed of noodles. The meals often conclude with a dozen or so girls linking arms in a tight circle, swaying, singing, shouting, *"Hoop Phi!"*

Even though they beat Hamp in the Western Mass Regional finals, they weren't really champions—not yet. Do they have what it takes, these sweet-looking girls reared in maple syrup country on land that includes the Robert Frost trail? Playing before a few thousand fans in what is almost your own backyard is nothing compared with a stadium that seats 13,800, where real pros play. Rocking Feiker is one thing, but the Centrum?

When the bus finally pulls in front of the Centrum and it is time to leap off, the girls have faces like masks. To the world, they are a bunch of teen-age girls; inside their heads, they are commandos. To the world, these teen-agers have pretty names: Patri, Kristin, Jen, Kathleen, Kim, Jamila, Sophie, Jade, Emily J., Emily S., Jan, Lucia, Carrie, Rita, Jessi, Julie. But as far as the girls are concerned, they *are* the codes that encapsulate their rare and superb skills, their specialty plays, their personal styles. They are Cloudy and Cougar and Jones-bones and Gumby and Grace and Skippy and Predator. They are warriors.

The girls crowd into a locker room. With much less commotion than usual, they dress in their baggy knee-length uniforms. They slap hands and stand tall. Meanwhile, the arena is redolent of hot dogs, popcorn, sweat and anticipation, one side of the bleachers filled with their people and the other side with the fans from Haverhill.

The girls walk out wordlessly. They look up.

You have to live in a small town for a while before you can read a crowd, especially in New England, where fences are deep in the soil.[8] But if you've been in a town like Amherst for a while, you can go to an

---

8. **fences are deep in the soil:** people keep their lives and emotions private from others.

out-of-town game, even one in as imposing and cavernous a facility as the Centrum, and you can feel this sudden lurch of well-being that comes from the soothing familiarity of faces that are as much a part of your landscape as falling leaves, as forsythia in season, as rhubarb in June. You scan the rows, and for better, and sometimes for worse, you know who's who. You know whose parents don't talk to whom else and you know why. You know who has had troubles that never get discussed.

You see the lawyer that represented your folks or one of their friends in a land dispute or a custody case. You see the realtor who tried to sell a house next to the landfill to the new kids in town. You see the doctor who was no help for your asthma and the one who was. You see the teacher who declared your baby brother a complete mystery and the teacher who always stops to ask what your remarkable brother is up to now. You know which man is the beloved elementary-school principal, now retired. You recognize the plump-cheeked ladies from the cafeteria who specialize in home-made cinnamon buns for 65 cents. You see your family and you see the fathers and mothers and stepfathers and stepmothers of your teammates. You know whose brother flew in from Chicago for the game; whose step-grandparents came from Minnesota.

But what is most important about all this is how mute it is. The commonality is something that is understood, as tacit as the progression of the summer to fall to winter to spring, and just as comforting.

Usually there is a buzz of cheering at the start of a game, but this time the Amherst crowd is nearly silent as the referee tosses the ball.

The Haverhill center taps the ball backward to her point guard. She comes down the court, swings the ball to the wing, who instantly dishes it inside to the center. Easy layup. Amherst blinks first. Two-nothing. In the Haverhill stands, the crowd cheers. It is the only pure cheer they will get.

Within a few seconds, the score is 6–4 Amherst, and something truly remarkable takes place. The Hurricanes enter into a zone where all of them rate all-Americas. It's a kind of controlled frenzy that can overtake a group of athletes under only the most elusive of circumstances. It's not certain what triggers it, perhaps it's Jamila's gentle three-pointer from the wing, or more likely, when Jen drives the baseline and as she swoops beneath the basket like a bird of prey she releases the ball back over her head, placing it like an egg against the backboard and through the hoop. It may have been 10 seconds later when Jamila steals the ball, pushing it down court in a three-on-one break, makes a no-look pass to Jen who just as quickly fires the ball across the lane to Kathleen for an uncontested layup. Whatever it is that started it, there is nothing Haverhill can do to stop it, and time-outs repeatedly called for by their hapless coach only fuel Amherst's frenzy further.

Even the sportscasters can't remember a 37 to 0 run in a state championship game. The halftime score is 51–6.

An astonished Amherst can hardly even cheer. One Amherst fan shouts: "Where's Dr. Kevorkian?" Another makes the very un-Amherst comment: "They should bring on the Haverhill boys for the second half."

Among the spectators is Kathleen's father, Donald Poe, an associate professor of psychology at Hampshire College, who saw how her defense, along with that of Kristin and Emily Shore, kept Haverhill's score so low.

When his son, Chris, was an infant, Donald Poe tried to teach him to say "ball" as his first word, until he was told that "b" is hard sound for a baby. He expected a son to be an athlete, and when Kathleen came along he didn't have that expectation. Yet whenever they go into the yard and she pitches a ball to him, it takes only five minutes before his hand hurts. She throws a heavy ball.

To him, what's important is not that Amherst win, but that the spirit of girls' sports endures. Next year, it doesn't have to be Amherst; it might be Westside in Springfield. Its junior varsity is undefeated. When he was in W. T. Woodson High School in Fairfax, Va., the girls were not allowed to use the boys' gym, which was fancy and varnished with a log in the middle of the floor. The girls had a little back gym, without bleachers. After a game, whenever he saw the little kids asking his daughter for autographs, he was glad to see the girls, pleased that they now had models. But he was just as glad to see the boys asking: to him their respect for the girls' team was just as important.

The final score is 74–36.

After receiving the trophies and after collapsing in one huge hysterical teen-age heap, they all stand up. First they sing "Happy Birthday" to Kristin Marvin, who turns 18 this day. Then they extend their arms toward their parents, teachers, brothers, sisters, even to some of those 140 little girls whose parents have allowed them a school night of unprecedented lateness, and in one final act as a team, these girls shout, in the perfect unison that has served them so well on the court, *"Thank you."*

Back in the locker room, Kristin Marvin sucks on orange slices and sloshes water on her face. She then stands on a back bench, raises her right fist, turns to her comrades and shouts: "Holy #@&*! We're the *#&*@# champions!" And then she loses it. For the next half-hour, she throws herself into the arms of one teammate after another. She cries and hugs, and hugs and cries, and so do they.

Coach keeps knocking at the door, trying to roust the stragglers. Finally, he announces he is coming in, and what greets him is a roomful of girls who return his level gaze with eyes that are rheumy and red as they sputter "last . . . final . . . never again."

He looks right at them and says: "You're wrong. This isn't the last. There will be more basketball." His tone is conversational, almost adult to adult.

"But. . . ." they start to say.

"I promise you. There will be lots more basketball."

Still they regard him with disbelief. They can't decipher his real message, at least not at this moment. They can't fathom how the word "basketball" might have more than one meaning.

Over, the game was over. On the way home, they watched a videotape of the game. Jen was stunned at how it had all fallen into place: We were so fluid it was scary. While they watched themselves, television viewers all over the state were witnessing recaps of the highlights and hearing the verdicts of professional commentators who claimed these girls had wandered into the wrong league: They shoulda been playing Calipari's men at U Mass; they coulda taught the Celtics a thing or two.

The girls would hear all that in the days to come, but at this moment they were mostly thinking about the present—when truth itself had become a dream. The bus was going backward, retracing its earlier path, down the Pike back through Palmer, where the only sense of abundance is in the fast-food stores, then through Bondsville with its gin mill and the sunken rusty playground with a metal fence, back through the center of Belchertown, a singularly flat stretch in a town with a singularly unfortunate name, and back in and out of Pelham—thanks to Jen, on the map at last.

Kathleen Poe wished that the whole team could sleep that night in the gym at the high school, the coziest, most homey, softest place she could now imagine, that they could all sink into its floor, become part of it forever. She kept trying out rhymes in her head, phrases popping into her mind like sudden rebounds: top and stop, pride and ride, forever and sever, heart, smart, true, you.

*Hoop Phi is of an intangible, untouchable breed.*
*It satisfies the soul, and a life-long need.*
*We represented our school, represented our sex,*
*Now maybe both will get some well-earned respect.*

No one really wanted the ride to end. The bare trees, the velvety night air, the cocoon of the bus itself.

At the town line there waited another police escort, this time back into town. The cruiser was once again full of proud, slow ceremony. At the corner of Main and Triangle, the cruiser seemed to lurch right to take the short-cut, back to the school, but then as if that was only a feint, it continued to move forward, so that the girls would be brought through town the long way.

The bus, boisterous in its very bigness, moved past the red-bricked Dickinson homestead with its top-heavy trees, tall and thin with a crown of green: *We're somebody; who are you?* Downtown was almost empty save for a couple of pizza eaters in the front window of Antonio's and a lone worker sweeping in the back shadows of Bart's Ice Cream. As the strobe lights from the cruiser bounced off the storefronts, the bus wheezed past St. Bridget's and the bagel place, turning right, then left, finally pulling into the school parking lot a few minutes shy of midnight.

All of a sudden one of the players shouted: "There are people there, waiting for us!" And, indeed, in the distance was a small crowd standing in the cold and in the dark, clapping.

When the bus came to a stop, Coach stood up. "I promise it won't be mushy. There's just one thing you should know. When you're the state champions, the season never ever ends. I love you. Great job. And now, I'd like everybody else on the bus to please wait so that the team can get off first."

Often the Hurricanes will bound off a bus in a joyous squealing clump. On this night, they rose from their seats, slowly, in silence. *State champs!* For the final time this season, with great care bordering on tenderness, the teammates gathered their stuff, their uniforms, their shoes, their socks, their game faces and their courage. And then in a decision that was never actually articulated but seemed to have evolved as naturally as the parabola of a perfect three-pointer, the Hurricanes waited for captain Jen Pariseau to lead the way, which she did, and one by one the rest of the women followed, with captain Jamila Wideman the last of the Hurricanes to step off the bus into the swirling sea of well-wishers and winter coats.

Overhead the sky was as low-hanging and as opaque as it had been earlier in the evening, but it didn't need the stars to make it shine.

---

## Responding to the Article

1. Think of several different words that describe this team as a unit. Are these the same terms you would apply to the team members individually? If not, what other words would you use?
2. Why, to the Amherst fans, was *JennyandJamila* one word?
3. Why does Diane Stanton, mother of the star of the boys' basketball team, write to the girls?
4. Do you think the team members will ever feel the same amount of closeness again? Why or why not?

## Exploring the Author's Craft

**Setting** is the general time and place in which a story occurs. In this article, the action moves to various specific locales within the more general setting (the Amherst area), and the author uses well-chosen details to bring those locales to life. How does the author describe each of the following?
a. the route of the bus
b. the gym during the championship game

## Writer's Workshop

This is an extended assignment. Find some group activity that will be going on for at least two weeks' time. Now cover it as a journalist, as Madeleine H. Blais did with the Amherst girls' basketball team. Be sure that each locale in your story is carefully described, and make individual people come alive through character sketches that reveal unique aspects of their lives. The word *I* should not appear in your writing unless you are quoting someone else.

## James Dickey

James Dickey, who was born in Atlanta in 1923, was a college football and track star who graduated *magna cum laude* from Vanderbilt University. Dickey wrote several novels, including the well-known *Deliverance*, and published many volumes of poetry. According to Lance Morrow writing in *Time* magazine, several months before his death in 1997 Dickey told a friend, "I had a dream last night. I was back in high school playing football. I scored three touchdowns, including the winning touchdown, and I ended up with the most beautiful girl in the school. I said to her, 'This is the most wonderful day of my life. Too bad it's only a dream.' And she said, 'Yes, but in the dream it's real.'" Much of Dickey's writing contains themes of struggle and conflict.

*To you it may be just a football game, but to the quarterback it's war.*

# In the Pocket

Going backward

All of me and some

Of my friends are forming a shell  my arm is looking

Everywhere and some are breaking

5              In  breaking down

And out  breaking

Across, and one is going deep  deeper

Than my arm.  Where is Number one hooking

Into the violent green alive

10          With linebackers?  I cannot find him he cannot beat

His man  I fall back more

Into the pocket[1] it is raging and breaking

Number Two has disappeared into the chalk

Of the sideline  Number Three is cutting with half

15          A step of grace  my friends are crumbling

Around me the wrong color

Is looming  hands are coming

Up and over between

My arm and Number Three:  throw it hit him in

20                              the middle

Of his enemies  hit move scramble

Before death and the ground

Come up LEAP STAND KILL DIE STRIKE

Now.

---

1. **pocket:** area where the quarterback stands to throw a pass.

---

## Responding to the Poem

1.  Explain exactly what is happening in this poem.
2.  Is the football-as-war metaphor that James Dickey employs in the
    poem a valid one? Explain.

## Exploring the Author's Craft

**Diction** is the language chosen by a writer. List all the words selected by James Dickey—the diction—that contribute to the atmosphere of violence and danger in this poem.

## Writer's Workshop

Describe a moment in sports in terms of something else. In other words, create an extended metaphor as James Dickey did with his war metaphor in "In the Pocket." You may write in prose or in poetry.

## Alternate Media Response

Use any medium—art, photography, film, videotape—to do two things at once: report about a dramatic moment in sport and also comment on that moment, as did James Dickey in "In the Pocket."

## Melva Prahl

Melva Prahl wrote this story for a creative writing class at her high school, Northern Highlands Regional High School in Allendale, New Jersey.

*There are many kinds of competition, many ways of winning.*

# Athletes and Other Artists

**H**ey, Mr. Forester, could you open the library door for me? I have a research paper due tomorrow and I need some info!" Mr. Forester slowly dragged his feet down the hall together with his long, brown pants that had grown larger as he grew older. He looked at Billy through his dull, lifeless eyes and murmured, "You know I'm not supposed to do this, Billy, but I gotta go and clean up anyway." His fingers shook and fumbled as he turned the master key. "There ya go. Be sure to put the books back where you found them."

"Yeah, sure. It shouldn't take me long. I want to get back to the basketball game in time for the third quarter." Billy had always been asking favors of Mr. Forester since he was a freshman. One time he had to get Mr. Forester to cut off his lock from his street locker when he left both keys inside. Then there was the time when a couple of his friends flung his sneakers on top of the school roof and he had to get Mr. Forester to take a ladder and get them down. Mr. Forester was the school's handyman. Nobody was sure how long he had been at the school, but he was there when Billy's oldest brother graduated and it seemed like he'd still be there when Billy's youngest sister would graduate.

Billy grabbed the "G" encyclopedia and promptly started copying. Mr. Forester found a dirty, old dust rag and was sliding it along the book shelves.

"Hey, Billy, you a junior or a senior?"

"A senior," Billy said as his eyes searched for the place where he had left off.

"You know what you're gonna do when you get out of high school?" Mr. Forester asked.

"Yeah, I was thinking about going into biology. Maybe I'll be a doctor. I don't know." Billy laughed to himself. He knew he wouldn't be able to hack all the work and schooling it would take to be a doctor, but it made his parents feel good when he said it.

"Now that's a good idea!" Mr. Forester said decidedly. "That way you're sure to get a good paying job. People always get sick, you know."

Billy nodded as Mr. Forester started to unwind the vacuum cord. "My son would've made a good doctor. He was always fixin' up old Blue's war wounds, but he had a knack for dancin', too. He wouldn't have known it if his mother hadn't enrolled him in a ballet school when he was five years old. She was always after him to dance. Now how many boys do you know spend their free time practicing *pirouettes* and some kind of *jeté*[1] leaps instead of free shots on a basketball court? I never could understand him. He could've gone out with any girl he wanted to. God knows he danced with enough of 'em. But he always hung around home saying that none of the boys really liked him and that the girls were all stuck up. Now when I was a boy I didn't care how stuck up the girl was, as long as she had a good build, you know what I mean?" He reached down and plugged in the vacuum cleaner; it started with a loud hum as he pushed it along the carpet in between the tables and chairs. "Could ya pick up your feet, Billy? Yeah, I had it pretty good with the girls and I was a darn good basketball player, if I do say so myself." Billy's feet slowly began sinking to the floor, but Mr. Forester continued paying no attention. "Every December I take the train into New York and see him perform in *The Nutcracker*. The first time I went I couldn't for the life of me figure out why they would make a ballet about a guy who cracks nuts." He chuckled to himself, "I guess that shows ya how much culture I got. You can put your feet down now, Billy." Billy let his feet drop to the floor. "I can't help but wonder what would've happened if my wife hadn't taken him to that first ballet lesson. He would never have known he had such a talent in him. He might have

---

1. *jeté*: a leap forward, backward, or to the side, from one foot to another.

become a lawyer or a doctor or even a star basketball player. You know, I bet a lot of people have something special in them and they don't even know it. Oh, well, I guess I'll never know. At least he makes good money. Why, he's even gone all the way around the world on a ballet tour. Can't do that when you're a janitor." Mr. Forester sighed as he put the empty trash can back in the corner. "Well, Billy, looks like I'm through in here, how 'bout you?"

"Just one more line, Mr. Forester!" Billy said hastily. Billy scribbled the final sentence on the paper and desperately hoped he made the wording from the encyclopedia sound like his own. "Thanks a lot, Mr. Forester. I don't know what I would've done if you hadn't let me in."

"That's all right, Billy. I can remember a few times I got into trouble 'cause I didn't hand in a report on time."

As they entered the hall, they could hear applause coming from the gymnasium. "Must be the team's back from the locker room. Why don't we go in and take a look at the scoreboard," Mr. Forester said with a bit of excitement.

"Great! I'm sure glad I made it back in time," said Billy.

When they stepped inside, they were met by a wave of heat and noise. The gymnasium was filled with the familiar faces that passed Mr. Forester each day in the halls. The team was now taking its practice shots with balls flying everywhere. The ball flew right to Mr. Forester. Feeling a spark of energy, he dribbled the ball up to the basket and leaped up doing a perfect jeté as the ball sank into the basket.

## Responding to the Story

What do you think of this story? Did you like it? What do you think the high school student who wrote it was trying to do?

## Exploring the Author's Craft

One mark of a good fiction writer is that a story doesn't necessarily go in the direction the reader expects. Explain how the writer fooled the reader's expectations throughout this story.

## Writer's Workshop

Take an unlikely situation—such as this one, a student having a friendship with a custodian—and give it a creative shape in a sketch, story, or poem. End it with a phrase or line that ties the work in with something earlier, as Melva Prahl did with the ballet term *jeté*.

## Making Connections in

# PART TWO

Complete one or more of the following assignments as your teacher directs.

1. In classic five-paragraph essay format (explained in "Making Connections" at the end of Part One), write an essay about three different kinds of competition dramatized in this unit. Make each of the three middle paragraphs be about a different kind of competition, and use specific examples to make your points.

2. How do "Through the Tunnel" and "Athletes and Other Artists" deal with different approaches to relating to one's peers? Write an essay explaining your ideas.

3. Are different qualities required in sports competitions than in other types of competitions? Explain your opinion, and then give reasons why you think as you do. Use examples from the selections in Part Two to help you make your points.

4. In your view, which character in Part Two had the most difficult job competing? Explain your answer in detail.

# Realizing

In Part One of this book we met characters your age who are searching for something in life. In Part Three we will be involved with the results of that search— coming to insights and conclusions.

This section introduces characters who reach important realizations about their parents, about society's prejudices, about the need for security of various kinds, about themselves. Among others, you will encounter a young girl who realizes she can write a poem and a young man who comes to recognize his family's values in his own relationships. Some of the characters you will meet are writing in the present; others are looking back with happiness—or regret.

As you read, you will see that realizing is one more important part of the process of coming of age.

## Two Perspectives

### Frank McCourt

Frank McCourt was born in Brooklyn, New York, in 1930, but did most of his growing up amid the poverty of Limerick, Ireland. He wrote about this childhood in *Angela's Ashes,* a vivid memoir that won the Pulitzer Prize in 1996 and that remained on the best seller list for well over a year. McCourt taught writing for many years in a high school in New York City and credits his students with teaching him much of what he knows.

### Glenn W. Dresbach

Born in 1889, Glenn W. Dresbach published poems in such places as *The New York Times, The Saturday Evening Post,* and *The Atlantic Monthly.* Before his death in 1968 Dresbach won many awards, including the bronze medallion of United Poets Laureate International. "The Cave" was written at least thirty years ago; does it still communicate in our time?

*How do people cope when everything is going badly?*

# from Angela's Ashes

Frank McCourt

**W**hen Dad gets a job Mam is cheerful and she sings,

*Anyone can see why I wanted your kiss,*
*It had to be and the reason is this*
*Could it be true, someone like you*
*Could love me, love me?*

When Dad brings home the first week's wages Mam is delighted she can pay the lovely Italian man in the grocery shop and she can hold her head up again because there's nothing worse in the world than to owe and be beholden to anyone. She cleans the kitchen, washes the mugs and plates, brushes crumbs and bits of food from the table, cleans out the icebox and orders a fresh block of ice from another Italian. She buys toilet paper that we can take down the hall to the lavatory and that, she says, is better than having the headlines from the *Daily News* blackening your arse. She boils water on the stove and spends a day at a great tin tub washing our shirts and socks, diapers for the twins, our two sheets, our three towels. She hangs everything out on the clotheslines behind the apartment house and we can watch the clothes dance in wind and sun. She says you wouldn't want the neighbors to know what you have in the way of a wash but there's nothing like the sweetness of clothes dried by the sun.

When Dad brings home the first week's wages on a Friday night we know the weekend will be wonderful. On Saturday night Mam will boil water on the stove and wash us in the great tin tub and Dad will dry us. Malachy will turn around and show his behind. Dad will pretend to be shocked and we'll all laugh. Mam will make hot cocoa and we'll be able to stay up while Dad tells us a story out of his head. All we have to do is say a name, Mr. MacAdorey or Mr. Leibowitz down the hall, and Dad will have the two of them rowing up a river in Brazil chased by Indians with green noses and puce shoulders. On nights like that we can drift off to sleep knowing there will be a breakfast of eggs, fried tomatoes and fried bread, tea with lashings of sugar and milk and, later in the day, a big dinner of mashed potatoes, peas and ham, and a trifle Mam makes, layers of fruit and warm delicious custard on a cake soaked in sherry.

When Dad brings home the first week's wages and the weather is fine Mam takes us to the playground. She sits on a bench and talks to Minnie MacAdorey. She tells Minnie stories about characters in Limerick and Minnie tells her about characters in Belfast and they laugh because there are funny people in Ireland, North and South. Then they teach each other sad songs and Malachy and I leave the swings and seesaws to sit with them on the bench and sing,

> *A group of young soldiers one night in a camp*
> *Were talking of sweethearts they had.*
> *All seemed so merry except one young lad,*
> *And he was downhearted and sad.*
> *Come and join us, said one of the boys,*
> *Surely there's someone for you.*
> *But Ned shook his head and proudly he said*
> *I am in love with two, Each like a mother to me,*
> *From neither of them shall I part.*
> *For one is my mother, God bless her and love her,*
> *The other is my sweetheart.*

Malachy and I sing that song and Mam and Minnie laugh till they cry at the way Malachy takes a deep bow and holds his arms out to Mam at the end. Dan MacAdorey comes along on his way home from work and says Rudy Vallee[1] better start worrying about the competition.

When we go home Mam makes tea and bread and jam or mashed potatoes with butter and salt. Dad drinks the tea and eats nothing. Mam says, God above, How can you work all day and not eat? He says, The tea is enough. She says, You'll ruin your health, and he tells her again that food is a shock to the system. He drinks his tea and tells us stories and shows us letters and words in the *Daily News* or he smokes a cigarette, stares at the wall, runs his tongue over his lips.

When Dad's job goes into the third week he does not bring home the wages. On Friday night we wait for him and Mam gives us bread and

---

1. **Rudy Vallee:** American singer and performer who was extremely popular during the 1920s and 1930s.

tea. The darkness comes down and the lights come on along Classon Avenue. Other men with jobs are home already and having eggs for dinner because you can't have meat on a Friday.[2] You can hear the families talking upstairs and downstairs and down the hall and Bing Crosby is singing on the radio, Brother, can you spare a dime?[3]

Malachy and I play with the twins. We know Mam won't sing Anyone can see why I wanted your kiss. She sits at the kitchen table talking to herself, What am I going to do? till it's late and Dad rolls up the stairs singing Roddy McCorley. He pushes in the door and calls for us, Where are my troops? Where are my four warriors?

Mam says, Leave those boys alone. They're gone to bed half hungry because you have to fill your belly with whiskey.

He comes to the bedroom door. Up, boys, up. A nickel for everyone who promises to die for Ireland.

> Deep in Canadian woods we met
> From one bright island flown.
> Great is the land we tread, but yet
> Our hearts are with our own.

Up, boys, up. Francis, Malachy, Oliver, Eugene. The Red Branch Knights, the Fenian Men, the IRA.[4] Up, up.

Mam is at the kitchen table, shaking, her hair hanging damp, her face wet. Can't you leave them alone? she says. Jesus, Mary and Joseph, isn't it enough that you come home without a penny in your pocket without making fools of the children on top of it?

She comes to us. Go back to bed, she says.

I want them up, he says. I want them ready for the day Ireland will be free from the center to the sea.

Don't cross me, she says, for if you do it'll be a sorry day in your mother's house.

---

2. **can't have meat on a Friday:** a regulation of the Catholic Church until the 1960s.
3. **Bing Crosby . . . spare a dime?:** Bing Crosby (1904–1977) was a famous American singer and film star. "Brother, can you spare a dime?" was a popular song during the Great Depression of the 1930s.
4. **Red Branch . . . IRA:** various groups devoted to freeing Ireland from English rule.

He pulls his cap down over his face and cries, My poor mother. Poor Ireland. Och, what are we going to do?

Mam says, You're pure stone mad, and she tells us again to go to bed.

On the morning of the fourth Friday of Dad's job Mam asks him if he'll be home tonight with his wages or will he drink everything again? He looks at us and shakes his head at Mam as if to say, Och, you shouldn't talk like that in front of the children.

Mam keeps at him. I'm asking you, Are you coming home so that we can have a bit of supper or will it be midnight with no money in your pocket and you singing Kevin Barry and the rest of the sad songs?

He puts on his cap, shoves his hands into his trouser pockets, sighs and looks up at the ceiling. I told you before I'll be home, he says.

Later in the day Mam dresses us. She puts the twins into the pram and off we go through the long streets of Brooklyn. Sometimes she lets Malachy sit in the pram when he's tired of trotting along beside her. She tells me I'm too big for the pram. I could tell her I have pains in my legs from trying to keep up with her but she's not singing and I know this is not the day to be talking about my pains.

We come to a big gate where there's a man standing in a box with windows all around. Mam talks to the man. She wants to know if she can go inside to where the men are paid and maybe they'd give her some of Dad's wages so he wouldn't spend it in the bars. The man shakes his head. I'm sorry, lady, but if we did that we'd have half the wives in Brooklyn storming the place. Lotta men have the drinking problem but there's nothing we can do long as they show up sober and do their work.

We wait across the street. Mam lets me sit on the sidewalk with my back against the wall. She gives the twins their bottles of water and sugar but Malachy and I have to wait till she gets money from Dad and we can go to the Italian for tea and bread and eggs.

When the whistle blows at half five men in caps and overalls swarm through the gate, their faces and hands black from the work. Mam tells us watch carefully for Dad because she can hardly see across the street herself, her eyes are that bad. There are dozens of men, then a few, then none. Mam is crying, Why couldn't ye see him? Are ye blind or what?

She goes back to the man in the box. Are you sure there wouldn't be one man left inside?

No, lady, he says. They're out. I don't know how he got past you.

We go back through the long streets of Brooklyn. The twins hold up their bottles and cry for more water and sugar. Malachy says he's hungry and Mam tells him wait a little, we'll get money from Dad and we'll all have a nice supper. We'll go to the Italian and get eggs and make toast with the flames on the stove and we'll have jam on it. Oh, we will, and we'll all be nice and warm.

It's dark on Atlantic Avenue and all the bars around the Long Island Railroad Station are bright and noisy. We go from bar to bar looking for Dad. Mam leaves us outside with the pram while she goes in or she sends me. There are crowds of noisy men and stale smells that remind me of Dad when he comes home with the smell of the whiskey on him.

The man behind the bar says, Yeah, sonny, whaddya want? You're not supposeta be in here, y'know.

I'm looking for my father. Is my father here?

Naw, sonny, how'd I know dat? Who's your fawdah?

His name is Malachy and he sings Kevin Barry.

Malarkey?

No, Malachy.

Malachy? And he sings Kevin Barry?

He calls out to the men in the bar, Youse guys, youse know guy Malachy what sings Kevin Barry?

Men shake their heads. One says he knew a guy Michael sang Kevin Barry but he died of the drink which he had because of his war wounds.

The barman says, Jeez, Pete, I didn't ax ya to tell me history o' da woild, did I? Naw, kid. We don't let people sing in here. Causes trouble. Specially the Irish. Let 'em sing, next the fists are flying. Besides, I never hoid a name like dat Malachy. Naw, kid, no Malachy here.

The man called Pete holds his glass toward me. Here, kid, have a sip, but the barman says, Whaddya doin', Pete? Tryina get the kid drunk? Do that again, Pete, an' I'll come out an' break y'ass.

Mam tries all the bars around the station before she gives up. She leans against a wall and cries. Jesus, we still have to walk all the way to Classon Avenue and I have four starving children. She sends me back into the bar where Pete offered me the sip to see if the barman would fill the twins' bottles with water and maybe a little sugar in each. The men in the bar think it's very funny that the barman should be filling baby bottles but he's big and he tells them shut their lip. He tells me babies should be drinking milk not water and when I tell him Mam doesn't have the money he empties the baby bottles and fills them with milk. He says, Tell ya mom they need that for the teeth an' bones. Ya drink water en' sugar an' all ya get is rickets. Tell ya Mom.

Mam is happy with the milk. She says she knows all about teeth and bones and rickets but beggars can't be choosers.

When we reach Classon Avenue she goes straight to the Italian grocery shop. She tells the man her husband is late tonight, that he's probably working overtime, and would it be at all possible to get a few things and she'll be sure to see him tomorrow?

The Italian says, Missus, you always pay your bill sooner or later and you can have anything you like in this store.

Oh, she says, I don't want much.

Anything you like, missus, because I know you're an honest woman and you got a bunch o' nice kids there.

We have eggs and toast and jam though we're so weary walking the long streets of Brooklyn we can barely move our jaws to chew. The twins fall asleep after eating and Mam lays them on the bed to change their diapers. She sends me down the hall to rinse the dirty diapers in the lavatory so that they can be hung up to dry and used the next day. Malachy helps her wash the twins' bottoms though he's ready to fall asleep himself.

I crawl into bed with Malachy and the twins. I look out at Mam at the kitchen table, smoking a cigarette, drinking tea, and crying. I want to get up and tell her I'll be a man soon and I'll get a job in the place with the big gate and I'll come home every Friday night with money for eggs and toast and jam and she can sing again Anyone can see why I wanted your kiss.

The next week Dad loses the job. He comes home that Friday night, throws his wages on the table and says to Mam, Are you happy now? You hang around the gate complaining and accusing and they sack me. They were looking for an excuse and you gave it to them.

He takes a few dollars from his wages and goes out. He comes home late roaring and singing. The twins cry and Mam shushes them and cries a long time herself.

# The Cave

Glenn W. Dresbach

Sometimes when the boy was troubled, he would go
    To a little cave of stone above the brook
And build a fire just big enough to glow
    Upon the ledge outside, then sit and look.
5  Below him was the winding silver trail
    Of water from the upland pasture springs,
And meadows where he heard the calling quail;
    Before him was the sky, and passing wings.

The tang of willow twigs he lighted there,
10    Fragrance of meadows breathing slow and deep,
The cave's own musky coolness on the air,
    The scent of sunlight . . . all were his to keep.
We had such places—cave or tree or hill . . .
    And we are lucky if we keep them still.

---

## Responding to the Selections

1. Name five specific things that the family in *Angela's Ashes* does as a result of the good news of Dad's earning a salary.
2. Name five specific occurrences that show how things change when the family is struggling for money.

3.  What kind of realization does Frank come to at the end of this episode?
4.  What function did the cave provide for the boy in the poem "The Cave"? How would having such a place have helped young Frank McCourt?

## Exploring the Authors' Craft

1.  **Tone** in a piece of writing is the author's attitude toward the subject matter.
    a.  Find the exact place in *Angela's Ashes* where the tone begins to change from light and upbeat to dark and somber. What is the reason for the change?
    b.  What is the tone of "The Cave"? What images created and words chosen by the author help create that tone?
2.  "The Cave" is a **sonnet,** a fourteen-line poem with a very specific line format and rhyme scheme. Examine "The Cave" to see its structure.
    a.  How many syllables are in each line? What is the rhyme scheme?
    b.  What function do the last two lines of the poem serve?

## Writer's Workshop

Frank McCourt's recollections are particularly powerful because he includes so many details from his childhood. Your task here is to try to be as detailed as McCourt is. Take a moment from your own childhood—or a several-day segment as McCourt does—and place the reader there through your inclusion of very specific details and dialogue.

## Alternate Media Assignment

For those of you who can illustrate . . .

1. Take any one of the vivid scenes that McCourt has created and draw or paint it yourself. What kinds of colors will you use? Why?
2. Draw or paint how you picture the setting of "The Cave." What kinds of colors will you use here?

## Paula Dan

Paula Dan was born in Romania in 1970, the oldest of nine children. She and her family emigrated to the United States when she was nine years old. Of "Faces," written when she was a student, Paula Dan says, "This essay was inspired by an incident that took place when I was fifteen. Our neighbor was a friendly and charming man well liked by everyone. Unfortunately there was a dark side to his personality which I discovered one night when, awakened by crying, pajama-clad children, we found a totally out of control Mr.——. I was naive enough to try to calm him down and he almost hit me, too. In the essay I tried to describe the two sides of his personality, the side the public saw and the side his family knew."

***Can someone's mood change in an instant?***

# Faces

**G**ood afternoon," the soft, low voice drifted over to where Dad and I were weeding in the garden.

"You're home from work already?" Dad asked as he stood up.

"Yes, it's been a long day," Mr. Stavros answered. "How are the vegetables doing?" As Mr. Stavros and Dad talked, I continued to weed and every once in a while, I listened to their conversation.

Mr. Stavros was our new neighbor. He was a very small man, but his arms were very thick and his shoulders were wide and heavily muscled. He was smiling and his even, white teeth stood out against his tanned face.

"Do you like roses?" I realized that he'd addressed the question to me.

"Yes," I answered, "but I can't seem to grow them too well."

"I have some extra bushes," Mr. Stavros said, thoughtfully. "If you want them I'll get Joanna to bring them down later on."

"Oh, yes, I'd love to have them." I thought of how they'd look in the front of the house with my other rose bush.

"I have enough flowers already," Mr. Stavros chuckled. "My wife complains that nobody even notices the house because of the flowers."

All three of us weeded in silence for a while, then Mr. Stavros started talking again. "Flowers are beautiful," he said, staring dreamily at something Dad and I could not see. "The vegetables are food for your stomach, but flowers are food for your eyes." His eyes came back into focus and he grinned at Dad. "Stop looking at me like I'm crazy," he said through his smile.

"I'm sorry," Dad laughed, "but I don't understand what you're talking about."

"She does." Mr. Stavros turned his small brown face toward me. "Ask her to explain."

As we talked, a shadow fell over us, and we looked up at Joanna who had come upon us silently. Without a word to either Dad or me, she turned her commanding voice to her father.

"I need money."

"What for?" All the dreaminess was gone from his voice. It sounded cold and businesslike now.

"I need new shoes; these are falling apart." She lifted up one foot and presented one mangled sneaker to her dad.

"When they fall off your feet I'll buy you new ones; you're walking fine as far as I can see."

Joanna stretched herself up to her full height, about one half a foot taller than her dad. "I need money now."

"Later." Mr. Stavros's face was a light shade of gray under his tan.

"I'm going to work later," Joanna whined.

"Go ask your mother."

"You don't let me and mom have any money or I wouldn't be begging you."

Mr. Stavros answered her in a furious voice, spitting out every individual word into her face. "I'm the boss in my house."

Joanna's eyes filled with tears. "I hate you."

He hit her so fast I couldn't follow his hand. All I saw was Joanna holding the side of her face, her eyes tearing as she started toward her house. Mr. Stavros followed her. He walked slowly, as if it took a great effort to lift each foot.

Joanna never came to bring me the roses, but I didn't want them anymore.

---

## Responding to the Essay

At what point did the change in Mr. Stavros occur? Did the change surprise you? Why or why not?

## Exploring the Author's Craft

A symbol is an object, place, character, or event that stands for some abstract quality or idea. Sometimes, as in this story, the meaning of a symbol can change to reflect the changes in a character or a situation. What do rose bushes stand for at the beginning of this story? In what way do they stand for something different at the end?

## Writer's Workshop

In any creative writing form you wish to employ—story, drama, or poetry—show contrasting "faces" of one person as Paula Dan does in this piece of writing.

## Alternate Media Response

This very short selection could easily be adapted into a script; the dialogue is already written. Videotape "Faces." Be sure to include the flowers as a symbol in your script.

## Gary Soto

Gary Soto was born in 1952 in Fresno, California. A prolific writer, he has produced nine poetry collections for adults, including *New and Selected Poems*, a 1995 finalist for the National Book Award. He has also written nonfiction for young adults, a play, and a movie script. Most interestingly, one of his recent projects was an opera called *Nerd-landia* commissioned by the Los Angeles Opera. Soto creates works that are fresh, alive, and vivid, evoking his Mexican heritage and the California of his youth. Taken together, his books for adults and young people have sold over a million copies; one can almost see and hear and taste and touch the places Gary Soto evokes in them.

*When you get beyond surface differences, people are often pretty much alike.*

# Like Mexicans

**M**y grandmother gave me bad advice and good advice when I was in my early teens. For the bad advice, she said that I should become a barber because they made good money and listened to the radio all day. "Honey, they don't work como burros,"[1] she would say every time I visited her. She made the sound of donkeys braying. "Like that, honey!" For the good advice, she said that I should marry a Mexican girl. "No Okies, hijo"[2]—she would say—"Look my son. He marry one and they

---

1. **como burros:** like donkeys. [Spanish]
2. **No Okies, hijo:** Not Okies, son. ("Okies" is a derogatory term for people from Oklahoma.)

fight every day about I don't know what and I don't know what." For her, everyone who wasn't Mexican, black, or Asian were Okies. The French were Okies, the Italians in suits were Okies. When I asked about Jews, whom I had read about, she asked for a picture. I rode home on my bicycle and returned with a calendar depicting the important races of the world. "Pues sí, son Okies también!"[3] she said, nodding her head. She waved the calendar away and we went to the living room where she lectured me on the virtues of the Mexican girl: first, she could cook and, second, she acted like a woman, not a man, in her husband's home. She said she would tell me about a third when I got a little older.

I asked my mother about it—becoming a barber and marrying Mexican. She was in the kitchen. Steam curled from a pot of boiling beans, the radio was on, looking as squat as a loaf of bread. "Well, if you want to be a barber—they say they make good money." She slapped a round steak with a knife, her glasses slipping down with each strike. She stopped and looked up. "If you find a good Mexican girl, marry her of course." She returned to slapping the meat and I went to the backyard where my brother and David King were sitting on the lawn.

I ignored them and climbed the back fence to see my best friend, Scott, a second-generation Okie. I called him, and his mother pointed to the side of the house where his bedroom was a small aluminum trailer, the kind you gawk at when they're flipped over on the freeway, wheels spinning in the air. I went around to find Scott pitching horseshoes.

I picked up a set of rusty ones and joined him. While we played, we talked about school and friends and record albums. The horseshoes scuffed up dirt, sometimes ringing the iron that threw out a meager shadow like a sundial. After three argued-over games, we pulled two oranges apiece from his tree and started down the alley still talking school and friends and record albums. We pulled more oranges from the alley and talked about who we would marry. "No offense, Scott," I said with an orange slice in my mouth, "but I would never marry an Okie." We walked in step, almost touching. "No offense, Gary," Scott said, "but I would *never* marry a Mexican." I looked at him: a fang of

---

3. **Pues sí, . . . también:** Well yes, they are Okies, too! [Spanish]

orange slice showed from his munching mouth. I didn't think anything of it. He had his girl and I had mine. But our seventh-grade vision was the same: to marry, get jobs, buy cars and maybe a house if we had money left over.

We talked about our future lives until, to our surprise, we were on the downtown mall, two miles from home. We bought a bag of popcorn at Penney's and sat on a bench near the fountain watching Mexican and Okie girls pass. "That one's mine," I pointed with my chin when a girl with eyebrows arched into black rainbows ambled by. "She's cute," Scott said about a girl with yellow hair and a mouthful of gum. We dreamed aloud, our chins busy pointing out girls. We agreed that we couldn't wait to become men and lift them onto our laps.

But the woman I married was not Mexican but Japanese. It was a surprise to me. For years, I went about wide-eyed in my search for the brown girl in a white dress at a dance. I searched the playground at the baseball diamond. When the girls raced for grounders, their hair bounced like something that couldn't be caught. When they sat together in the lunchroom, heads pressed together, I knew they were talking about us Mexican guys. I saw them and dreamed them. I threw my face into my pillow, making up sentences that were good as in the movies.

But when I was twenty, I fell in love with this other girl who worried my mother, who had my grandmother asking once again to see the calendar of the Important Races of the World. I told her I had thrown it away years before. I took a much-glanced-at snapshot from my wallet. We looked at it together, in silence. Then grandma reclined in her chair, lit a cigarette, and said, "Es pretty."[4] She blew and asked with all her worry pushed up to her forehead: "Chinese?"

I was in love and there was no looking back. She was the one. I told my mother who was slapping hamburger into patties. "Well, sure if you want to marry her," she said. But the more I talked, the more concerned she became. Later I began to worry. Was it all a mistake? "Marry a Mexican girl," I heard my mother say in my mind. I heard it at breakfast. I heard it over math problems, between Western Civilization

---

4. **Es pretty:** She is pretty.

and cultural geography. But then one afternoon while I was hitchhiking home from school, it struck me like a baseball in the back: my mother wanted me to marry someone of my own social class—a poor girl. I considered my fiancée, Carolyn, and she didn't look poor, though I knew she came from a family of farm workers and pull-yourself-up-by-the-bootstraps ranchers. I asked my brother, who was marrying Mexican poor that fall, if I should marry a poor girl. He screamed "Yeah" above his terrible guitar playing in his bedroom. I considered my sister who had married Mexican. Cousins were dating Mexican. Uncles were remarrying poor women. I asked Scott, who was still my best friend, and he said, "She's too good for you, so you better not."

I worried about it until Carolyn took me home to meet her parents. We drove in her Plymouth until the houses gave way to farms and ranches and finally her house fifty feet from the highway. When we pulled into the drive, I panicked and begged Carolyn to make a U-turn and go back so we could talk about it over a soda. She pinched my cheek, calling me a "silly boy." I felt better, though, when I got out of the car and saw the house: the chipped paint, a cracked window, boards for a walk to the back door. There were rusting cars near the barn. A tractor with a net of spiderwebs under a mulberry. A field. A bale of barbed wire like children's scribbling leaning against an empty chicken coop. Carolyn took my hand and pulled me to my future mother-in-law who was coming out to greet us.

We had lunch: sandwiches, potato chips, and iced tea. Carolyn and her mother talked mostly about neighbors and the congregation at the Japanese Methodist Church in West Fresno. Her father, who was in khaki work clothes, excused himself with a wave that was almost a salute and went outside. I heard a truck start, a dog bark, and then the truck rattle away.

Carolyn's mother offered another sandwich, but I declined with a shake of my head and a smile. I looked around when I could, when I was not saying over and over that I was a college student, hinting that I could take care of her daughter. I shifted my chair. I saw newspapers piled in corners, dusty cereal boxes and vinegar bottles in corners. The wallpaper was bubbled from rain that had come in from a bad roof. Dust. Dust lay on lamp shades and window sills. These people are just like Mexicans, I thought. Poor people.

Carolyn's mother asked me through Carolyn if I would like a *sushi*.[5]
A plate of black and white things were held in front of me. I took one,
wide-eyed, and turned it over like a foreign coin. I was biting into one
when I saw a kitten crawl up the window screen over the sink. I chewed
and the kitten opened its mouth in terror as she crawled higher, wanting
in to paw the leftovers from our plates. I looked at Carolyn, who said
that the cat was just showing off. I looked up in time to see it fall. It
crawled up, then fell again.

We talked for an hour and had apple pie and coffee, slowly. Finally,
we got up with Carolyn taking my hand. Slightly embarrassed, I tried to
pull away but her grip held me. I let her have her way as she led me
down the hallway with her mother right behind me. When I opened the
door, I was startled by a kitten clinging to the screen door, its mouth
screaming "cat food, dog biscuits, *sushi*. . . ." I opened the door and the
kitten, still holding on, whined in the language of hungry animals. When
I got into Carolyn's car, I looked back: the cat was still clinging. I asked
Carolyn if it was possibly hungry, but she said the cat was being silly.
She started the car, waved to her mother, and bounced us over the rain-
pocked drive, patting my thigh for being her lover baby. Carolyn waved
again. I looked back, waving, then gawking at a window screen where
there were now three kittens clawing and screaming to get in. Like
Mexicans, I thought. I remembered the Molinas and how the cats clung
to their screens—cats they shot down with squirt guns. On the highway,
I felt happy, pleased by it all. I patted Carolyn's thigh. Her people were
like Mexicans, only different.

---

5. **sushi:** Japanese dish consisting of small portions of rice, raw fish, and sometimes seaweed.

## Responding to the Memoir

1.  Name five or six things that the narrator observes that convince him that Carolyn's people are "just like Mexicans."
2.  What difference do you see between the grandmother's and the mother's attitudes toward non-Mexicans? Do you think this difference in attitude is common in America today? Discuss.
3.  Why is the narrator "happy, pleased by it all" at the end of the visit to Carolyn's house?

## Exploring the Author's Craft

Gary Soto is one of the most readable of contemporary American writers. His stories move at a rapid pace, and they are full of the stuff of daily life: record albums, boyfriends and girlfriends, a Penney's store, cats climbing up a kitchen screen.

   This story is also highly readable because of its effective similes—comparisons between dissimilar objects using connecting words such as "like" or "as." Find and list three of them and explain how they work. Are the comparisons in them valid?

## Writer's Workshop

Getting to know someone of a different nationality or ethnic background can be a positive, broadening experience. Write a personal narrative about such an occurrence and what you learned from it.

## Janis Ian

Janis Ian, who was born in 1951, stands unique in that she has received Grammy Award nominations for her records in the '60s, '70s, '80s , and '90s. She actually won a Grammy for "At Seventeen."

"Society's Child," (Polygram *Janis Ian—The Verve Years*) Ian says, "was written when I was about 14. . . . I was living in an all-black area at the time, and saw the problem happening in reverse with my friends' parents. I think the song's nationwide banning after its initial two releases, coupled with the furor it created when it finally was a hit (radio stations burned, disk jockeys fired for playing it), only proves what a deep chord it struck. I learned a lot from that song, chiefly that songs have a great and terrible power that is not to be trifled with. . . . The record's more than 30-year life span attests to this."

Ian continues, "I started 'At Seventeen' (Sony CD *Between the Lines*) sitting at my mother's dining room table, playing guitar while reading *The New York Times Magazine*. In it was an article that began, 'I learned the truth at eighteen,' about a debutante. 'Eighteen' didn't scan, so it became 'seventeen.' The song took a long time (three months) to finish, mainly because I was trying to be really honest with myself throughout the writing, and still find a way to connect to everyone listening. The first year I sang it onstage, I sang it with my eyes closed; I was so convinced I'd see everyone laughing at me otherwise. Now of course I realize that all of us feel this way, especially the debutantes and basketball heroes."

*Sometimes the realizations of adolescence can be bitter pills to swallow.*

# Society's Child

Come to my door, baby
Face is clean and shining black as night
My mama went to answer
You know that you looked so fine
5    Well, I could understand your tears and your shame
She called you Boy instead of your name
When she wouldn't let you inside
When she turned and said
"But honey, he's not our kind"

10    She says I can't see you anymore, baby
Can't see you anymore

Walk me down to school, baby
Everybody's acting deaf and blind
but I can hear 'em thinking
15    "Why don't they just stick to their own kind?"
My teachers all laugh, their smirking stares
cutting deep down in our affairs
Preachers of equality
Think they believe it?
20    then why won't they just let us be?

They say I can't see you anymore, baby
Can't see you anymore

One of these days I'm gonna stop my listening
Gonna raise my head up high
25  One of these days I'm gonna
    raise up my glistening wings and fly
    But that day will have to wait for a while
    Baby, I'm only society's child
    When we're older, things may change
30  but for now, this is the way
    they must remain

    I say I can't see you anymore, baby
    Can't see you anymore
    No, I don't want to see you anymore baby

# At Seventeen

I learned the truth at seventeen
That love was meant for beauty queens
and high school girls with clear-skinned smiles
who married young and then retired

5   The valentines I never knew
    The Friday night charades of youth
    were spent on one more beautiful
    At seventeen, I learned the truth

And those of us with ravaged faces

10    lacking in the social graces

desperately remained at home

inventing lovers on the phone

who called to say "Come dance with me"

and murmured vague obscenities

15    It isn't all it seems, at seventeen


A brown-eyed girl in hand-me-downs

whose name I never could pronounce

said "Pity please the ones who serve

They only get what they deserve"

20  The rich-relationed home town queens

marry into what they need

with a guarantee of company

and haven for the elderly


Remember those who win the game

25    lose the love they sought to gain

In debentures[1] of quality

and dubious integrity

Their small-town eyes will gape at you

in dull surprise, when payment due

30    exceeds accounts received, at seventeen

---

1. **debentures:** written statements that money or some other quantity is owed as a debt.

To those of us who knew the pain
of valentines that never came
and those whose names were never called
when choosing sides for basketball
35  It was long ago and far away
The world was younger than today
when dreams were all they gave for free
to ugly duckling girls like me

We all play the game, and when we dare
40   we cheat ourselves at solitaire
inventing lovers on the phone
repenting other lives unknown
that call and say "Come on, dance with me"
and murmur vague obscenities
45   at ugly girls like me, at seventeen

---

## Responding to the Song Lyrics

1. Both of these "poems" are really song lyrics. What view of
   adolescence do they present? Is it a valid view? Support your answer
   with examples from your own experience.
2. In both "Society's Child" and "At Seventeen" Ian does allow some
   hope that things will look better in the future. What exactly does
   she anticipate in each?

## Exploring the Author's Craft

Like other poets, writers of song lyrics must make their points through a limited number of carefully chosen words and word pictures. Identify at least three phrases from "At Seventeen" that you think vividly capture the experiences of adolescence.

## Writer's Workshop

Write a song lyric that captures at least one issue involving adolescence. Spend some time constructing lines that succinctly express the emotions you are trying to communicate.

## Alternate Media Response

Actually compose the music to accompany the lyric you wrote in Writer's Workshop.

## Gish Jen

Born in 1956 of Chinese immigrant parents, Gish Jen grew up in Scarsdale, New York. Her writing has appeared in *The Atlantic Monthly*, *The New Yorker*, and *Best American Short Stories* of both 1988 and 1995; and her first novel, *Typical American*, was nominated for the National Book Critics' Circle Award. Of Jen's 1996 novel *Mona in the Promised Land*, fellow Asian-American writer Amy Tan asks, "Can a novel be both hilariously funny and seriously important?" Tan answers "yes," and you might say "yes" to the same question about "The Water-Faucet Vision."

*Not all of the world's problems can be solved by miracles.*

# The Water-Faucet Vision

To protect my sister Mona and me from the pains—or, as they pronounced it, the "pins"—of life, my parents did their fighting in Shanghai dialect, which we didn't understand; and when my father one day pitched a brass vase through the kitchen window, my mother told us he had done it by accident.

"By accident?" said Mona.

My mother chopped the foot off a mushroom.

"By accident?" said Mona. "By *accident?*"

Later I tried to explain to her that she shouldn't have persisted like that, but it was hopeless.

"What's the matter with throwing things?" she shrugged. "He was *mad.*"

That was the difference between Mona and me: Fighting was just fighting to her. If she worried about anything, it was only that she might turn out too short to become a ballerina, in which case she was going to be a piano player.

I, on the other hand, was going to be a martyr. I was in fifth grade then, and the hyperimaginative sort—the kind of girl who grows morbid in Catholic school, who longs to be chopped or frozen to death but then has nightmares about it from which she wakes up screaming and clutching a stuffed bear. It was not a bear that I clutched, though, but a string of three malachite[1] beads that I had found in the marsh by the old aqueduct one day. Apparently once part of a necklace, they were each wonderfully striated[2] and swirled, and slightly humped toward the center, like a jellyfish; so that if I squeezed one, it would slip smoothly away, with a grace that altogether enthralled and—on those dream-harrowed nights—soothed me, soothed me as nothing had before or has since. Not that I've lacked occasion for soothing: Though it's been four months since my mother died, there are still nights when sleep stands away from me, stiff as a well-paid sentry. But that is another story. Back then I had my malachite beads, and if I worried them long and patiently enough, I was sure to start feeling better, more awake, even a little special—imagining, as I liked to, that my nightmares were communications from the Almighty Himself, preparation for my painful destiny. Discussing them with Patty Creamer, who had also promised her life to God, I called them "almost visions"; and Patty, her mouth wadded with the three or four sticks of doublemint she always seemed to have going at once, said, "I bet you'll be doin' miracleth by seventh grade."

Miracles. Today Patty laughs to think she ever spent good time stewing on such matters, her attention having long turned to rugs, and artwork, and antique Japanese bureaus—things she believes in.

"A good bureau's more than just a bureau," she explained last time we had lunch. "It's a hedge against life. I tell you, if there's one thing I believe, it's that cheap stuff's just money out the window. Nice stuff, on the other hand—now *that* you can always cash out, if life gets rough. *That* you can count on."

In fifth grade, though, she counted on different things.

"You'll be doing miracles too," I told her, but she shook her shaggy head and looked doleful.

---

1. **malachite:** a green mineral used for ornamental articles.
2. **striated:** striped; streaked.

"Na' me," she chomped. "Buzzit's okay. The kin' things I like, prayers work okay on."

"Like?"

"Like you 'member that dreth I liked?"

She meant the yellow one, with the criss-cross straps.

"Well gueth what."

"Your mom got it for you."

She smiled. "And I only jutht prayed for it for a week," she said.

As for myself, though, I definitely wanted to be able to perform a wonder or two. Miracle-working! It was the carrot of carrots: It kept me doing my homework, taking the sacraments; it kept me mournfully on key in music hour, while my classmates hiccuped and squealed their carefree hearts away. Yet I couldn't have said what I wanted such powers *for*, exactly. That is, I thought of them the way one might think of, say, an ornamental sword—as a kind of collectible, which also happened to be a means of defense.

But then Patty's father walked out on her mother, and for the first time, there was a miracle I wanted to do. I wanted it so much I could see it: Mr. Creamer made into a spitball; Mr. Creamer shot through a straw into the sky; Mr. Creamer unrolled and re-plumped, plop back on Patty's doorstep. I would've cleaned out his mind and given him a shave en route. I would've given him a box of peanut fudge, tied up with a ribbon, to present to Patty with a kiss.

But instead all I could do was try to tell her he'd come back.

"He will not, he will not!" she sobbed. "He went on a boat to Rio Deniro.[3] To Rio Deniro!"

I tried to offer her a stick of gum, but she wouldn't take it.

"He said he would rather look at water than at my mom's fat face. He said he would rather look at water than at me." Now she was really wailing, and holding her ribs so tightly that she almost seemed to be hurting herself—so tightly that just looking at her arms wound around her like snakes made my heart feel squeezed.

I patted her on the arm. A one-winged pigeon waddled by.

"He said I wasn't even his kid, he said I came from Uncle Johnny. He said I was garbage, just like my mom and Uncle Johnny. He said I wasn't

---

**3. Rio Deniro:** Patty is mispronouncing Rio de Janeiro, a coastal city in Brazil.

even his kid, he said I wasn't his Patty, he said I came from Uncle Johnny!"

"From your Uncle Johnny?" I said stupidly.

"From Uncle Johnny," she cried. "From Uncle Johnny!"

"He said that?" I said. Then, wanting to go on, to say *something*, I said, "Oh Patty, don't cry."

She kept crying.

I tried again. "Oh Patty, don't cry," I said. Then I said, "Your dad was a jerk anyway."

The pigeon produced a large runny dropping.

It was a good twenty minutes before Patty was calm enough for me just to run to the girls' room to get her some toilet paper; and by the time I came back she was sobbing again, saying "To Rio Deniro, to Rio Deniro" over and over again, as though the words had stuck in her and couldn't be gotten out. As we had missed the regular bus home and the late bus too, I had to leave her a second time to go call my mother, who was only mad until she heard what had happened. Then she came and picked us up, and bought us each a fudgsicle.

Some days later, Patty and I started a program to work on getting her father home. It was a serious business. We said extra prayers, and lit votive candles; I tied my malachite beads to my uniform belt, fondling them as though they were a rosary, I a nun. We even took to walking about the school halls with our hands folded—a sight so ludicrous that our wheeze of a principal personally took us aside one day.

"I must tell you," she said, using her nose as a speaking tube, "that there is really no need for such peee-ity."[4]

But we persisted, promising to marry God and praying to every saint we could think of. We gave up gum, then gum and slim jims both, then gum and slim jims and ice cream—and when even that didn't work, we started on more innovative things. The first was looking at flowers. We held our hands beside our eyes like blinders as we hurried by the violets by the flagpole, the window box full of tulips outside the nurse's office. Next it was looking at boys: Patty gave up angel-eyed Jamie Halloran and I, gymnastic Anthony Rossi. It was hard, but in the end our efforts paid off. Mr. Creamer came back a month later, and though he brought

---

4. **peee-ity:** piety, or devoutness.

with him nothing but dysentery, he was at least too sick to have all that much to say.

Then, in the course of a fight with my father, my mother somehow fell out of their bedroom window.

Recently—thinking a mountain vacation might cheer me—I sublet my apartment to a handsome but somber newlywed couple, who turned out to be every bit as responsible as I'd hoped. They cleaned out even the eggshell chips I'd sprinkled around the base of my plants as fertilizer, leaving behind only a shiny silverplate cake server and a list of their hopes and goals for the summer. The list, tacked precariously to the back of the kitchen door, began with a fervent appeal to God to help them get their wedding thank-yous written in three weeks or less. (You could see they had originally written "two weeks" but scratched it out—no miracles being demanded here.) It went on:

*Please help us, Almighty Father in Heaven Above, to get Ann a teaching job within a half-hour drive of here in a nice neighborhood.*

*Please help us, Almighty Father in Heaven Above, to get John a job doing anything where he won't strain his back and that is within a half-hour drive of here.*

*Please help us, Almighty Father in Heaven Above, to get us a car.*

*Please help us, A.F. in H.A., to learn French.*

*Please help us, A.F. in H.A., to find seven dinner recipes that cost less than 60 cents a serving and can be made in a half-hour. And that don't have tomatoes, since You in Your Heavenly Wisdom made John allergic.*

*Please help us, A.F. in H.A., to avoid books in this apartment such as You in Your Heavenly Wisdom allowed John, for Your Heavenly Reasons, to find three nights ago (June 2nd).*

Et cetera. In the left hand margin they kept score of how they had fared with their requests, and it was heartening to see that nearly all of them were marked "Yes! Praise the Lord!" (sometimes shortened to PTL), with the sole exception of learning French, which was mysteriously marked "No! PTL to the Highest."

That note touched me. Strange and familiar both, it seemed like it had been written by some cousin of mine—some cousin who had stayed home to grow up, say, while I went abroad and learned what I had to, though the learning was painful. This, of course, is just a manner of speaking; in fact, I did my growing up at home, like anybody else.

But the learning *was* painful: I never knew exactly how it happened that my mother went hurtling through the air that night years ago, only that the wind had been chopping at the house, and that the argument had started about the state of the roof. Someone had been up to fix it the year before, but it wasn't a roofer, it was some man my father had insisted could do just as good a job for a quarter of the price. And maybe he could have, had he not somehow managed to step through a knot in the wood under the shingles and break his uninsured ankle. Now the shingles were coming loose again, and the attic insulation was mildewing besides, and my father was wanting to sell the house altogether, which he said my mother had wanted to buy so she could send pictures of it home to her family in China.

"The Americans have a saying," he said. "They saying, 'You have to keep up with the Jones family.' I'm saying if the Jones family in Shanghai, you can send any picture you want, *an-y* picture. Go take picture of those rich guys' house. You want to act like rich guys, right? Go take picture of those rich guys' house."

At that point my mother sent Mona and me to wash up, and started speaking Shanghaiese. They argued for some time in the kitchen, while we listened from the top of the stairs, our faces wedged between the bumpy Spanish scrolls of the wrought iron railing. First my mother ranted, then my father, then they both ranted at once until finally there was a thump, followed by a long quiet.

"Do you think they're kissing now?" said Mona. "I bet they're kissing, like this." She pursed her lips like a fish and was about to put them to the railing when we heard my mother locking the back door. We hightailed it into bed; my parents creaked up the stairs. Everything at that point seemed fine. Once in their bedroom, though, they started up again, first softly, then louder and louder, until my mother turned on a radio to try to disguise the noise. A door slammed; they began shouting at one another; another door slammed; a shoe or something banged the wall behind Mona's bed.

"How're we supposed to *sleep?*" said Mona, sitting up.

There was another thud, more yelling in Shanghaiese, and then my mother's voice pierced the wall, in English. "So what you want I should do? Go to work like Theresa Lee?"

My father rumbled something back.

"You think you're big shot because you have job, right? You're big shot, but you never get promotion, you never get raise. All I do is spend money, right? So what do you do, you tell me. So what do you do!"

Something hit the floor so hard that our room shook.

"So kill me," screamed my mother. "You know what you are? You are failure. Failure! You are failure!"

Then there was a sudden, terrific, bursting crash—and after it, as if on a bungled cue, the serene blare of an a cappella[5] soprano, picking her way down a scale.

By the time Mona and I knew to look out the window, a neighbor's pet beagle was already on the scene, sniffing and barking at my mother's body, his tail crazy with excitement; then he was barking at my stunned and trembling father, at the shrieking ambulance, the police, at crying Mona in her bunny-footed pajamas, and at me, barefoot in the cold grass, squeezing her shoulder with one hand and clutching my malachite beads with the other.

My mother wasn't dead, only unconscious, the paramedics figured that out right away, but there was blood everywhere, and though they were reassuring about her head wounds as they strapped her to the stretcher, commenting also on how small she was, how delicate, how light, my father kept saying, "I killed her, I killed her" as the ambulance screeched and screeched headlong, forever, to the hospital. I was afraid to touch her, and glad of the metal rail between us, even though its sturdiness made her seem even frailer than she was; I wished she was bigger, somehow, and noticed, with a pang, that the new red slippers we had given her for Mother's Day had been lost somewhere along the way. How much she seemed to be leaving behind, as we careened along—still not there, still not there—Mona and Dad and the medic and I taking up the whole ambulance, all the room, so there was no room for anything else; no room even for my mother's real self, the one who should have been pinching the color back to my father's gray face, the one who should have been calming Mona's cowlick—the one who should have been bending over us, to help us to be strong, to help us get through, even as we bent over her.

_____

5. **a cappella:** singing without instrumental accompaniment.

Then suddenly we were there, the glowing square of the emergency room entrance opening like the gates of heaven; and immediately the talk of miracles began. Alive, a miracle. No bones broken, a miracle. A miracle that the hemlocks cushioned her fall, a miracle that they hadn't been trimmed in a year and a half. It was a miracle that all that blood, the blood that had seemed that night to be everywhere, was from one shard of glass, a single shard, can you imagine, and as for the gash in her head, the scar would be covered by hair. The next day my mother cheerfully described just how she would part it so that nothing would show at all.

"You're a lucky duck-duck," agreed Mona, helping herself, with a little *pirouette*, to the cherry atop my mother's chocolate pudding.

That wasn't enough for me, though. I was relieved, yes, but what I wanted by then was a real miracle, not for her simply to have survived but for the whole thing never to have happened—for my mother's head never to had to have been shaved and bandaged like that, for her high, proud forehead to never have been swollen down over her eyes, for her face and neck and hands never to have been painted so many shades of blue-black, and violet, and chartreuse. I still want those things—for my parents not to have had to live with this affair like a prickle-bush between them, for my father to have been able to look my mother in her swollen eyes and curse the madman, the monster that could have dared do this to the woman he loved. I wanted to be able to touch my mother without shuddering, to be able to console my father, to be able to get that crash out of my head, the sound of that soprano—so many things that I didn't know how to pray for them, that I wouldn't have known where to start even if I had the power to work miracles, right there, right then.

A week later, when my mother was home, and her head beginning to bristle with new hairs, I lost my malachite beads. I had been carrying them in a white cloth pouch that Patty had given me, and was swinging the pouch on my pinky on my way home from school, when I swung just a bit too hard, and it went sailing in a long arc through the air, whooshing like a perfectly thrown basketball through one of those holes of a nearby sewer. There was no chance of fishing it out: I looked and looked, crouching on the sticky pavement until the asphalt had crazed the skin of my hands and knees, but all I could discern was an evil-smelling musk, glassy and smug and impenetrable.

My loss didn't quite hit me until I was home, but then it produced an agony all out of proportion to my string of pretty beads. I hadn't cried at all during my mother's accident, and now I was crying all afternoon, all through dinner, and then after dinner too, crying past the point where I knew what I was crying for, wishing dimly that I had my beads to hold, wishing dimly that I could pray but refusing, refusing, I didn't know why, until I finally fell into an exhausted sleep on the couch, where my parents left me for the night—glad, no doubt, that one of the more tedious of my childhood crises seemed to be finally winding off the reel of life, onto the reel of memory. They covered me, and somehow grew a pillow under my head, and, with uncharacteristic disregard for the living-room rug, left some milk and pecan sandies on the coffee table, in case I woke up hungry. Their thoughtfulness was prescient:[6] I did wake up in the early part of the night; and it was then, amid the unfamiliar sounds and shadows of the living room, that I had what I was sure was a true vision.

Even now what I saw retains an odd clarity: the requisite strange light flooding the room, first orange, and then a bright yellow-green, then a crackling bright burst like a Roman candle going off near the piano. There was a distinct smell of coffee, and a long silence. The room seemed to be getting colder. Nothing. A creak; the light starting to wane, then waxing again, brilliant pink now. Still nothing. Then, as the pink started to go a little purple, a perfectly normal middle-aged man's voice, speaking something very like pig latin, told me quietly not to despair, not to despair, my beads would be returned to me.

That was all. I sat a moment in the dark, then turned on the light, gobbled down the cookies—and in a happy flash understood I was so good, really, so near to being a saint that my malachite beads would come back through the town water system. All I had to do was turn on all the faucets in the house, which I did, one by one, stealing quietly into the bathroom and kitchen and basement. The old spigot by the washing machine was too gunked up to be coaxed very far open, but that didn't matter. The water didn't have to be full blast, I understood that. Then I gathered together my pillow and blanket and trundled up to my bed to sleep.

---

6. **prescient:** foreseeing; knowing beforehand.

By the time I woke up in the morning I knew that my beads hadn't shown up, but when I knew it for certain, I was still disappointed; and as if that weren't enough, I had to face my parents and sister, who were all abuzz with the mystery of the faucets. Not knowing what else to do, I, like a puddlebrain, told them the truth. The results were predictably painful.

"Callie had a *vision*," Mona told everyone at the bus stop. "A vision with lights, and sinks in it!"

Sinks, visions. I got it all day, from my parents, from my classmates, even some sixth and seventh graders. Someone drew a cartoon of me with a halo over my head in one of the girls' room stalls; Anthony Rossi made gurgling noises as he walked on his hands at recess. Only Patty tried not to laugh, though even she was something less than unalloyed understanding.

"I don't think miracles are thupposed to happen in *thewers*," she said.

Such was the end of my saintly ambitions. It wasn't the end of all holiness; the ideas of purity and goodness still tippled my brain, and over the years I came slowly to grasp of what grit true faith was made. Last night, though, when my father called to say that he couldn't go on living in our old house, that he was going to move to a smaller place, another place, maybe a condo—he didn't know how, or where—I found myself still wistful for the time religion seemed all I wanted it to be. Back then the world was a place that could be set right: One had only to direct the hand of the Almighty and say, just here, Lord, we hurt here—and here, and here, and here.

## Responding to the Story

1. What common experiences of growing up does Gish Jen present in this story? Consider that for something to be a "common experience" you presumably have lived it yourself or observed it.

2. How does the narrator's view of religion change from the beginning to the end of the story?

## Exploring the Author's Craft

**Humor** is basically anything that causes laughter or amusement, often through exaggeration or unexpected turns of events. There is a humorous tone to this short story, even as the narrator tells of some rather significant and dramatic events. Point out four different moments or lines of humor in the story.

## Writer's Workshop

One technique that can really help you as a beginning fiction writer is to try to create a distinctive first-person voice, a voice that might be quite different from your own. Creating that different voice might liberate you to go beyond your own experiences and actually create fiction.

Your challenge here, inspired by Gish Jen's humorous narrator, is to create a first-person voice that is humorous yet tells about events that are far more significant than silly. Write at least five hundred words; what you produce may serve as the beginning of something much more developed.

## Robert Cormier

Robert Cormier changed the face of literature for young adults with his novel *The Chocolate War*. Published in 1974, the book was realistic and also brutal, and it didn't have a happy ending. Cormier, who was born in 1925 in a small town in Massachusetts, specializes in this kind of writing. He says that, prompted by watching his children grow up, he can remember countless details of his own adolescence. One of the hallmarks of his writing is his skillful use of figurative language.

*Do people in nursing homes just sit there vacantly, or do they, too, have their memories and regrets?*

# The Moustache

At the last minute Annie couldn't go. She was invaded by one of those twenty-four-hour flu bugs that sent her to bed with a fever, moaning about the fact that she'd also have to break her date with Handsome Harry Arnold that night. We call him Handsome Harry because he's actually handsome, but he's also a nice guy, cool, and he doesn't treat me like Annie's kid brother, which I am, but like a regular person. Anyway, I had to go to Lawnrest alone that afternoon. But first of all I had to stand inspection. My mother lined me up against the wall. She stood there like a one-man firing squad, which is kind of funny because she's not like a man at all, she's very feminine, and we have this great relationship—I mean, I feel as if she really likes me. I realize that sounds strange, but I know guys whose mothers love them and cook special stuff for them and worry about them and all but there's something missing in their relationship.

Anyway. She frowned and started the routine.

"That hair," she said. Then admitted: "Well, at least you combed it."

I sighed. I have discovered that it's better to sigh than argue.

"And that moustache." She shook her head. "I still say a seventeen-year-old has no business wearing a moustache."

"It's an experiment," I said. "I just wanted to see if I could grow one." To tell the truth, I had proved my point about being able to grow a decent moustache, but I also had learned to like it.

"It's costing you money, Mike," she said.

"I know, I know."

The money was a reference to the movies. The Downtown Cinema has a special Friday night offer—half-price admission for high school couples, seventeen or younger. But the woman in the box office took one look at my moustache and charged me full price. Even when I showed her my driver's license. She charged full admission for Cindy's ticket, too, which left me practically broke and unable to take Cindy out for a hamburger with the crowd afterward. That didn't help matters, because Cindy has been getting impatient recently about things like the fact that I don't own my own car and have to concentrate on my studies if I want to win that college scholarship, for instance. Cindy wasn't exactly crazy about the moustache, either.

Now it was my mother's turn to sigh.

"Look," I said, to cheer her up. "I'm thinking about shaving it off." Even though I wasn't. Another discovery: You can build a way of life on postponement.

"Your grandmother probably won't even recognize you," she said. And I saw the shadow fall across her face.

Let me tell you what the visit to Lawnrest was all about. My grandmother is seventy-three years old. She is a resident—which is supposed to be a better word than *patient*—at the Lawnrest Nursing Home. She used to make the greatest turkey dressing in the world and was a nut about baseball and could even quote batting averages, for crying out loud. She always rooted for the losers. She was in love with the Mets until they started to win. Now she has arteriosclerosis, which the dictionary says is "a chronic disease characterized by abnormal thickening and hardening of the arterial walls." Which really means that she can't live at home anymore or even with us, and her memory has betrayed her as well as her body. She used to wander off and sometimes didn't recognize people. My mother visits her all the time, driving the thirty miles to Lawnrest almost every day. Because Annie was home for a semester break from college, we had decided to make a special Saturday visit. Now Annie was in bed, groaning theatrically—she's a drama major—but I told my mother I'd go anyway. I hadn't seen my grandmother since she'd been admitted to Lawnrest. Besides, the place is located on the Southwest Turnpike, which meant I could barrel along in my father's new LeMans. My ambition was to see the speedometer hit seventy-five. Ordinarily, I used the old station wagon, which can barely stagger up to fifty.

Frankly, I wasn't too crazy about visiting a nursing home. They reminded me of hospitals and hospitals turn me off. I mean, the smell of ether makes me nauseous, and I feel faint at the sight of blood. And as I approached Lawnrest—which is a terrible cemetery kind of name, to begin with—I was sorry I hadn't avoided the trip. Then I felt guilty about it. I'm loaded with guilt complexes. Like driving like a madman after promising my father to be careful. Like sitting in the parking lot, looking at the nursing home with dread and thinking how I'd rather be with Cindy. Then I thought of all the Christmas and birthday gifts my grandmother had given me and I got out of the car, guilty as usual. Inside, I was surprised by the lack of hospital smell, although there was another odor or maybe the absence of an odor. The air was antiseptic, sterile. As if there was no atmosphere at all or I'd caught a cold suddenly and couldn't taste or smell.

A nurse at the reception desk gave me directions—my grandmother was in East Three. I made my way down the tiled corridor and was glad to see that the walls were painted with cheerful colors like yellow and pink. A wheelchair suddenly shot around a corner, self-propelled by an old man, white-haired and toothless, who cackled merrily as he barely missed me. I jumped aside—here I was, almost getting wiped out by a two-mile-an-hour wheelchair after doing seventy-five on the pike. As I walked through the corridor seeking East Three, I couldn't help glancing into the rooms, and it was like some kind of wax museum—all these figures in various stances and attitudes, sitting in beds or chairs, standing at windows, as if they were frozen forever in these postures. To tell the truth, I began to hurry because I was getting depressed. Finally, I saw a beautiful girl approaching, dressed in white, a nurse or an attendant, and I was so happy to see someone young, someone walking and acting normally, that I gave her a wide smile and a big hello and I must have looked like a kind of nut. Anyway, she looked right through me as if I were a window, which is about par for the course whenever I meet beautiful girls.

I finally found the room and saw my grandmother in bed. My grandmother looks like Ethel Barrymore.[1] I never knew who Ethel Barrymore was until I saw a terrific movie, *None But the Lonely Heart*, on TV, starring Ethel Barrymore and Cary Grant. Both my grandmother and Ethel Barrymore have these great craggy faces like the side of a mountain and wonderful voices like syrup being poured. Slowly. She was propped up in bed, pillows puffed behind her. Her hair had been combed out and fell upon her shoulders. For some reason, this flowing hair gave her an almost girlish appearance, despite its whiteness.

She saw me and smiled. Her eyes lit up and her eyebrows arched and she reached out her hands to me in greeting. "Mike, Mike," she said. And I breathed a sigh of relief. This was one of her good days. My mother had warned me that she might not know who I was at first.

I took her hands in mine. They were fragile. I could actually feel her bones, and it seemed as if they would break if I pressed too hard. Her skin was smooth, almost slippery, as if the years had worn away all the roughness the way the wind wears away the surfaces of stones.

"Mike, Mike, I didn't think you'd come," she said, so happy, and she was still Ethel Barrymore, that voice like a caress. "I've been waiting all this time." Before I could reply, she looked away, out the window. "See the birds? I've been watching them at the feeder. I love to see them come. Even the blue jays. The blue jays are like hawks—they take the food that the small birds should have. But the small birds, the chickadees, watch the blue jays and at least learn where the feeder is."

She lapsed into silence, and I looked out the window. There was no feeder. No birds. There was only the parking lot and the sun glinting on car windshields.

She turned to me again, eyes bright. Radiant, really. Or was it a medicine brightness? "Ah, Mike. You look so grand, so grand. Is that a new coat?"

"Not really," I said. I'd been wearing my Uncle Jerry's old army-fatigue jacket for months, practically living in it, my mother said. But

---

1. **Ethel Barrymore:** (1879–1959) a distinguished stage and film actor; member of a famous family of actors that included her brothers Lionel and John.

she insisted that I wear my raincoat for the visit. It was about a year old but looked new because I didn't wear it much. Nobody was wearing raincoats lately.

"You always loved clothes, didn't you, Mike?" she said.

I was beginning to feel uneasy because she regarded me with such intensity. Those bright eyes. I wondered—are old people in places like this so lonesome, so abandoned that they go wild when someone visits? Or was she so happy because she was suddenly lucid and everything was sharp and clear? My mother had described those moments when my grandmother suddenly emerged from the fog that so often obscured her mind. I didn't know the answers, but it felt kind of spooky, getting such an emotional welcome from her.

"I remember the time you bought the new coat—the Chesterfield," she said, looking away again, as if watching the birds that weren't there. "That lovely coat with the velvet collar. Black, it was. Stylish. Remember that, Mike? It was hard times, but you could never resist the glitter."

I was about to protest—I had never heard of a Chesterfield, for crying out loud. But I stopped. Be patient with her, my mother had said. Humor her. Be gentle.

We were interrupted by an attendant who pushed a wheeled cart into the room. "Time for juices, dear," the woman said. She was the standard forty- or fifty-year-old woman: glasses, nothing hair, plump cheeks. Her manner was cheerful but a businesslike kind of cheerfulness. I'd hate to be called "dear" by someone getting paid to do it. "Orange or grape or cranberry, dear? Cranberry is good for the bones, you know."

My grandmother ignored the interruption. She didn't even bother to answer, having turned away at the woman's arrival, as if angry about her appearance.

The woman looked at me and winked. A conspiratorial[2] kind of wink. It was kind of horrible. I didn't think people winked like that anymore. In fact, I hadn't seen a wink in years.

"She doesn't care much for juices," the woman said, talking to me as if my grandmother weren't even there. "But she loves her coffee. With lots of cream and two lumps of sugar. But this is juice time, not coffee

---

2. **conspiratorial:** as if involved together in some secret plot or plan.

time." Addressing my grandmother again, she said, "Orange or grape or cranberry, dear?"

"Tell her I want no juices, Mike," my grandmother commanded regally, her eyes still watching invisible birds.

The woman smiled, patience like a label on her face. "That's all right, dear. I'll just leave some cranberry for you. Drink it at your leisure. It's good for the bones."

She wheeled herself out of the room. My grandmother was still absorbed in the view. Somewhere a toilet flushed. A wheelchair passed the doorway—probably that same old driver fleeing a hit-run accident. A television set exploded with sound somewhere, soap-opera voices filling the air. You can always tell soap-opera voices.

I turned back to find my grandmother staring at me. Her hands cupped her face, her index fingers curled around her cheeks like parenthesis marks.

"But you know, Mike, looking back, I think you were right," she said, continuing our conversation as if there had been no interruption. "You always said, 'It's the things of the spirit that count, Meg.' The spirit! And so you bought the baby-grand piano—a baby grand in the middle of the Depression.[3] A knock came on the door and it was the deliveryman. It took five of them to get it into the house." She leaned back, closing her eyes. "How I loved that piano, Mike. I was never that fine a player, but you loved to sit there in the parlor, on Sunday evenings, Ellie on your lap, listening to me play and sing." She hummed a bit, a fragment of melody I didn't recognize. Then she drifted into silence. Maybe she'd fallen asleep. My mother's name is Ellen, but everyone always calls her Ellie. "Take my hand, Mike," my grandmother said suddenly. Then I remembered—my grandfather's name was Michael. I had been named for him.

"Ah, Mike," she said, pressing my hands with all her feeble strength. "I thought I'd lost you forever. And here you are, back with me again. . . ."

Her expression scared me. I don't mean scared as if I were in danger but scared because of what could happen to her when she realized the mistake she had made. My mother always said I favored her side of the

---

3. **the Depression:** period during the 1930s when the economy was very bad and many people were out of work.

family. Thinking back to the pictures in the old family albums, I recalled my grandfather as tall and thin. Like me. But the resemblance ended there. He was thirty-five when he died, almost forty years old. And he wore a moustache. I brought my hand to my face. I also wore a moustache now, of course.

"I sit here these days, Mike," she said, her voice a lullaby, her hand still holding mine, "and I drift and dream. The days are fuzzy sometimes, merging together. Sometimes it's like I'm not here at all but somewhere else altogether. And I always think of you. Those hours we had. Not enough years, Mike, not enough. . . ."

Her voice was so sad, so mournful that I made sounds of sympathy, not words exactly but the kind of soothings that mothers murmur to their children when they awaken from bad dreams.

"And I think of that terrible night, Mike, that terrible night. Have you ever really forgiven me for that night?"

"Listen . . . , " I began. I wanted to say: "Nana, this is Mike your grandson, not Mike your husband."

"Sh . . . sh . . . ," she whispered, placing a finger as long and cold as a candle against my lips. "Don't say anything. I've waited so long for this moment. To be here. With you. I wondered what I would say if suddenly you walked in that door like other people have done. I've thought and thought about it. And I finally made up my mind—I'd ask you to forgive me. I was too proud to ask before." Her fingers tried to mask her face. "But I'm not proud anymore, Mike." That great voice quivered and then grew strong again. "I hate you to see me this way— you always said I was beautiful. I didn't believe it. The Charity Ball when we led the grand march and you said I was the most beautiful girl there . . ."

"Nana," I said. I couldn't keep up the pretense any longer, adding one more burden to my load of guilt, leading her on this way, playing a pathetic game of make-believe with an old woman clinging to memories. She didn't seem to hear me.

"But that other night, Mike. The terrible one. The terrible accusations I made. Even Ellie woke up and began to cry. I went to her and rocked her in my arms and you came into the room and said I was wrong. You were whispering, an awful whisper, not wanting to upset little Ellie but wanting to make me see the truth. And I didn't answer you, Mike. I was too proud. I've even forgotten the name of the girl. I sit here, wondering now—was it Laura or Evelyn? I can't remember. Later, I learned that you were telling the truth all the time, Mike. That I'd been wrong . . ." Her eyes were brighter than ever as she looked at me now, but tear-bright, the tears gathering. "It was never the same after that night, was it, Mike? The glitter was gone. From you. From us. And then the accident . . . and I never had the chance to ask you to forgive me . . ."

My grandmother. My poor, poor grandmother. Old people aren't supposed to have those kinds of memories. You see their pictures in the family albums and that's what they are: pictures. They're not supposed to come to life. You drive out in your father's LeMans doing seventy-five on the pike and all you're doing is visiting an old lady in a nursing home. A duty call. And then you find out that she's a person. She's *somebody*. She's my grandmother, all right, but she's also herself. Like my own mother and father. They exist outside of their relationship to me. I was scared again. I wanted to get out of there.

"Mike, Mike," my grandmother said. "Say it, Mike."

I felt as if my cheeks would crack if I uttered a word.

"Say you forgive me, Mike. I've waited all these years . . ."

I was surprised at how strong her fingers were.

"Say, *'I forgive you, Meg.'*"

I said it. My voice sounded funny, as if I were talking in a huge tunnel. "I forgive you, Meg."

Her eyes studied me. Her hands pressed mine. For the first time in my life, I saw love at work. Not movie love. Not Cindy's sparkling eyes when I tell her that we're going to the beach on a Sunday afternoon. But love like something alive and tender, asking nothing in return. She raised her face, and I knew what she wanted me to do. I bent and brushed my lips against her cheek. Her flesh was like a leaf in autumn, crisp and dry.

She closed her eyes and I stood up. The sun wasn't glinting on the cars any longer. Somebody had turned on another television set, and the voices were the show-off voices of the panel shows. At the same time you could still hear the soap-opera dialogue on the other television set.

I waited awhile. She seemed to be sleeping, her breathing serene and regular. I buttoned my raincoat. Suddenly she opened her eyes again and looked at me. Her eyes were still bright, but they merely stared at me. Without recognition or curiosity. Empty eyes. I smiled at her, but she didn't smile back. She made a kind of moaning sound and turned away on the bed, pulling the blankets around her.

I counted to twenty-five and then to fifty and did it all over again. I cleared my throat and coughed tentatively.[4] She didn't move; she didn't respond. I wanted to say, "Nana, it's me." But I didn't. I thought of saying, "Meg, it's me." But I couldn't.

Finally I left. Just like that. I didn't say goodbye or anything. I stalked through the corridors, looking neither to the right nor the left, not caring whether that wild old man with the wheelchair ran me down or not.

On the Southwest Turnpike I did seventy-five—no, eighty—most of the way. I turned the radio up as loud as it could go. Rock music—anything to fill the air. When I got home, my mother was vacuuming the living-room rug. She shut off the cleaner, and the silence was deafening. "Well, how was your grandmother?" she asked.

I told her she was fine. I told her a lot of things. How great Nana looked and how she seemed happy and had called me Mike. I wanted to ask her—hey, Mom, you and Dad really love each other, don't you? I mean—there's nothing to forgive between you, is there? But I didn't.

Instead I went upstairs and took out the electric razor Annie had given me for Christmas and shaved off my moustache.

---

4. **tentatively:** in an uncertain, hesitating manner.

---

## Responding to the Story

1.  Why does Mike shave off his moustache at the story's end? Explain your thoughts in some detail.
2.  Was Mike right in pretending to be his grandfather? Why or why not?
3.  What elements of your own experience were you reminded of as you read "The Moustache"?

## Exploring the Author's Craft

**Figurative language** is the general term for language making comparisons that are to be interpreted more imaginatively than realistically. Similes and metaphors are examples; so sometimes are analogies, more extended comparisons between two basically different things that have some points in common.

For the following examples of figurative language, tell what the author is trying to summon up in the reader's mind and whether or not you think he succeeded.

a. ". . . the corridor . . . was like some kind of wax museum—all these figures in various stances and attitudes, sitting in beds or chairs, standing at windows, as if they were frozen forever in these postures."

b. "Her skin was smooth, almost slippery, as if the years had worn away all the roughness the way the wind wears away the surfaces of stones."

c. ". . . and she was still Ethel Barrymore, that voice like a caress."

d. "Her flesh was like a leaf in autumn, crisp and dry."

## Writer's Workshop

By practicing with figurative language, you may begin to use it naturally and spontaneously in your writing. Take any experience of yours in the last full day and describe it. Include three figurative comparisons in the midst of three paragraphs of description and narration about your experience. Try to make one of your comparisons a rather extended one, as Cormier did in his description of the corridor as a wax museum.

## Alternate Media Response

In a creative form other than writing, deal with the topic of the elderly. You might paint or sculpt an image of an older person, or do a photographic collage on this theme, or videotape an interview with several older people.

# Maria Mazziotti Gillan

Maria Mazziotti Gillan is the director of the Poetry Center at Passaic County Community College in Paterson, New Jersey, and the editor of *Footwork: The Paterson Literary Review*. She has read her work on National Public Radio on *The Poet and the Poem* and *All Things Considered*. She says, "Increasingly my sense of myself as an Italian American has informed my work. I think of my work as a way of giving voice to people who could not speak for themselves, a way of making the Italian American person real for other Americans who are so influenced by stereotypical images of what it means to be Italian American."

Gillan, who was born in 1940, says, "I grew up in Paterson, New Jersey. I knew very few English words and was afraid to speak out because I was frightened that instead of using the English word, I would use the Italian one by mistake. I have written a great deal about silence and about finding the courage to speak." Of "Betrayals" she says, "In writing this poem, I tried to capture the way a moment in the present can make us remember something that we did or said when we were very young so that we are seeing that moment from the perspective of the person we have become."

*If your parents sometimes embarrass you, consider that one day you might embarrass your own children.*

# Betrayals

At thirteen, I screamed,
"You're disgusting,"
drinking your coffee from a saucer.
Your startled eyes darkened with shame.

5   You, one dead leg dragging,
counting your night-shift hours,
You, smiling past yellowed, gaping teeth,
You, mixing the egg nog for me yourself
in a fat dime store cup.

10  How I betrayed you,
over and over, ashamed of your broken tongue,
how I laughed, savage and innocent,
at your mutilations.[1]

Today, my son shouts,
15  "Don't tell anyone you're my mother,"
hunching down in the car
so the other boys won't see us together.

Daddy, are you laughing?
Oh, how things turn full circle,

---

1. **mutilations:** acts of destroying or wrecking—in this case, the English language.

20    My own words coming back

to slap my face.


I was sixteen when you called one night from your work.

I called you dear,

loving you in that moment

25    past all barriers of the heart.

You called again every night for a week.

I never said it again.

I wish I could say it now.


Dear, my Dear

30    with your twisted tongue

I did not understand you

dragging your burden of love.

---

## Responding to the Poem

1. In a sentence, summarize why you think the narrator was embarrassed about her father.
2. What do you think the narrator means by the last line, "dragging your burden of love"?

## Exploring the Author's Craft

**Irony** is a term that refers to the difference between what is expected and what really is. Often it involves the contrast between something that happens and its significance in the light of other things that happen.

Explain what is ironic about the events described in this poem. To what realizations does the irony lead the narrator?

## Writer's Workshop

Create a free-verse poem—no rhyme or fixed rhythm—that deals with a realization made about a parent or caregiver.

## Two Perspectives

### John Cheever

John Cheever was born in 1912. A master of the short story, Cheever published in a variety of magazines such as *The Atlantic Monthly* and *The New Yorker;* many stories were later collected into books. Cheever also wrote several novels and won both a National Book Award and a Pulitzer Prize for his fiction. Much of Cheever's writing is set in middle-class, suburban America, but the points he makes frequently seem relevant to a much wider audience. Cheever died in 1982.

### Gordon Hunt/Amanda McBroom

Stephen Holden of *The New York Times* says of cabaret singer Amanda McBroom, "[Her] rich warm contralto, which finds a perfect balance between intimate expression and theatrical interpretation, infuses her songs' first-person narrators with an open-hearted humanity that is uplifting for seeming utterly natural." The song that follows, "Errol Flynn," shows that humanity and naturalness as McBroom presents a recollection of her father. Gordon Hunt worked with Amanda McBroom on the lyrics of this song.

*What memories of their parents would children like to have?*

# Reunion

### John Cheever

**T**he last time I saw my father was in Grand Central Station. I was going from my grandmother's in the Adirondacks to a cottage on the Cape that my mother had rented, and I wrote my father that I would be in New York between trains for an hour and a half, and asked if we could have lunch together. His secretary wrote to say that he would meet me at the information booth at noon, and at twelve o'clock sharp I saw him coming through the crowd. He was a stranger to me—my mother divorced him three years ago and I hadn't been with him since—but as soon as I saw him I felt that he was my father, my flesh and blood, my future and my doom. I knew that when I was grown I would be something like him: I would have to plan my campaigns within his limitations. He was a big, good-looking man, and I was terribly happy to see him again. He struck me on the back and shook my hand. "Hi, Charlie," he said. "Hi, boy. I'd like to take you up to my club, but it's in the Sixties,[1] and if you have to catch an early train I guess we'd better get something to eat around here." He put his arm around me, and I smelled my father the way my mother sniffs a rose. It was a rich compound of whiskey, after-shave lotion, shoe polish, woolens, and the rankness of a mature male. I hoped that someone would see us together. I wished that we could be photographed. I wanted some record of our having been together.

We went out of the station and up a side street to a restaurant. It was still early, and the place was empty. The bartender was quarreling with a delivery boy, and there was one very old waiter in a red coat down by the kitchen door. We sat down, and my father hailed the waiter in a loud voice. *"Kellner!"* he shouted. *"Garçon! Cameriere![2] You!"* His boisterousness in the empty restaurant seemed out of place. "Could we have a little service here!" he shouted. "Chop chop." Then he clapped his hands. This caught the waiter's attention and he shuffled over to our table.

"Were you clapping your hands at me?" he asked.

---

1. **Sixties:** that is, somewhere between 60th and 69th streets.
2. *Kellner! . . . Garçon! Cameriere:* the German, French, and Italian words for waiter.

"Calm down, calm down, *sommelier*,"[3] my father said. "If it isn't too much to ask of you—if it wouldn't be too much above and beyond the call of duty, we would like a couple of Beefeater Gibsons."

"I don't like to be clapped at," the waiter said.

"I should have brought my whistle," my father said. "I have a whistle that is audible only to the ears of old waiters. Now, take out your little pad and your little pencil and see if you can get this straight: two Beefeater Gibsons. Repeat after me: two Beefeater Gibsons."

"I think you'd better go somewhere else," the waiter said quietly.

"That," said my father, "is one of the most brilliant suggestions I have ever heard. Come on, Charlie, let's get the hell out of here."

I followed my father out of that restaurant into another. He was not so boisterous this time. Our drinks came, and he cross-questioned me about the baseball season. He then struck the edge of his empty glass with his knife and began shouting again. "*Garçon! Kellner! Cameriere! You!* Could we trouble you to bring us two more of the same."

"How old is the boy?" the waiter asked.

"That," my father said, "is none of your God-damned business."

"I'm sorry, sir," the waiter said, "but I won't serve the boy another drink."

"Well, I have some news for you," my father said. "I have some very interesting news for you. This doesn't happen to be the only restaurant in New York. They've opened another on the corner. Come on, Charlie."

He paid the bill, and I followed him out of that restaurant into another. Here the waiters wore pink jackets like hunting coats, and there was a lot of horse tack on the walls. We sat down and my father began to shout again. "Master of the hounds! Tallyhoo and all that sort of thing! We'd like a little something in the way of a stirrup cup. Namely, two Bibson Geefeaters."

"Two Bibson Geefeaters?" the waiter asked, smiling.

"You know damned well what I want," my father said angrily. "I want to Beefeater Gibsons, and make it snappy. Things have changed in jolly old England. So my friend the duke tells me. Let's see what England can produce in the way of a cocktail."

"This isn't England," the waiter said.

"Don't argue with me," my father said. "Just do as you're told."

"I just thought you might like to know where you are," the waiter said.

---

3. *sommelier:* waiter in charge of wine and other liquors.

"If there is one thing I cannot tolerate," my father said, "it is an impudent domestic.[4] Come on, Charlie."

The fourth place we went to was Italian. *"Buon giorno,"* my father said. *"Per favore, possiamo avere due cocktail americani, forti, forti. Molto gin, poco vermut."*[5]

"I don't understand Italian," the waiter said.

"Oh, come off it," my father said. "You understand Italian, and you know damned well you do. *Vogliamo due cocktail americani. Subito."*[6]

The waiter left us and spoke with the captain, who came over to our table and said, "I'm sorry, sir, but this table is reserved."

"All right," my father said. "Get us another table."

"All the tables are reserved," the captain said.

"I get it," my father said. "You don't desire our patronage. Is that it? Well, the hell with you. *Vada all' inferno.* Let's go, Charlie."

"I have to get my train," I said.

"I'm sorry, sonny," my father said. "I'm terribly sorry." He put his arm around me and pressed me against him. "I'll walk you back to the station. If there had only been time to go up to my club."

"That's all right, Daddy," I said.

"I'll get you a paper," he said. "I'll get you a paper to read on the train."

Then he went up to a newsstand and said, "Kind sir, will you be good enough to favor me with one of your God-damned, no-good, ten-cent afternoon papers?" The clerk turned away from him and stared at a magazine cover. "Is it asking too much, kind sir," my father said, "is it asking too much for you to sell me one of your disgusting specimens of yellow journalism?"[7]

"I have to go, Daddy," I said. "It's late."

"Now, just wait a second, sonny," he said. "Just wait a second. I want to get a rise out of this chap."

"Goodbye, Daddy," I said, and I went down the stairs and got my train, and that was the last time I saw my father.

---

4. **domestic:** usually, a hired household servant.
5. ***Buon giorno . . . vermut:*** Good day. Please give us two American cocktails [martinis], very strong. A lot of gin, a little vermouth.[Italian]
6. ***Vogliamo . . . Subito:*** We want two American cocktails. Right now. [Italian]
7. **yellow journalism:** sensational brand of journalism given to screaming headlines, slanted reporting, and outright fraud, prevalent in the late nineteenth century.

# Errol Flynn

**Gordon Hunt /Amanda McBroom**

In a hall on a wall in a house in Reseda,
There's a poster held up by two nails and a pin.
It's my daddy, the actor 'bout to die with his boots on.
He's the man standing up there beside Errol Flynn.[1]

5  He got third or fourth billing at the end of each picture.
"That don't mean much," he would say with a grin.
But he held my hand tight as he pointed his name out
Only four or five names down below Errol Flynn.

Fame. It is fleeting and stars, they keep falling,
10  And staying right up there . . . that's the business of art.
And luck kisses some, and she passes by others.
Disappointment and bourbon are hard on the heart.

Now the women and beers and the years with old Errol
They took their toll and took me from his side.
15  He kissed me goodbye at the old Union Station.
That's the last time I saw him. The last time I cried.

Now I'm sitting alone in a house in Reseda,

---

1. **Errol Flynn:** actor famous for his portrayal of swashbuckling heroes in movies made from the 1930s to the 1950s.

Watching the late show as moonlight shines in,

And up on the screen . . . well, here comes my daddy.

20  It's a sad funny feeling. Now I'm older than him.


So, you daddys and daughters, you sons and you mothers,

Remember life's over before it begins.

So love one another and stand close together . . .

As close as my dad did to old Errol Flynn.

---

## Responding to the Selections

1.  Since the "reunion" in John Cheever's story was the last time the narrator saw his father, what is he most likely to remember about the man? Support your answer with evidence from the text.
2.  As Amanda McBroom thinks back about her father, character actor David Bruce, what kind of feelings does she express? Explain with references from the text.
3.  What advice about life does the writing team of Hunt and McBroom explicitly give us? What advice about being a parent might John Cheever's narrator give?


## Exploring the Authors' Craft

"Show, don't tell" is one of the oldest formulas ever given to writers. Explain how John Cheever employed that formula in creating "Reunion."

## Writer's Workshop

In any writing form you choose—a story, a script, a poem—produce your own creative writing about a parent and a child.

## Alternate Media Response

In any medium other than writing, create a work that deals with a parent and a child. Try to convey an attitude or point of view in the work, as Cheever and Hunt/McBroom did.

## Toni Cade Bambara

Toni Cade Bambara was born in 1939 in New York City. She worked as a film producer and was active in the civil rights movement in the 1960s and 1970s. Her short story collections, including *Gorilla, My Love* and *The Sea Birds Are Still Alive*, often deal with street-smart city characters who sometimes have to struggle to survive. She also edited two collections of stories by other African-American writers. Bambara, who wrote the widely anthologized short story "Raymond's Run," died in 1995.

*Some days, the world just doesn't look very beautiful.*

# Geraldine Moore the Poet

Geraldine paused at the corner to pull up her knee socks. The rubber bands she was using to hold them up made her legs itch. She dropped her books on the sidewalk while she gave a good scratch. But when she pulled the socks up again, two fingers poked right through the top of her left one.

"That stupid dog," she muttered to herself, grabbing at her books and crossing against traffic. "First he chews up my gym suit and gets me into trouble, and now my socks."

Geraldine shifted her books to the other hand and kept muttering angrily to herself about Mrs. Watson's dog, which she minded two days a week for a dollar. She passed the hot-dog man on the corner and waved. He shrugged as if to say business was very bad.

*Must be,* she thought to herself. *Three guys before you had to pack up and forget it. Nobody's got hot-dog money around here.*

Geraldine turned down her street, wondering what her sister Anita would have for her lunch. She was glad she didn't have to eat the free lunches in high school any more. She was sick of the funny-looking tomato soup and the dried-out cheese sandwiches and those oranges that were more green than orange.

When Geraldine's mother first took sick and went away, Geraldine had been on her own except when Miss Gladys next door came in on Thursdays and cleaned the apartment and made a meat loaf so Geraldine could have dinner. But in those days Geraldine never quite managed to get breakfast for herself. So she'd sit through social studies class, scraping her feet to cover up the noise of her stomach growling.

Now Anita, Geraldine's older sister, was living at home waiting for her husband to get out of the Army. She usually had something good for lunch—chicken and dumplings if she managed to get up in time, or baked ham from the night before and sweet-potato bread. But even if there was only a hot dog and some baked beans—sometimes just a TV dinner if those soap operas kept Anita glued to the TV set—anything was better than the noisy school lunchroom where monitors kept pushing you into a straight line or rushing you to the tables. Anything was better than that.

Geraldine was almost home when she stopped dead. Right outside her building was a pile of furniture and some boxes. That wasn't anything new. She had seen people get put out in the street before, but this time the ironing board looked familiar. And she recognized the big, ugly sofa standing on its arm, its underbelly showing the hole where Mrs. Watson's dog had gotten to it.

Miss Gladys was sitting on the stoop, and she looked up and took off her glasses. "Well, Gerry," she said slowly, wiping her glasses on the hem of her dress, "looks like you'll be staying with me for a while." She looked at the men carrying out a big box with an old doll sticking up over the edge. "Anita's upstairs. Go on up and get your lunch."

Geraldine stepped past the old woman and almost bumped into the superintendent. He took off his cap to wipe away the sweat.

"Darn shame," he said to no one in particular. "Poor people sure got a hard row to hoe."

"That's the truth," said Miss Gladys, standing up with her hands on her hips to watch the men set things on the sidewalk.

Upstairs, Geraldine went into the apartment and found Anita in the kitchen.

"I dunno, Gerry," Anita said. "I just don't know what we're going to do. But everything's going to be all right soon as Ma gets well." Anita's voice cracked as she set a bowl of soup before Geraldine.

"What's this?" Geraldine said.

"It's tomato soup, Gerry."

Geraldine was about to say something. But when she looked up at her big sister, she saw how Anita's face was getting all twisted as she began to cry.

That afternoon, Mr. Stern, the geometry teacher, started drawing cubes and cylinders on the board. Geraldine sat at her desk adding up a column of figures in her notebook—the rent, the light and gas bills, a new gym suit, some socks. Maybe they would move somewhere else, and she could have her own room. Geraldine turned the squares and triangles into little houses in the country.

"For your homework," Mr. Stern was saying with his back to the class, "set up your problems this way." He wrote GIVEN: in large letters, and then gave the formula for the first problem. Then he wrote TO FIND: and listed three items they were to include in their answers.

Geraldine started to raise her hand to ask what all these squares and angles had to do with solving real problems, like the ones she had. *Better not*, she warned herself, and sat on her hands. *Your big mouth got you in trouble last term.*

In hygiene class, Mrs. Potter kept saying that the body was a wonderful machine. Every time Geraldine looked up from her notebook, she would hear the same thing. "Right now your body is manufacturing all the proteins and tissues and energy you will need to get through tomorrow."

And Geraldine kept wondering, *How? How does my body know what it will need, when I don't even know what I'll need to get through tomorrow?*

As she headed down the hall to her next class, Geraldine remembered that she hadn't done the homework for English. Mrs. Scott had said to write a poem, and Geraldine had meant to do it at lunchtime. After all, there was nothing to it—a flower here, a raindrop there, moon, June, rose, nose. But the men carrying off the furniture had made her forget.

"And now put away your books," Mrs. Scott was saying as Geraldine tried to scribble a poem quickly. "Today we can give King Arthur's knights a rest. Let's talk about poetry."

Mrs. Scott moved up and down the aisles, talking about her favorite poems and reciting a line now and then. She got very excited whenever she passed a desk and could pick up the homework from a student who had remembered to do the assignment.

"A poem is your own special way of saying what you feel and what you see," Mrs. Scott went on, her lips moist. It was her favorite subject.

"Some poets write about the light that . . . that . . . makes the world sunny," she said, passing Geraldine's desk. "Sometimes an idea takes the form of a picture—an image."

For almost half an hour, Mrs. Scott stood at the front of the room, reading poems and talking about the lives of the great poets. Geraldine drew more houses, and designs for curtains.

"So for those who haven't done their homework, try it now," Mrs. Scott said. "Try expressing what it is like to be . . . to be alive in this . . . this glorious world."

"Oh, brother," Geraldine muttered to herself as Mrs. Scott moved up and down the aisles again, waving her hands and leaning over the students' shoulders and saying, "That's nice," or "Keep trying." Finally she came to Geraldine's desk and stopped, looking down at her.

"I can't write a poem," Geraldine said flatly, before she even realized she was going to speak at all. She said it very loudly, and the whole class looked up.

"And why not?" Mrs. Scott asked, looking hurt.

"I can't write a poem, Mrs. Scott, because nothing lovely's been happening in my life. I haven't seen a flower since Mother's Day, and the sun don't even shine on my side of the street. No robins come sing on my window sill."

Geraldine swallowed hard. She thought about saying that her father doesn't even come to visit any more, but changed her mind. "Just the rain comes," she went on, "and the bills come, and the men to move out our furniture. I'm sorry, but I can't write no pretty poem."

Teddy Johnson leaned over and was about to giggle and crack the whole class up, but Mrs. Scott looked so serious that he changed his mind.

"You have just said the most . . . the most poetic thing, Geraldine Moore," said Mrs. Scott. Her hands flew up to touch the silk scarf around her neck. "'Nothing lovely's been happening in my life.'" She repeated it so quietly that everyone had to lean forward to hear.

"Class," Mrs. Scott said very sadly, clearing her throat, "you have just heard the best poem you will ever hear." She went to the board and stood there for a long time staring at the chalk in her hand.

"I'd like you to copy it down," she said. She wrote it just as Geraldine had said it, bad grammar and all.

*Nothing lovely's been happening in my life.*
*I haven't seen a flower since Mother's Day,*
*And the sun don't even shine on my side of the street.*
*No robins come sing on my window sill.*
*Just the rain comes, and the bills come,*
*And the men to move out our furniture.*
*I'm sorry, but I can't write no pretty poem.*

Mrs. Scott stopped writing, but she kept her back to the class for a long time—long after Geraldine had closed her notebook.

And even when the bell rang, and everyone came over to smile at Geraldine or to tap her on the shoulder or to kid her about being the school poet, Geraldine waited for Mrs. Scott to put the chalk down and turn around. Finally Geraldine stacked up her books and started to leave. Then she thought she heard a whimper—the way Mrs. Watson's dog whimpered sometimes—and she saw Mrs. Scott's shoulders shake a little.

---

## Responding to the Story

1. According to Mrs. Scott's standards, are Geraldine's words poetry? Explain, with reference to Mrs. Scott's words in the text.
2. According to your own definition of, and standards for, poetry, are Geraldine's words poetry? Justify your answer.

## Exploring the Author's Craft

When a writer uses **parallel structure**, he or she begins several sentences in a row the same way—for example, subject-verb, subject-verb—and often repeats key words in each sentence. The repetition of the sentence structures creates a rhythmic effect, one that appeals to the reader and can become almost hypnotic. Parallel structure may also be established with repeated phrases or word forms: the titles of the five parts of this book—Searching, Competing, Realizing, Loving, Separating—are parallel.

In "Geraldine Moore the Poet," Toni Cade Bambara has created a poem that uses parallel structure. Explain where that structure occurs and what effect it has on you.

## Writer's Workshop

Write down exactly what you are feeling right now. Make your subject and reactions go beyond the classroom. Be honest and direct. Now try to rearrange those words in some poetic form, as Geraldine's teacher had the wisdom and creativity to do. Try to include some parallel structure in your finished work.

## Making Connections in
# PART THREE

Complete one or more of the following assignments as your teacher directs.

1.  Why are the pieces of writing in this section brought together under the title "Realizing"? Write in classic five-paragraph structure an essay in which you define *realizing* and show how three of the selections in Part Three involve situations of realization. (Note: the five-paragraph essay structure in explained in Making Connections in Part One.)

2.  Which two pieces of writing in Part Three are most true to life as you know it? Support your answer with specific references to the world you know.

3.  Gray Soto in "Like Mexicans" and Janis Ian's narrator in "Society's Child" both write about situations in which parents try to influence whom their children date. Write a comparison-and-contrast essay about how the situations are different in the two works. What realization did Soto come to that Ian was not allowed to reach?

4.  Sometimes our realizations are about the world in which we live; sometimes our realizations are about ourselves. Explain two situations in this section of the book in which the narrators or main characters learn something significant about themselves.

# PART FOUR

# Loving

Loving takes many forms. As adolescents we perhaps think of romantic love more than any other kind. But love between parent and child and between friend and friend are crucial parts of *all* ages in our lives.

In this section of the book we will meet characters who are learning about romantic love and are caught up in its wonder and possible pain. A short story, "Snowfall in Childhood," and a short essay, "Kissing," written almost fifty years apart, touch on universal aspects of romantic love. Vietnam, a place many of us associate with war, is the inspiration for two pieces of writing that deal with love of a different sort.

In this section of the book you will examine the varied ways that love can play a crucial part in people's lives.

## Ben Hecht

Ben Hecht lived from 1894 to 1964. Primarily a journalist and writer for the stage and screen, Hecht once stated, "There is a basic and never varying reason behind all my short story writing. It is this—I write to cheer myself up. My short stories are my chief social effort to escape the gloomy pits of information in my mind. My point of view in most of my stories is that of a child who finds the world full of exuberant and engrossing matters, who dramatizes what he sees so he many enjoy it more, and who asks as a reward for his labors only the illusion that existence is a fine thing." In "Snowfall in Childhood" Hecht certainly creates a narrator who "finds the world full of exuberant and engrossing matters."

*A snowstorm brings a new view of the world—and a first love.*

# Snowfall in Childhood

**I** got out of bed to see what had happened in the night. I was thirteen years old. I had fallen asleep watching the snow falling through the half-frosted window.

But though the snow had promised to keep falling for a long time, perhaps three or four days, on opening my eyes I was full of doubts. Snowstorms usually ended too soon.

While getting out of bed I remembered how, as I was nearly asleep, the night outside the frosted window had seemed to burst into a white jungle. I had dreamed of streets and houses buried in snow.

I hurried barefooted to the window. It was scribbled with a thick frost and I couldn't see through it. The room was cold and through the opened window came the fresh smell of snow like the moist nose of an animal resting on the ledge and breathing into the room.

I knew from the smell and the darkness of the window that snow was falling. I melted a peephole on the glass with my palms. I saw that this time the snow had not fooled me. There it was, still coming down white and silent and too thick for the wind to move, and the streets and houses were almost as I had dreamed. I watched, shivering and happy. Then I dressed, pulling on my clothes as if the house were on fire. I was finished with breakfast and out in the storm two hours before schooltime.

The world had changed. All the houses, fences, and barren trees had new shapes. Everything was round and white and unfamiliar.

I set out through these new streets on a voyage of discovery. The unknown surrounded me. Through the thick falling snow, the trees, houses, and fences looked like ghost shapes that had floated down out of the sky during the night. The morning was without light, but the snowfall hung and swayed like a marvelous lantern over the streets. The snowbanks, already over my head in places, glowed mysteriously.

I was pleased with this new world. It seemed to belong to me more than that other world which lay hidden.

I headed for the school, jumping like a clumsy rabbit in and out of snowbanks. It seemed wrong to spoil the smooth outlines of these snowdrifts and I hoped that nobody else would pass this way after me. In that case the thick falling snow would soon restore the damage. Reassured by this hope I continued on my devastations like some wanton[1] explorer. I began to feel that no one would dare the dangers of my wake. Then, as I became more aware of the noble proportions of this snowstorm, I stopped worrying altogether about the marring of the new and glowing world. Other snows had melted and been shoveled away, but this snow would never disappear. The sun would never shine again and the little Wisconsin town through which I plunged and tumbled to school on this dark storm-filled morning was from now on an arctic land full of danger and adventure.

When eventually, encased in snow, I arrived at the school, I found scores of white-covered figures already there. The girls had taken shelter inside, but the boys stayed in the storm. They jumped in and out of the snowdrifts and tumbled through the deep unbroken white fields in front of the school.

---

1. **wanton:** unrestrained; reckless.

Muffled cries filled the street. Someone had discovered how faraway our voices sounded in the snowfall and this started the screaming. We screamed for ten minutes, delighted with the fact that our voices no longer carried and that the snowstorm had made us nearly dumb.

Tired with two hours of such plunging and rolling, I joined a number of boys who like myself had been busy since dawn and who now stood for the last few minutes before the school bell with half-frozen faces staring at the heavily falling snow as if it were some game they couldn't bear to leave.

When we were finally seated in our grade room, we continued to watch the snowstorm through the windows. The morning had grown darker as we had all hoped it would, and it was necessary to turn on the electric lights in the room. This was almost as thrilling as the pale storm still floating outside the windows.

In this yellow light the school seemed to disappear and in its place a picnic spread around us. The teachers themselves seemed to change. Their eyes kept turning toward the windows and they kept looking at us behind our desks as if we were strangers. We grew excited and even the sound of our lessons—the sentences out of geography and arithmetic books—made us tremble.

Passing through the halls during recess we whispered to one another about the snowstorm, guessing at how deep the snowdrifts must be by this time. We looked nervously at our teachers who stood in the classroom doorways stiff and far removed from our secret whispers about the snow.

I felt sorry for these teachers, particularly for the one who had taught me several years ago when I was in the Fifth Grade. I saw her as I walked by the opened door of her room. She was younger than the other teachers, with two dark braids coiled around her head, a white starched shirtwaist, and soft dark eyes that had always looked kindly at me when I was younger. I saw her now sitting behind her large desk looking over the heads of her class out of the window and paying no attention to the whispers and giggles of her pupils.

As for my own teacher, a tall thin woman with a man's face, by afternoon I had become so happy I could no longer hear what she was saying. I sat looking at the large clock over her head. My feeling on the way to school that it would never be light again and that the snowstorm would keep on forever had increased so that it was something I now knew rather than hoped. My eagerness to get out into the world of wind, gloom, and perpetual snow, kept lifting me out of my seat.

At three o'clock we rushed into the storm. Our screams died as we reached the school entrance. What we saw silenced us. Under the dark sky the street lay piled in an unbroken bank of snow. And above it the snowfall still hung in a thick and moving cloud. Nothing was visible but snow. Everything else had disappeared. Even the sky was gone.

I saw the teachers come out and look around them, frowning. The children of the lower grades stood chattering and frightened near the teachers. I waited until the teacher with the two black braids saw me, and then, paying no attention to her warning, spoken in a gentle voice, I plunged into the storm. I felt brave but slightly regretful that Miss Wheeler could no longer see me as I pushed into the head-high piles of snow and vanished fearlessly into the storm. But I was certain that she was still thinking of me and worrying about my safety. This thought added excitement to the snowstorm.

After an hour I found myself alone. My legs were tired with jumping and my face burned. It had grown darker and the friendliness seemed to have gone out of the storm. The wind bit with a sharper edge and I turned toward my home.

I arrived at the house that now looked like a snowdrift and ploughed my way up to its front door. My heart was beating violently. I stopped to take a last look at the storm. It was hard to leave it. But for the first time in my life an adult logic instructed me. There would be even more snow tomorrow. And in this wind and snow-filled gloom, and even in the marvelously buried street, there was something now unplayful.

I entered the house, calling for something to eat, but as soon as I had taken my coat off and shaken myself clean, I was at the window again. The way this storm was keeping on was hard to believe.

At the table I was too excited to eat. I trembled and was unable to hear what was being said around me. In this room I could feel the night outside and the storm still blowing on my face. It seemed as if I were still in the street. My eyes kept seeing snow and my nose breathing it. The room and the people in it became far away. I left the table, taking a slice of bread and butter with me, and ran upstairs to my own room.

There were a lot of things to do, such as making my leather boots more waterproof by rubbing lard on them, putting my stamp collection in order, sharpening a deer's-foot knife I had recently acquired, winding tape on my new hockey stick, or reading one of the half-dozen new books I had bought with my last birthday money. But none of these activities or even redrawing the plans for the iceboat on which I was working was possible. I sat in a chair near the window, unable to think. The pale storm in the night seemed to spin like a top, and, keeping the window frost melted with my palms, I sat and watched it snowing for an hour. Then, becoming sleepy, I went to bed. I thought drowsily of how happy Miss Wheeler would be to see me alive on Monday after the way I had rushed into the storm.

There was no seeing through my window when I awoke. The furnace never got going until after seven, and before that hour on a winter's morning the house creaked with cold and the windows were sheeted thick with ice. But I knew as I dressed that the snowfall was over. There was too much wind blowing outside and the breath that came in from the snow-banked window ledge was no longer as fresh as it had been.

It was still dark. The bleak and gusty dawn lay over the snow like a guttering candle. The sky had finished with its snowing but now the wind set the snowbanks ballooning into the air and the roof tops burst into little snowstorms.

I went outside and explored for ten minutes. When I came back into the house, I needed no warning against going out to play. My skin was almost frozen and the wind was too strong to stand up in. I settled down as a prisoner in front of the fireplace for breakfast, lying on my stomach and turning the pages of a familiar oversized edition of Dante's *Inferno*. It was full of Doré's nightmarish pictures.[2]

The house bustled with cooking and cleaning. But these were the dim activities of grownups. I felt alone and took care of the fire to keep it from going out and leaving me to freeze to death. I carried logs all morning from the cellar and lay perspiring and half-scorched on the hearthstone. Every half-hour I went to the window to have a look at the enemy. The sight of the whirling snowbanks and the sound of the brutal wind as it hit against the house sent me back to the fireplace to scorch myself anew.

---

2. **Dante's *Inferno* . . . Doré's nightmarish pictures:** The *Inferno* is the first book of Dante Alighieri's (1265–1321) epic poem *The Divine Comedy*, about a journey through the afterworld. French artist Gustave Doré (1832-1883) made many engravings to illustrate Dante's poem.

In this way I spent the day until late afternoon. It grew dark early. The snow turned leaden. The wind stopped. The dead storm lay in the street and as far as I could see from the window there were no inhabitants in the world. The dark snow was empty. I shivered and went back to the fireplace.

A half-hour later our doorbell rang. Company had arrived for supper. They were the Joneses, who lived in the town of Corliss some eight miles away. They had brought their daughter Anna.

The lights went on in the house. Baked and dizzy with the fire's heat, I joined the two families in the larger parlor. They were talking excitedly about the damage done by the storm. Accounts of store windows blown in, roofs blown off, signs blown down, and wagons abandoned in the drifts were exchanged, and I listened happily. Later, when the talk turned to duller topics, I became aware of Anna.

She was sitting in a corner watching me. She was a blondish girl two years older than I was and she went to high school. I had known her for a long time but had never liked her because she was too calm, never laughing or running, but always looking at people with a sad smile or just a stare as if she had something important on her mind. But now that she was watching me that way, I felt suddenly interested in her. I wondered what she could be thinking of me and what made her smile in that half-sad way at me.

I sat next to her at the table, and after looking at her several times out of the side of my eyes and catching her eyes doing the same thing, my heart started beating faster. I lost interest in eating. I wanted to be alone with her so we could sit and look at each other without the others noticing.

After supper the two families let us go to the hall upstairs, where I kept most of my possessions, without asking us any questions. I found a deck of cards and a cribbage board and a lapboard for a table. Underneath the lapboard our knees touched.

She played cribbage better than I and smiled at me as I kept losing. But I was only half aware of the game. I kept looking at her, unable to talk, and the light pressure of her knees began to make me feel weak. Her face seemed to become brighter and more beautiful as we played. A mist appeared around her eyes and her smile became so close, as if it were moving swiftly toward me, that I began to tremble. I felt ashamed of being so tongue-tied and red-faced, but with a half-frightened, blissful indifference to everything—even Anna—I kept on playing.

We hardly spoke. I grew too nervous to follow the game and I wanted to stop. But I thought if we stopped, we could no longer sit this way with our knees touching. At moments when Anna withdrew her touch, I trembled and waited as if I were hanging from somewhere. When finally her knees returned to their place against mine, I caught my breath and frowned at the cards as if I were completely taken up with them.

As the hour passed, my face began to feel swollen and lopsided and it seemed to me my features had grown ugly beyond words. I tried to distract Anna's attention from this phenomenon by twisting my mouth, screwing up my eyes, and making popping noises with my cheeks as we played. But a new fear arrived to uncenter my attention. I became afraid now that Anna would notice her knees were touching mine and move them away. I began at once pretending a deeper excitement in the game, complaining against my bad luck and denouncing her for cheating. I was determined to keep her interested in the game at any cost, believing that her interest in what we were doing made her unaware of her knees touching mine.

Finally Anna said she was tired of the game. She pushed the cribbage board away. I waited, holding my breath, for her to realize where her knees were and to move them away. I tried not to look at her, but I was so frightened of this happening that I found myself staring at her. She seemed to be paying no attention to me. She was leaning back in her chair and her eyes were half closed. Her face was unsmiling and I felt she was thinking of something. This startled me. My throat filled with questions, but I was so afraid of breaking this hidden embrace of our knees under the lapboard that I said nothing.

The mist seemed to have spread from her eyes to her hair and over the rest of her face. Wherever I looked, this same glow rested around her. I noticed then that her hand was lying on the lapboard. I thought desperately of touching it, but there was something disillusioning in this thought. I watched her fingers begin to tap gently on the board as if she were playing the piano. There was something strange about her hand, as if it did not belong to the way her knees were touching mine or to the mist that rose from her eyes.

The minutes passed in silence and then Anna's mother called her from downstairs.

"I guess they're going home," I said, and Anna nodded. She pressed closer against me, but in my confusion I couldn't figure out whether this was the accidental result of her starting to get out of her chair or on purpose.

"Why don't you ride out with us?" she said. She leaned over the lapboard toward me. "We've got the wagon sleigh and there's plenty of room."

Before I could answer, she had stood up. My knees felt suddenly cold. I slid the lapboard to the floor, ashamed and sad. Anna, without looking back at me, had gone down the stairs. I kept myself from running after her. I was sure she was laughing at me and that she was saying to herself, He's a big fool. He's a big fool.

The Joneses were ready to leave when I came into the parlor. Anna's mother smiled at me.

"Why don't you come and visit us over Sunday?" she said. "There's even more snow in Corliss than here."

"More snow than you can shake a stick at," said another member of the Jones family. They all laughed, and while they were laughing, my mother hustled me off for my wraps. I was to drive away with the Jones family in the sleigh drawn by the two strong horses that stood in front of our house.

I pulled on my leather boots, sweater, and overcoat while the good-bys were being made. I kept trying to catch Anna's attention, but she was apparently unaware that I was in the room. This made me sad, and slowly my eagerness to go to Corliss left me. I wanted instead to go up to my room and slam the door forever on all the Joneses. Anna's gayety, the way she said good-by over and over again and laughed and kissed all the members of my family as if nothing had happened to her, as if she hadn't sat with her eyes closed pressing against my knees in the hallway upstairs, made me almost ill. I felt abandoned and forgotten.

Finally I stood muffled and capped and scowling as my family offered some final instructions for my behavior. I heard nothing of what was said but turned over and over in my mind what I was going to do on the ride and after we got to Corliss. Chiefly I was going to ignore Anna, neither speak to her nor show her by a single look that I knew she was alive.

At this point Anna, having said good-by to everybody several times, seized my arm unexpectedly and whispered against my ear.

"Come, hurry," she said. "We want to get a good place."

Without a word I rushed out of the house, slipping down the snow-caked steps and tumbling headlong into a snowdrift. I scrambled after Anna into the wagon sleigh. It was a low-sided farm wagon placed on wide, heavy wooden runners and piled with warm hay and horse blankets. There was room for only one on the seat. The rest of the Joneses, seven including me, would have to lie in the hay, covered by the robes.

Anna was already in the wagon half-buried in the hay, a blanket over her. She gave me excited orders to brush the snow from my clothes, to cover myself well and not to get out and run alongside the horses when we were going up hill.

"It doesn't help any," she said. "They can pull just the same if you stay in here. And besides, I don't want you to."

The rest of the Joneses came out and crowded into the wagon around us. Anna's father took his place on the driver's seat, assuring my mother, who had come out with a shawl over her head, that there was no danger because the state plow had cleared the road even to way beyond Corliss. I heard my mother ask where I was. Mrs. Jones answered that I was buried somewhere in the hay and Anna whispered close to me not to answer or say anything. I obeyed her.

The sleigh started off. I heard the horses thumping in the snow and the harness bells falling into a steady jingling. Lying on my back, I looked into the night. Stars filled the sky and a white glare hung over the housetops. The street was silent. I could no longer see the snow-covered houses with their lighted windows. My nose filled with the fresh smell of snow and the barn smells of hay and horse blankets, I lay, listening to the different sounds—the harness bells and the snow crunching under the runners.

The stillness of this winter's night was as intense as the storm that had raged for three days. I felt that all the wind and snow there was had blown themselves out forever and that the night as far as the highest star had been emptied by the storm. This emptiness as I lay looking into it was like being hypnotized. It was something to run out into, to fly up into, as the snowfall had been. I began to want to see further, and the star-filled sky that had seemed so vast a few minutes ago now didn't seem vast enough.

I had almost forgotten about Anna when I felt a now familiar warmth press against me. She had moved closer, as if joggled by the sleigh. I held my breath waiting for her to order me to move away and give her room, but she was silent.

My hand at my side touched her fingers. Now I forgot the sky and the great sprinkle of stars that seemed like a thin, far-away snowfall that had stopped moving. The night, the glare of snow, the jingling harness bells died away; only my fingers were alive.

When I had looked at her hand tapping gently on the lapboard, it had seemed strange, and the thought of touching it somehow disillusioning.[3] But now under the horse blankets, hidden in the hay, this hand seemed more breathing and mysterious and familiar than anything about her. I lay unable to move closer to it, our fingertips barely touching. I grew dizzy wishing to reach her hand, but I felt as powerless to move toward it as to fly.

The minutes passed. Two of the Joneses started singing. The thump of the horses, the jingling of the sleighbells, and the crunching of the snow under the runners seemed part of this soft singing. I too wished to sing, to stand up suddenly in this sweeping-along sleigh and bellow at the silent night.

Then the fingers for which I had been wishing until I was dizzy seemed to start walking under the horse blankets, seemed to be running toward me in the warm hay. They came as far as my hand, closed around it, and I felt the throb of their tips against my palm. The night turned into a dream. I opened my eyes to the wide sprinkle of stars and a mist seemed to have come over them. The snow-covered hills over which we were gliding sparkled behind a mist, and suddenly the night into which I was looking lost its hours. It stretched away without time as if it were not something that was passing like our sleigh over the snow, but a star-filled winter's night that would never change and never move.

Lying beside Anna, her hand in mine, with the sleigh now flying in a whirl of snow down the white hill, I thought this night would never end.

---

3. **disillusioning:** not as good as imagined.

## Responding to the Story

1. Reread the paragraph on page 221 that begins, "I pulled on my leather boots, sweater, and overcoat. . . ." What universal aspect of romantic love is being dealt with in this passage?
2. Now reread the story's two final paragraphs. What aspects of romantic love are being dealt with here?
3. What role does the snowstorm play in this story and in what happens between the narrator and Anna?

## Exploring the Author's Craft

When a writer uses **description**, he or she names as many details as possible to bring alive a situation or place or object. Contrary to what you might think, good description (and good writing of all kinds) relies on nouns more than adjectives. A beginning writer and a weak writer pile on adjectives. But a good writer continues to name things. That is what description is all about.

In this short story Ben Hecht is shown as a master of description. Reread the first eighteen paragraphs. Find at least five sentences in which Hecht uses primarily nouns to bring the story alive.

## Writer's Workshop

Ben Hecht obviously knew what a mammoth snowstorm is like. Describe something that you know equally well. Write at least five paragraphs all on the same topic, developing a description in the same way Hecht kept expanding his description of the snowstorm. Concentrate on using well-chosen nouns to create a strong picture in your description.

## Alternate Media Response

In some art form other than the printed word, capture a snowstorm as vividly as Hecht did in "Snowfall in Childhood."

# Two Perspectives

## John Logan

Born in Iowa in 1923, John Logan taught at many colleges and universities. Although his name is not widely known outside the community of American poets, his work is highly regarded by his contemporaries. "The Picnic" appears in a collection called *Ghosts of the Heart*, published in 1960. John Logan died in 1987.

## Mari Evans

Mari Evans was born in 1923. A poet and playwright as well as a prose writer for children, early in her writing career she began to look on poet Langston Hughes as a model. Evans has published several collections of her own work and is also the editor of *Black Women Writers (1950–1980): A Critical Evaluation*. As one critic said of her poetry, "Her language is spare and uncomplicated, but her simplicity is deceptive."

*Love can make your heart soar—or it can break it.*

# The Picnic

**John Logan**

It is the picnic with Ruth in the spring.
Ruth was third on my list of seven girls
But the first two were gone (Betty) or else
Had someone (Ellen has accepted Doug).
5   Indian Gully the last day of school;
Girls make the lunches for the boys too.
I wrote a note to Ruth in algebra class
Day before the test. She smiled, and nodded.
We left the cars and walked through the young corn,
10  The shoots green as paint and the leaves like tongues
Trembling. Beyond the fence where we stood
Some wild strawberry flowered by an elm tree
And Jack-in-the-pulpit[1] was olive ripe.
A blackbird fled as I crossed, and showed
15  A spot of gold or red under its quick wing.
I held the wire for Ruth and watched the whip
Of her long, striped skirt as she followed.
Three freckles blossomed on her thin, white back
Underneath the loop where the blouse buttoned.
20  We went for our lunch away from the rest,
Stretched in the new grass, our heads close
Over unknown things wrapped up in wax papers.

---

**1. Jack-in-the-pulpit:** purplish-brown flower that grows with a leaf arched over it.

Ruth tried for the same, I forget what it was,
And our hands were together. She laughed,

25    And a breeze caught the edge of her little
Collar and the edge of her brown, loose hair
That touched my cheek. I turned my face in-
to the gentle fall. I saw how sweet it smelled.
She didn't move her head or take her hand.

30    I felt a soft caving in my stomach
As at the top of the highest slide
When I had been a child, but was not afraid,
And did not know why my eyes moved with wet
As I brushed her cheek with my lips and brushed

35    Her lips with my own lips. She said to me
Jack, Jack, different than I had ever heard,
Because she wasn't calling me, I think,
Or telling me. She used my name to
Talk in another way I wanted to know.

40    She laughed again and then she took her hand;
I gave her what we both had touched—can't
Remember what it was, and we ate the lunch.
Afterward we walked in the small, cool creek
Our shoes off, her skirt hitched, and she smiling,

45    My pants rolled, and then we climbed up the high
Side of Indian Gully and looked
Where we had been, our hands together again.
It was then some bright thing came in my eyes,
Starting at the back of them and flowing

50  Suddenly through my head and down my arms
    And stomach and my bare legs that seemed not
    To stop in feet, not to feel the red earth
    Of the Gully, as though we hung in a
    Touch of birds. There was a word in my throat
55  With the feeling and I knew the first time
    What it meant and I said, it's beautiful.
    Yes, she said, and I felt the sound and word
    In my hand join the sound and word in hers
    As in one name said, or in one cupped hand.
60  We put back on our shoes and socks and we
    Sat in the grass awhile, crosslegged, under
    A blowing tree, not saying anything.
    And Ruth played with shells she found in the creek,
    As I watched. Her small wrist which was so sweet
65  To me turned by her breast and the shells dropped
    Green, white, blue, easily into her lap,
    Passing light through themselves. She gave the pale
    Shells to me, and got up and touched her hips
    With her light hands, and we walked down slowly
70  To play the school games with the others.

# Where Have You Gone?

Mari Evans

where have you gone . . .

with your confident
walk . . . with
your crooked smile . . .

5   why did you leave
me
when you took your
laughter
and departed
10  Are you aware that
with you
went the sun
all light
and what few stars
15  there were . . . ?

where have you gone
with your confident
walk your
crooked smile the
20  rent money

in one pocket and

my heart

in

another. . . .

_____

## Responding to the Poems

1.  What kind of feelings are you left with after reading "The Picnic"?
    Explain in your own words.
2.  What kind of feelings are you left with after reading "Where Have
    You Gone?" Explain in your own words.

## Exploring the Authors' Craft

The overall feeling or atmosphere that a piece of writing conveys is
called its **mood**. Mood doesn't just happen; instead, it is created
carefully and artistically through the words chosen and the images
created by the writer. Explain how the moods of both "The Picnic" and
"Where Have You Gone?" were created and conveyed to the reader.
Obviously, you must be very specific.

## Writer's Workshop

Write a piece of poetry or prose on the topic of romantic love. Choose
words and images to create a mood similar to that of "The Picnic" or of
"Where Have You Gone?"

## Al Capp

Cartoonist Al Capp was born in 1909 and died in 1979. He created the cartoon character and strip "Li'l Abner," which Charles M. Schultz, creator of "Peanuts," called "one of the great comic strips of all time."

Capp once wrote and illustrated a cartoon for World War II veterans who were amputees; Capp could identify with them since he had lost a leg in an accident when he was nine. In that cartoon he makes the point that "Mistah Capp haint no *bettern'n* nobody else, nor *no diff'rent*. One laig more or less didn't change *him* or *his* life, jest like it don't hafta change *nobody else's*." Read this memoir to see if losing a leg did change his life.

*Disability or not, Capp was determined to meet that girl.*

# from My Well-Balanced Life on a Wooden Leg

**I** became a candidate for a wooden leg on August 21, 1919, when I was nine years old. That day my father, a vague and unworldly man, gave me fifty cents to get a haircut: thirty-five cents for the haircut, five cents for a tip, ten cents for trolley fare. At least that was the way he figured it. I, a calculating and worldly kid, figured it a little differently. I had seen a tantalizing offer on a sign in a downtown New Haven window: PROF. AMOROSO, BARBER ACADEMY—HAIRCUTS 15 CENTS— NO TIPPING. By hitching a ride on the back of an ice wagon I could step into Professor Amoroso's with fifty cents and, with luck, step out again with most of the money (and possibly some of my scalp) intact. Clutching that fifty-cent piece, blinded with dreams of riches and power, I hopped off the ice cart in front of the barber academy—and directly into the path of a huge old-fashioned trolley car. I was caught under the wheels and before the car could be stopped my left leg was severed at the thigh.

During the ride to the hospital and later, while I was under anesthetic, I never once unclutched that half dollar. My mother finally took it from me. For years afterward she kept that coin, the kind of melancholy memento that only mothers understand, in the drawer of her sewing machine. I used to find her now and then, staring into the open drawer and quietly weeping. (A dozen years later, during the Depression and a particularly severe family financial crisis, she opened the drawer again, stared at the coin for the last time, and marched to the grocery store with it.)

Losing a leg at nine is not all loss. For one thing it made me a celebrity among the other kids, to whom I had previously been merely another vague and grubby menace. True, I was not much good at baseball, wrestling, or apple-orchard raiding, but then I never had been much good at them, and now I was spared the embarrassment of displaying my awkwardness. As for grownups, they suddenly noticed the spiritual qualities in me as a slow-moving, one-legged boy, which had been totally hidden from them when I was a hooting, howling, fast-moving two-legger. Gifts poured in from formerly unenchanted, unprofitable, and unheard-of relatives. Yes, at nine, I reveled in the drama and distinction of that shocking pinned-up pants leg and those swagger crutches. With two legs I had been a nobody. With one leg I was somebody.

Then came the day that had been hailed so glowingly by my doctor, my parents, and the local wooden leg salesman—the day when I could strap on my new leg and walk around again like everyone else. It was one of the most shattering letdowns of my life. I damn well did not walk around like everyone else. I went through weeks of stumbling, of toppling, of aching, cursing and weeping before I mastered the gadget. And still I did not walk around like everyone else. I walked like everyone else who had a wooden leg. I swayed and I dragged.

For a while the other kids were even more fascinated by the wooden leg than they had been by the absence of the real one, and that made a satisfying unique figure of me for as long as it lasted. But the novelty wore off and the years wore on. I became a teenager with all the routine problems of teenagers—and one special problem: namely, how to get myself treated by girls in their teens as though I did not have a special problem.

A teenager wants more than anything else in life to look, act, and be treated like all other teenagers. On the first two counts I did fine. I am sure that I looked and behaved as oddly as all the other teenagers at Central High School in Bridgeport, Connecticut, where I then lived. But I got different and special treatment, especially from the girls, and that made life hell for me. My rooster roughness and rowdiness was forgiven with sweet understanding, when what I wanted was the same thrilled contempt that was accorded two-legged rowdies for the same behavior.

So I took to hanging out on street corners. Every afternoon I would leave the high school world, limp a half-dozen blocks along Main Street, and prop myself against the corner of D. M. Read's store at the city's busiest intersection. I was then in a different world, and I was then a different guy. As long as I stayed in one place, the girls I stared at and whistled at treated me like any other street-corner wise guy—with the exaggerated disdain that a nicely behaved girl uses to tell a boy on a street corner who is not behaving very nicely that she would not dream of acknowledging him because she is terribly interested in him. If a girl did look back invitingly, I would look away, pleased but immobile. On a good afternoon there might be as many as a dozen look-backs and look-aways before the streets thinned out. I would go home delighted, having had a remarkable few hours of being treated ordinarily.

Then one day three teenage girls stopped for traffic in what was then called a roadster,[1] and I aimed a brassy leer their way. Two of them turned up their noses. But the third and prettiest smiled at me—and then, to my joy and dismay, dropped her school pad over the side and motioned me with an inviting smile to pick up the pad and, possibly, her too. My triumph filled me with panic. If I moved she'd find out. So I stared stonily in the other direction until at last they were forced to move on. When I turned back the pad still lay in the street. I limped over and snatched it up. Inside was a girl's name and address. The address was in Brooklawn, then the best residential section of Bridgeport, an area of great houses, all with verandas—and all with steps.

Now to a man who has lost his leg above the knee, steps are an endless horror. On level ground he can make reasonable progress,

---

1. **roadster:** an open car with a single wide seat and sometimes an extra folding seat—commonly called a rumble seat—in the back.

striding forward with his good leg and rhythmically swinging the wooden one up behind. On steps, however, he must rise on the good leg, stop, pull up the wooden one, rise again with the good leg—pull and stop, pull and stop. It is a slow and unappealing process, the only experience with my wooden leg that irritates me to this day. When I was a boy, it was a humiliation I'd go to any length to avoid.

But I wanted to meet that girl. I phoned her. She had driven off before I could return the pad, I explained gravely, but I would be glad to deliver it to her tonight. She said that was awfully nice of me and maybe if I had no other plans I could have lemonade with her—say at seven o'clock? She would be waiting on the porch.

At a quarter to seven I hurried up the walk to her house. I was deliberately early: if I reached the veranda before her, she would find me seated and would not see me climbing the stairs, or even walking. My plan worked fine, and when she opened the door a few minutes before seven, I was waiting. There was a long pause.

"I'm sorry," she said at last from the doorway. "But I can't see you tonight. I have to go away. Thank you for returning the pad. Please leave it on the chair." She turned back in, and the door closed behind her.

I dropped the pad and hurried down the stairs and away as fast as I could. I never saw her again. It would have been too much for both of us to bear, for we had both been playing the same game. I had arrived early so she would not see me walk. She had planned to be waiting on the porch so I would not see her walk. For in the instant of her turning away at the door, I had seen the stiffening of her shoulder, the outthrust movement of her hip—the sure signs that she, too, of all the sad, shy girls on earth, had an artificial leg.

## Responding to the Memoir

1. What point does Al Capp make when he says, "With two legs I had been a nobody. With one leg I was somebody"? Do you think it is a valid point? Why or why not?
2. "A teenager wants more than anything else in life to look, act, and be treated like all other teenagers." Respond to these words of Al Capp.
3. What point about romantic relationships does Capp make with the way this story ends?

## Exploring the Author's Craft

Al Capp explains in a very matter-of-fact way how his accident affected his growing up. Find two or three sentences that you think are good examples of his realistic, down-to-earth style.

## Writer's Workshop

Relate an autobiographical incident that is similar to Capp's in its bluntness and frankness. Try to end, as did Capp, with a surprise for the reader.

## Alternate Media Response

In a library find and look through books of Al Capp's cartoons. Then create your own comic strip of at least eight panels or sections. In it deal with some aspect of romantic love from a teenager's point of view.

## Two Perspectives

### Gary Paulsen

Gary Paulsen, born in 1939, is a prolific writer of stories and novels for young people. Some of his best known works are *Hatchet* and *Dogsong*. Paulsen's writings are always vividly real and filled with details of the natural world; he himself has twice raced in the Iditarod, the 1,180-mile dogsled race across Alaska. In 1997 Paulsen won the American Library Association's Margaret T. Edwards Award for lifetime contribution in writing books for teenagers.

### Anonymous

"'Dear Sir . . .': Vietnam Memories" is a portion of a letter left at the Vietnam Veterans Memorial in Washington, D.C., and collected in an exhibit produced by a partnership that includes the National Park Service, the [New] Jersey Explorer Children's Museum and NJ Youth Corps, and AmeriCorps at Jersey City State College.

*Sometimes to love you must understand and forgive.*

# Stop the Sun

Gary Paulsen

Terry Erickson was a tall boy, 13, starting to fill out with muscle but still a little awkward. He was on the edge of being a good athlete, which meant a lot to him. He felt it coming too slowly, though, and that bothered him.

But what bothered him even more was when his father's eyes went away.

Usually it happened when it didn't cause any particular trouble. Sometimes during a meal his father's fork would stop halfway to his mouth, just stop, and there would be a long pause while the eyes went away, far away.

After several minutes his mother would reach over and take the fork and put it gently down on his plate, and they would go back to eating—or try to go back to eating—normally.

They knew what caused it. When it first started, Terry had asked his mother in private what it was, what was causing the strange behavior.

"It's from the war," his mother had said. "The doctors at the veterans' hospital call it Vietnam syndrome."[1]

"Will it go away?"

"They don't know. Sometimes it goes away. Sometimes it doesn't. They are trying to help him."

"But what happened? What actually caused it?"

"I told you. Vietnam."

"But there had to be something," Terry persisted. "Something made him like that. Not just Vietnam. Billy's father was there, and he doesn't act that way."

"That's enough questions," his mother said sternly. "He doesn't talk about it, and I don't ask. Neither will you. Do you understand?"

"But, Mom."

"That's enough."

---

1. **syndrome:** group of symptoms characteristic of a disease.

And he stopped pushing it. But it bothered him whenever it happened. When something bothered him, he liked to stay with it until he understood it, and he understood no part of this.

Words. His father had trouble, and they gave him words like Vietnam syndrome. He knew almost nothing of the war, and when he tried to find out about it, he kept hitting walls. Once he went to the school library and asked for anything they might have that could help him understand the war and how it affected his father. They gave him a dry history that described French involvement, Communist involvement, American involvement. But it told him nothing of the war. It was all numbers, cold numbers, and nothing of what had *happened*. There just didn't seem to be anything that could help him.

Another time he stayed after class and tried to talk to Mr. Carlson, who taught history. But some part of Terry was embarrassed. He didn't want to say why he wanted to know about Vietnam, so he couldn't be specific.

"What do you want to know about Vietnam, Terry?" Mr. Carlson had asked. "It was a big war."

Terry had looked at him, and something had started up in his mind, but he didn't let it out. He shrugged. "I just want to know what it was like. I know somebody who was in it."

"A friend?"

"Yessir. A good friend."

Mr. Carlson had studied him, looking into his eyes, but didn't ask any other questions. Instead he mentioned a couple of books Terry had not seen. They turned out to be pretty good. They told about how it felt to be in combat. Still, he couldn't make his father be one of the men he read about.

And it may have gone on and on like that, with Terry never really knowing any more about it except that his father's eyes started going away more and more often. It might have just gone the rest of his life that way except for the shopping mall.

It was easily the most embarrassing thing that ever happened to him.

It started as a normal shopping trip. His father had to go to the hardware store, and he asked Terry to go along.

When they got to the mall they split up. His father went to the hardware store, Terry to a record store to look at albums.

Terry browsed so long that he was late meeting his father at the mall's front door. But his father wasn't there, and Terry looked out to the car to make sure it was still in the parking lot. It was, and he supposed his father had just gotten busy, so he waited.

Still his father didn't come, and he was about to go to the hardware store to find him when he noticed the commotion. Or not a commotion so much as a sudden movement of people.

Later, he thought of it and couldn't remember when the feeling first came to him that there was something wrong. The people were moving toward the hardware store and that might have been what made Terry suspicious.

There was a crowd blocking the entry to the store, and he couldn't see what they were looking at. Some of them were laughing small, nervous laughs that made no sense.

Terry squeezed through the crowd until he got near the front. At first he saw nothing unusual. There were still some people in front of him, so he pushed a crack between them. Then he saw it: His father was squirming along the floor on his stomach. He was crying, looking terrified, his breath coming in short, hot pants like some kind of hurt animal.

It burned into Terry's mind, the picture of his father down on the floor. It burned in and in, and he wanted to walk away, but something made his feet move forward. He knelt next to his father and helped the owner of the store get him up on his feet. His father didn't speak at all but continued to make little whimpering sounds, and they led him back into the owner's office and put him in a chair. Then Terry called his mother and she came in a taxi to take them home. Waiting, Terry sat in a chair next to his father, looking at the floor, wanting only for the earth to open and let him drop in a deep hole. He wanted to disappear.

Words. They gave him words like Vietnam syndrome, and his father was crawling through a hardware store on his stomach.

When the embarrassment became so bad that he would cross the street when he saw his father coming, when it ate into him as he went to sleep, Terry realized he had to do something. He had to know this thing, had to understand what was wrong with his father.

When it came, it was simple enough at the start. It had taken some courage, more than Terry thought he could find. His father was sitting in the kitchen at the table and his mother had gone shopping. Terry wanted it that way; he wanted his father alone. His mother seemed to try to protect him, as if his father could break.

Terry got a soda out of the refrigerator and popped it open. As an afterthought, he handed it to his father and got another for himself. Then he sat at the table.

His father smiled. "You look serious."

"Well . . ."

It went nowhere for a moment, and Terry was just about to drop it altogether. It may be the wrong time, he thought, but there might never be a better one. He tightened his back, took a sip of pop.

"I was wondering if we could talk about something, Dad," Terry said.

His father shrugged. "We already did the bit about girls. Some time ago, as I remember it."

"No. Not that." It was a standing joke between them. When his father finally got around to explaining things to him, they'd already covered it in school. "It's something else. "

"Something pretty heavy, judging by your face."

"Yes."

"Well?"

I still can't do it, Terry thought. Things are bad, but maybe not as bad as they could get. I can still drop this thing.

"Vietnam," Terry blurted out. And he thought, there, it's out. It's out and gone.

"No!" his father said sharply. It was as if he had been struck a blow. A body blow.

"But, Dad."

"No. That's another part of my life. A bad part. A rotten part. It was before I met your mother, long before you. It has nothing to do with this family, nothing. No."

So, Terry thought, so I tried. But it wasn't over yet. It wasn't started yet.

"It just seems to bother you so much," Terry said, "and I thought if I could help or maybe understand it better. . . ." His words ran until he foundered,[2] until he could say no more. He looked at the table, then out the window. It was all wrong to bring it up, he thought. I blew it. I blew it all up. "I'm sorry."

But now his father didn't hear him. Now his father's eyes were gone again, and a shaft of something horrible went through Terry's heart as

---

2. **foundered:** broke down; failed.

he thought he had done this thing to his father, caused his eyes to go away.

"You can't know," his father said after a time. "You can't know this thing."

Terry said nothing. He felt he had said too much.

"This thing that you want to know—there is so much of it that you cannot know it all, and to know only a part is . . . is too awful. I can't tell you. I can't tell anybody what it was really like."

It was more than he'd ever said about Vietnam, and his voice was breaking. Terry hated himself and felt he would hate himself until he was an old man. In one second he had caused such ruin. And all because he had been embarrassed. What difference did it make? Now he had done this, and he wanted to hide, to leave. But he sat, waiting, knowing that it wasn't done.

His father looked to him, through him, somewhere into and out of Terry. He wasn't in the kitchen anymore. He wasn't in the house. He was back in the green places, back in the hot places, the wet-hot places.

"You think that because I act strange, that we can talk and it will be all right," his father said. "That we can talk and it will just go away. That's what you think, isn't it?"

Terry started to shake his head, but he knew it wasn't expected.

"That's what the shrinks say," his father continued. "The psychiatrists tell me that if I talk about it, the whole thing will go away. But they don't know. They weren't there. You weren't there. Nobody was there but me and some other dead people, and they can't talk because they couldn't stop the morning."

Terry pushed his soda can back and forth, looking down, frightened at what was happening. *The other dead people*, he'd said, as if he were dead as well. *Couldn't stop the morning.*

"I don't understand, Dad."

"No. You don't." His voice hardened, then softened again, and broke at the edges. "But see, see how it was. . . ." He trailed off, and Terry thought he was done. His father looked back down to the table, at the can of soda he hadn't touched, at the tablecloth, at his hands, which were folded, inert[3] on the table.

---

3. **inert:** without power to move or act.

"We were crossing a rice paddy[4] in the dark," he said, and suddenly his voice flowed like a river breaking loose. "We were crossing the paddy, and it was dark, still dark, so black you couldn't see the end of your nose. There was a light rain, a mist, and I was thinking that during the next break I would whisper and tell Petey Kressler how nice the rain felt, but of course I didn't know there wouldn't be a Petey Kressler."

He took a deep, ragged breath. At that moment Terry felt his brain swirl, a kind of whirlpool pulling, and he felt the darkness and the light rain because it was in his father's eyes, in his voice.

"So we were crossing the paddy, and it was a straight sweep, and then we caught it. We began taking fire from three sides, automatic weapons, and everybody went down and tried to get low, but we couldn't. We couldn't get low enough. We could never get low enough, and you could hear the rounds hitting people. It was just a short time before they brought in the mortars and we should have moved, should have run, but nobody got up, and after a time nobody *could* get up. The fire just kept coming and coming, and then incoming mortars, and I heard screams as they hit, but there was nothing to do. Nothing to do."

"Dad?" Terry said. He thought, maybe I can stop him. Maybe I can stop him before . . . before it gets to be too much. Before he breaks.

"Mortars," his father went on, "I hated mortars. You just heard them *wump* as they fired, and you didn't know where they would hit, and you always felt like they would hit your back. They swept back and forth with the mortars, and the automatic weapons kept coming in, and there was no radio, no way to call for artillery. Just the dark to hide in. So I crawled to the side and found Jackson, only he wasn't there, just part of his body, the top part, and I hid under it and waited, and waited, and waited.

"Finally the firing quit. But see, see how it was in the dark with nobody alive but me—I yelled once, but that brought fire again, so I shut up, and there was nothing, not even the screams."

His father cried, and Terry tried to understand, and he thought he could feel part of it. But it was so much, so much and so strange to him.

"You cannot know this," his father repeated. It was almost a chant. "You cannot know the fear. It was dark, and I was the only one left alive

---

4. **rice paddy:** flooded, enclosed field where rice is grown.

out of 54 men, all dead but me, and I knew that the Vietcong were just waiting for light. When the dawn came, 'Charley'[5] would come out and finish everybody off, the way they always did. And I thought if I could stop the dawn, just stop the sun from coming up, I could make it."

Terry felt the fear, and he also felt the tears coming down his cheeks. His hand went out across the table, and he took his father's hand and held it. It was shaking.

"I mean I actually thought that if I could stop the sun from coming up, I could live. I made my brain work on that because it was all I had. Through the rest of the night in the rain in the paddy, I thought I could do it. I could stop the dawn." He took a deep breath. "But you can't, you know. You can't stop it from coming, and when I saw the gray light, I knew I was dead. It would just be minutes, and the light would be full, and I just settled under Jackson's body, and hid."

He stopped, and his face came down into his hands. Terry stood and went around the table to stand in back of him, his hands on his shoulders, rubbing gently.

"They didn't shoot me. They came, one of them poked Jackson's body and went on, and they left me. But I was dead. I'm still dead, don't you see? I died because I couldn't stop the sun. I died. Inside where I am—I died."

Terry was still in back of him, and he nodded, but he didn't see. Not that. He understood only that he didn't understand, and that he would probably never know what it was really like, would probably never understand what had truly happened. And maybe his father would never be truly normal.

But Terry also knew that it didn't matter. He would try to understand, and the trying would have to be enough. He would try hard from now on, and he would not be embarrassed when his father's eyes went away. He would not be embarrassed no matter what his father did. Terry had knowledge now. Maybe not enough and maybe not all that he would need.

But it was a start.

---

5. 'Charley': term American soldiers used for the North Vietnamese and the South Vietnamese Vietcong, their adversaries in the Vietnam War.

# "Dear Sir . . .": Vietnam Memories

**Anonymous**

**D**ear Sir,

For twenty-two years I have carried your picture in my wallet. I was only eighteen years old that day when we faced one another on the trail in Chu Lai, Vietnam. Why you didn't take my life I'll never know. You stared at me for so long, armed with your AK-47, and yet you did not fire. Forgive me for taking your life. I was reacting just the way I was trained to kill V.C. . . .

So many times over the years I have stared at your picture and your daughter, I suspect. Each time my heart and guts would burn with the pain of guilt. I have two daughters myself now. . . . I perceive you as a brave soldier defending his home. Above all else, I can now respect the importance that life held for you. I suppose that is why I am able to be here today. . . . It is time for me to continue the life process and release my pain and guilt.

Forgive me, Sir.

## Responding to the Selections

1. Describe Terry's feelings about his father in "Stop the Sun." How do they change during the story?
2. Explain how these two pieces of writing concerning Vietnam—one fictional, one very factual—connect with each other.
3. Why do you think that these two texts are in a section of the book called "Loving"?

## Exploring the Authors' Craft

The point of view that a story is told from affects the way we understand the action. A first-person narrator is a character who tells his or her own story; a third-person narrator tells *about* the characters but is not a participant in the action. In some cases, as in "Stop the Sun," the third-person narrator may know the thoughts of one or more characters.

1. What do you learn about Terry from the narrator in "Stop the Sun"? Do you think you understand Terry better than if he had told the story himself?
2. Why do you think Gary Paulsen doesn't use the third-person narrator to tell about Terry's father's thoughts?
3. Both Terry's father and the "Dear Sir" author present powerful first-person statements. What similarities are there between these statements?

## Writer's Workshop

Terry's father's retelling of his Vietnam experience is particularly strong because it is explained in his own words. Create a first-person narrative of at least eight paragraphs that also conveys a significant story; it certainly doesn't have to be about war.

## Laura Cunningham

Laura Cunningham, who was born in 1947, is a novelist, playwright, and journalist. Her pieces have appeared in *The New Yorker, The Atlantic Monthly,* and *Esquire.* Her 1989 memoir, *Sleeping Arrangements,* tells of being brought up by two uncles; "Kissing," originally published in the "Hers" column in *The New York Times,* is another recollection of her youth.

*That first real kiss was not a private matter, but something to be shared in detail with friends.*

# Kissing

**I** saw them on the street. The boy appeared to be 15, the girl a few years younger. They were kissing—lightly and frequently—as if to punctuate their conversation. How happy and easy they seemed to be, I thought, how unlike myself at that age.

At 13 I both longed for and feared my first date. I had no doubt that it would change my life, throwing me headlong into romance and sensation. Certain girls at my high school spoke knowingly of the pros and cons of "soul kissing," but my experience was still limited to kissing games, savage rites that had occurred between the ages of 10 and 12.

Among the kissing games my favorite had been Blindfold, in which each girl was blindfolded in turn, then kissed by all the boys at the party. For the finale the girl had to identify, by number, the boy who had been the best kisser. Postman, too, could be exciting, although often when closeted in a bathroom with the appointed postman—he was to "deliver de letter de sooner de better"—both parties would chicken out. Conspirators, boy and girl, would observe a five-minute silence to titillate[1]

---

1. **titillate:** interest; excite.

the imagination of those waiting outside, then leave the room with a pact "not to tell."

But kissing games didn't count. Tingles and sparks, the "molten passion" that I had read about in love comics, could only be expected during the emotional involvement of a date.

Finally, at 13, I had a date, blind, of course. In preparation I bought a dress—a brown and white checked shirtwaist—and made endless decisions. Should I wear my hair up or down? Heels or flats? Lipstick or not? I debated longest whether to wear a padded bra; I finally wore it. I tried to tamp down my excitement, recalling my one phone conversation with the boy, during which he had stuttered, his voice trembling over the "d" in date: "Can we go out on a d-d-d-d-d-date?" Yes, he had a problem with the letter d, my unknown love, but still he had been able to make me nervous.

Boys scared me. They had to be dealt with, certainly spoken to. And speaking to a boy was not something easily accomplished. The highest accolade at my all-girls' high school was "She can talk to boys."

I could not. On my early encounters I was so agitated by the actual presence of boyness that I'd be struck mute. On the street corner or at the luncheonette I would stare helplessly ahead: the world, life itself, swept suddenly bare of subjects. This difficulty of conversation impressed me so much that I wrote in my diary, "I am convinced that people go all the way because they can't think of anything to say."

Was it any wonder that when my first date called I clutched the phone receiver and felt sweat beads big as tears roll down my skin? And hadn't I prepared for the call by jotting down a list of Topics and keeping it near the phone?

Anxious? Of course I was anxious. On the actual night, when the downstairs buzzer sounded, it seemed to ring up my spine. I pressed the button, then poised myself in the foyer. When he rang the doorbell, I counted to 20, then yanked open the door.

A young Paul Newman! Robert Sidell (for that was his name), a TV repair major from an all-boys' vocational high school, was good-looking. I wish my friends could see him—slim, tall, with curling blond hair and dark blue eyes. In our all-girls' classification system, this Robert Sidell would rank high. We invariably described boys in terms of movie stars. At their young age the boys seemed too amorphous[2] on their own, so we likened them to celebrities and amended the description to fit. Ours was a world peopled by "short Troy Donahues," "Tab Hunter but with brown hair" and "Jewish George Maharises."[3] A Jewish George Maharis rated high, but nothing could top a young Paul Newman except perhaps "Troy Donahue and a 1960 Impala."

In a daze I moved through the introductions, the door, the lobby, the walk to the movie house, two hours of "Inherit the Wind," and the walk home. The walk home was dramatic: a 75-mile-an-hour wind sprang up, but in my determination to keep the conversation going (I feared a one-minute pause like a death sentence), I babbled on without any mention of wind or rain. Robert Sidell, too, ignored the hurricane. We walked 20 blocks, heads bowed, bodies straining against the gale force, and spoke only of evolution, movies and our life goals. I was going to be an actress; he was going to be a TV repairman. "Maybe someday I'll fix a set just when you are on a program," he mused. Throughout this conversation my lips moved stiffly. I was wondering what they'd have to do next. I pursed and pointed toward that ultimate moment: Would he kiss me good night?

At the door, without asking, Robert Sidell pressed his lips to mine. I tensed. Where were the sparks, the molten aches? I felt only a cold pressure, Robert Sidell's teeth behind his lip. He ground toward me. I waited for more—the dart of a tongue, the implement of soul kissing. Would he? He did. His tongue stabbed through my lips, heavy, cold, with the feel of grit. The tongue entered, then just as abruptly withdrew. "We'll save the rest for when we're married," he said and was gone.

I spun inside, into the dark living room where I slept on a Castro Convertible.[4] Planning to throw myself on the mattress and cry, I sailed through the air and hit hard wood. I lay on the floor, the wind knocked out of me, and checked to see if anything was broken or paralyzed. When it was established that I was unharmed, I allowed my original reaction to register. As my eyes became accustomed to the dark—I

---

2. **amorphous:** having no definite form or pattern.
3. **Troy Donahues . . .George Maharises:** Donahue, Hunter, and Meharis were idols of many teenage girls in the 1950s.
4. **Castro Convertible:** a brand of sofa that folds out into a bed.

could see the unconverted couch sitting smugly against the wall—I tried to adjust to what I was: *frigid*.

Frigid. I accepted a second date with Robert Sidell. Maybe I would yet thaw out, but that was not my primary motivation. The very existence of a boyfriend, the possibility that my friends might see me with him, was too delicious to abandon on the ground of romantic disfunction. At my school your word about a date was not enough; you were required to show proof. Indeed, the proof—the evidence that we were attractive to boys—seemed more crucial than the boys themselves. Class rings, bracelets, Photomaton[5] shots of yourself as part of a kissing couple—these items were satisfying. I don't believe we really needed or wanted the boys; they were demanding and frightening strangers. They panted, pawed, drooled, refused to take girls home or spend money on them. No, boys were risky. It was the talisman, the evidence, that was desired.

On the second date I secretly ran a tape recorder behind the couch while Robert Sidell repeated the proposal and his hard, cold kiss. His tongue probed a bit deeper this time, then rested on my own before retreating. I didn't believe he really wanted to marry me, but I wanted the tape recording as proof to my friends that a boy had mouthed the words. The kiss itself did not record, which was just as well.

Robert Sidell disappeared, and I rejoined my friends in the after-school gatherings at the luncheonette. There our conversation usually centered on "getting someone." Our fears festered years ahead of schedule. We would be dateless for all the big ones: "Sweet 16," the prom, every New Year's Eve. "Why can't we find someone?" my best friend, Sheila, would wail. "What's wrong with us?" After crunching through sacks of potato chips, guzzling gallons of soda, we could come to only one conclusion: "We're too beautiful. We frighten boys away."

Most of our fears were fulfilled. We *were* dateless for the big ones. Yet over the years I somehow racked up what Sheila called experience. I became a promiscuous kisser. I kissed 36 boys, most of them in my doorway, a few in the incinerator room of the apartment building.

---

5. **Photomaton:** photo booth where, for a small amount of money, one could take three or four instant candid photographs of oneself and one's friends.

There, with background sound effects of thundering garbage and belching flame, it was not hard to imagine where it would all lead: *hell*.

I kissed one boy there for six hours. We kissed so long that the boy's stubble grew in and scraped my cheeks. Afterward I confronted myself in the medicine-chest mirror and saw that my skin was hanging off my face in long horror movie strips. He had seen me that way too! I wept.

Thank goodness rites of passage are just that: you get to pass through them. Adolescence ends. And all I could say in favor of my first experience was: at least they can't be repeated. Adolescence circa 1960? I was glad to kiss it goodbye.

---

## Responding to the Essay

1. Laura Cunningham attributes many of her reactions to the fact that she went to an all-girls' high school. In your opinion, are the girls she describes any different from those in a coed school? Explain.
2. Although this essay recalls events of a different era, what elements of it reflect life today, too?

## Exploring the Author's Craft

Every good writer knows that he or she must be specific, not general, in his or her writing. Name five specific aspects of "adolescence circa 1960" that Laura Cunningham captures and details in this essay.

## Writer's Workshop

In writing about herself as a teenager "circa 1960," Laura Cunningham also captured the values of that era. Write a piece of prose about dating and romance in the society that you know. Be sure that as you are writing about dating and romance you are also capturing the values of the society you are living in.

## Two Perspectives

### Robert Hayden

Poet Robert Hayden was born in 1913 in Detroit. He worked as a college professor for much of his life and was also a consultant in poetry to the Library of Congress. Though interested in and influenced by African-American history, Hayden said, "Afro-American poets ought to be looked at as poets first, if that's what they truly are. I dare to hope that if my work means anything, if it's any good at all, it's going to have a human impact, not a narrowly racial, ethnic, or political and over-specialized impact." Hayden, whose poetry has been described as "flawless" and having "perfect pitch," died in 1980.

### Simon Ortiz

Born in 1941, Simon J. Ortiz is a major Native American author of poetry, short fiction, essays, and screenplays. Ortiz says, "In *Going for the Rain* [from which "My Father's Song" is taken] and later *A Good Journey*, I was very aware of trying to instill that sense of continuity essential to the poetry and stories in the books, essential to Native American life in fact, and making it as strongly apparent as possible." Ortiz, an Acoma, grew up in New Mexico and has degrees from the University of New Mexico and the University of Iowa.

*There are many different ways to appreciate a father.*

# Those Winter Sundays

**Robert Hayden**

Sundays too my father got up early
and put his clothes on in the blueblack cold,
then with cracked hands that ached
from labor in the weekday weather made
5   banked fires blaze. No one ever thanked him.

I'd wake and hear the cold splintering, breaking.
When the rooms were warm, he'd call,
and slowly I would rise and dress,
fearing the chronic angers of that house,

10   Speaking indifferently to him,
who had driven out the cold
and polished my good shoes as well.
What did I know, what did I know
of love's austere and lonely offices?

# My Father's Song

**Simon Ortiz**

Wanting to say things,
I miss my father tonight.
His voice, the slight catch,
the depth from his thin chest,
5   the tremble of emotion
in something he has just said
to his son, his song:

We planted corn one Spring at Acu[1]—
we planted several times
10   but this one particular time
I remember the soft damp sand
in my hand.

My father had stopped at one point
to show me an overturned furrow;
15   the plowshare had unearthed
the burrow nest of a mouse
in the soft moist sand.

Very gently, he scooped tiny pink animals
into the palm of his hand

---

1. **Acu:** Ortiz's childhood home in New Mexico.

20      and told me to touch them.
        We took them to the edge
        of the field and put them in the shade
        of a sand moist clod.


        I remember the very softness
25      of cool and warm sand and tiny alive mice
        and my father saying things.

---

## Responding to the Poems

1. What are some similarities and differences between the views of fathers in these two poems?
2. How does "My Father's Song" contribute to the sense of "continuity" Ortiz wishes to instill in all his readers? Is continuity an issue that interests Hayden here? Explain.

## Exploring the Authors' Craft

1. **Assonance** is a writing technique in which two or more middle vowel sounds are repeated for effect. In "Those Winter Sundays" notice how in the line ". . . put his clothes on in the blueblack cold" a number of similar *o* sounds are repeated. There are repeated *a* sounds, too, in a phrase like "cracked hands that ached" and repeated *i* sounds, in Simon Ortiz's line "tiny alive mice." Aside from the fact that assonance is appealing to the ear, writers sometimes use this technique to connect sound to meaning. How do the repeated *o* sounds in "Those Winter Sundays" reflect the poem's mood and tone?
2. **Personification** occurs when a nonliving thing is given human characteristics. In "Those Winter Sundays" the house is given the capability of feeling "angers." How does this personification contribute to the poem's meaning?

## Writer's Workshop

In both these poems the narrator comes to understand his father's way of showing love. Write a poem without rhyme about the love you get from a parent or caregiver. Try to use assonance and/or personification to help communicate your message—in other words, use these poetic devices as integral parts of the poem, parts that actually help convey the meaning.

## Jane Yolen

Jane Yolen, who was born in 1939, has published over 150 books, winning a variety of awards for her own writing as well as for editing collections of others' work. *Newsweek* magazine has called her "America's Hans Christian Andersen" and *The New York Times* has referred to her as "the Aesop of the 20th century." Both comments attest to Yolen's story-telling capabilities as well as her talent for finding good stories by other people.

*What did Katie's mother mean by giving her that box?*

# Birthday Box

**I** was ten years old when my mother died. Ten years old on that very day. Still she gave me a party of sorts. Sick as she was, Mama had seen to it, organizing it at the hospital. She made sure the doctors and nurses all brought me presents. We were good friends with them all by that time, because Mama had been in the hospital for so long.

The head nurse, V. Louise Higgins (I never did know what that *V* stood for), gave me a little box, which was sort of funny because she was the biggest of all the nurses there. I mean she was tremendous. And she was the only one who insisted on wearing all white. Mama had called her the great white shark when she was first admitted, only not to V. Louise's face. "All those needles," Mama had said. "Like teeth." But V. Louise was sweet, not sharklike at all, and she'd been so gentle with Mama.

I opened the little present first. It was a fountain pen, a real one, not a fake one like you get at Kmart.

"Now you can write beautiful stories, Katie," V. Louise said to me.

I didn't say that stories come out of your head, not out of a pen. That wouldn't have been polite, and Mama—even sick—was real big on politeness.

"Thanks, V. Louise," I said.

The Stardust Twins—which is what Mama called Patty and Tracey-lynn because they reminded her of dancers in an old-fashioned ballroom—gave me a present together. It was a diary and had a picture of a little girl in pink, reading in a garden swing. A little young for me, a little too cute. I mean, I read Stephen King and want to write like him. But as Mama always reminded me whenever Dad finally remembered to send me something, it was the thought that counted, not the actual gift.

"It's great," I told them. "I'll write in it with my new pen." And I wrote my name on the first page just to show them I meant it.

They hugged me and winked at Mama. She tried to wink back but was just too tired and shut both her eyes instead.

Lily, who is from Jamaica, had baked me some sweet bread. Mary Margaret gave me a gold cross blessed by the pope, which I put on even though Mama and I weren't churchgoers. That was Dad's thing.

Then Dr. Dann, the intern who was on days, and Dr. Pucci, the oncologist (which is the fancy name for a cancer doctor), gave me a big box filled to the top with little presents, each wrapped up individually. All things they knew I'd love—paperback books and writing paper and erasers with funny animal heads and colored paper clips and a rubber stamp that printed FROM KATIE'S DESK and other stuff. They must have raided a stationery store.

There was one box, though, they held out till the end. It was about the size of a large top hat. The paper was deep blue and covered with stars; not fake stars but real stars, I mean, like a map of the night sky. The ribbon was two shades of blue with silver threads running through. There was no name on the card.

"Who's it from?" I asked.

None of the nurses answered, and the doctors both suddenly were studying the ceiling tiles with the kind of intensity they usually saved for X rays. No one spoke. In fact the only sound for the longest time was Mama's breathing machine going in and out and in and out. It was a harsh, horrible, insistent sound, and usually I talked and talked to cover up the noise. But I was waiting for someone to tell me.

At last V. Louise said, "It's from your mama, Katie. She told us what she wanted. And where to get it."

I turned and looked at Mama then, and her eyes were open again. Funny, but sickness had made her even more beautiful than good health had. Her skin was like that old paper, the kind they used to write on with quill pens, and stretched out over her bones so she looked like a model. Her eyes, which had been a deep, brilliant blue, were now like the fall sky, bleached and softened. She was like a faded photograph of herself. She smiled a very small smile at me. I knew it was an effort.

"It's you," she mouthed. I read her lips. I had gotten real good at that. I thought she meant it was a present for me.

"Of course it is," I said cheerfully. I had gotten good at that, too, being cheerful when I didn't feel like it. "Of course it is."

I took the paper off the box carefully, not tearing it but folding it into a tidy packet. I twisted the ribbons around my hand and then put them on the pillow by her hand. It made the stark white hospital bed look almost festive.

Under the wrapping, the box was beautiful itself. It was made of a heavy cardboard and covered with a linen material that had a pattern of cloud-filled skies.

I opened the box slowly and . . .

"It's empty," I said. "Is this a joke?" I turned to ask Mama, but she was gone. I mean, her body was there, but she wasn't. It was as if she was as empty as the box.

Dr. Pucci leaned over her and listened with a stethoscope, then almost absently patted Mama's head. Then, with infinite care, V. Louise closed Mama's eyes, ran her hand across Mama's cheek, and turned off the breathing machine.

"Mama!" I cried. And to the nurses and doctors, I screamed, "Do something!" And because the room had suddenly become so silent, my voice echoed back at me. "Mama, do something."

I cried steadily for, I think, a week. Then I cried at night for a couple of months. And then for about a year I cried at anniversaries, like Mama's birthday or mine, at Thanksgiving, on Mother's Day. I stopped writing. I stopped reading except for school assignments. I was pretty mean to my half brothers and totally rotten to my stepmother and Dad. I felt empty and angry, and they all left me pretty much alone.

And then one night, right after my first birthday without Mama, I woke up remembering how she had said, "It's you." Not, "It's for you," just "It's you." Now Mama had been a high school English teacher and a writer herself. She'd had poems published in little magazines. She didn't use words carelessly. In the end she could hardly use any words at all.

So—I asked myself in that dark room—why had she said, "It's you"? Why were they the very last words she had ever said to me, forced out with her last breath?

I turned on the bedside light and got out of bed. The room was full of shadows, not all of them real.

Pulling the desk chair over to my closet, I climbed up and felt along the top shelf, and against the back wall, there was the birthday box, just where I had thrown it the day I had moved in with my dad.

I pulled it down and opened it. It was as empty as the day I had put it away.

"It's you," I whispered to the box.

And then suddenly I knew.

Mama had meant *I* was the box, solid and sturdy, maybe even beautiful or at least interesting on the outside. But I had to fill up the box to make it all it could be. And I had to fill me up as well. She had guessed what might happen to me, had told me in a subtle way. In the two words she could manage.

I stopped crying and got some paper out of the desk drawer. I got out my fountain pen. I started writing, and I haven't stopped since. The first thing I wrote was about that birthday. I put it in the box, and pretty soon that box was overflowing with stories. And poems. And memories.

And so was I.

And so was I.

## Responding to the Story

1. What were your feelings after reading this story? Explain what you liked or did not like about it.
2. In one sentence, how would you describe the mother's love for her daughter?

## Exploring the Author's Craft

Generally, a short story plot builds to a peak moment or **climax** that comes close to the end of the action; then there is usually a period of **resolution** or **dénouement**—a French word meaning "untying"—in which the plot more or less winds down. Where does the climax come in "Birthday Box"? What happens in the dénouement?

## Writer's Workshop

"Birthday Box" is brief but very effective. Try writing a story that has the characteristics listed below:
a. no more than two settings
b. at least one strong character, vividly portrayed
c. a plot that builds up to a climax somewhere before the story's ending

## Angela Patrick

This short story won a national award for Angela Patrick in the 1975 Scholastic Magazines Art and Writing Competition. When she wrote the story Angela was a student at Montgomery County High School in Mount Sterling, Kentucky. When the story was published, Angela wrote, "A year ago, the boy in that story was my first love. When it was over, but not really dead, I wrote down the magic of that day."

*The day was beautiful, and so were the feelings they shared.*

# First Love

**H**e was my first love.

The day was beautiful. The temperature zoomed to the eighties, unseasonal for early March weather, and the sun was brilliant. We had the windows down in the car all the way to my house. The heat made the hair around my face wet and I stroked it smoothly behind my ears. The radio just seemed to play all our favorite songs and I smiled at him so much that he asked me what was wrong. He already knew, though, and smiled back.

My house is far out in the country. Even our small town is ten miles away. I didn't mind the length that day, though, not as long as I was with him.

He's not like other guys his age. He's not a show-off. He doesn't rev the motor or screech the tires on his car, and he thinks about things. He doesn't just accept something because everyone else says it's true. He thinks about it for himself, and if he believes a certain way, he knows why. He's a real person, not just what you see on the outside, but much, much more. He's smart, too. He knows a great deal about a lot of things, but he realizes he doesn't know everything there is to learn and because of this he is constantly searching for the answers. It makes me excited because I want to help him find those answers.

He smiled at me when we turned into the driveway. I like the way he smiles: it makes me feel as bright and warm on the inside as it is in the little pockets between the hills around my house.

We took all my school books to the house and then took off to play basketball. We goofed off with the ball a while. He did funny shots off the backboard and I made goofy ones from far away. Then we even played a game and he beat me: twenty to two.

"Let's go for a walk," he said to me, placing the ball on the ground. His cheeks were shiny with perspiration and his eyes glistened.

"Sure," I answered as we started up a crooked little path.

We talked along between two lean, grassy hills. The sun was hot on my back. There was a forest on one side of us, but there wasn't very much shade because it was too early for the trees to have leaves. There was water running across a curve in the path. He jumped to the other side and held out his hand. I took it and made it safely across.

We started up one hillside. He put his arm around my shoulders and I put mine around his waist. His T-shirt was damp from the warmth of his body and I could feel him breathing as his sides moved gently against the palm of my hand.

There were far-off birds singing in the woods and their song melted with the rhythmic crunch of our tennis shoes on the brittle winter grass. We were silent and from time to time I laid my head on his shoulder and felt his warmth against my cheek. We reached the crest of the ridge and stopped.

"Wow, I like this!" he said, linking his arms around my waist. A cool, gusty, little breeze was blowing along the hill top and it cooled us from the long walk. He gently kissed the top of my forehead, turned me around and we walked on.

We came to the edge of a bank that was built up to form the sides of a pond. He stopped and touched my arm.

"You know, you're a punk," he said teasingly. And in one motion he scooped me up like a child and ran up the bank to the water's edge. I threw my arms around his neck and laughed aloud.

"Put me down," I commanded.

"No," he said and swung me out over the water. "I'm going to throw you in!"

I strengthened my hold on his neck and laughed. "If I go—you go, too."

He didn't care. He swung me out over the water again and pretended to be letting go.

"Put me down," I gasped, squeezing him very hard.

He lowered my feet to the ground in front of him and I tried to run. He caught me almost at once, though, and pulled me close, laughing gently to himself as he stroked my hair.

I squeezed him hard and rested my head against his cheek. His breath, warm and misty, touched my neck and his heart beat against me.

I stepped back, my hands still linked about his neck, and looked at him. The wind tossed his hair and the early sun caressed his forehead. And inside of me my heart grew until I could hardly breathe.

We wandered around the pond's edge, threw pebbles in the water, and hunted for frogs. He called me the "queen of nature" and said that all the animals were at my command. I sat down on the bank beside him and chuckled while he told me to command the cows to quit staring at him. But I was a haughty queen and wouldn't stoop to such a menial task. He persuaded me, however, and after he was satisfied I was rewarded.

We were both in a crazy, light mood and after a few minutes he said, "I bet I can climb that tree to the top."

"Oh," I laughed, "you can not."

"Wait and see," he said, and started up.

I smiled to myself. Sitting cross-legged under the boughs of that tree, I leaned my head back and watched him go up. He got smaller and smaller as he neared the top and he began to look more like a child than a man. All six feet of him looked dwarfed. His T-shirt and tennis shoes no longer appeared athletic but rather added to the child-like quality. It came to me that I was seeing him as the little boy he must have been— the little boy that all his seventeen years couldn't disguise.

"How's that?" he yelled at me from the top.

"That's not the top," I yelled back, for there was one more branch above him.

"You're so hard to please," he said, and moved up.

"Come on down," I cried, "you'll get hurt."

The wind was swinging him around in the top of that tree and he looked so cute. He laughed, his voice floating down to me from far away, and he started down.

Suddenly looking at him up there next to the sky, I got a lump in my throat and before I could stop myself two tears trickled down my cheeks. I blinked hard but everything about me blurred.

That was all. I gained control of myself before he came down and he never knew that I had cried for some strange emotion that I didn't understand.

I didn't know why I cried then but I know now. Deep down inside of me I knew even then that the happiness of that day wouldn't last. Tomorrow, or next week, or next month the joy would all be gone— gone to someone else and so would he.

And I was right.

---

## Responding to the Story

1.  Is the story's ending believable? Why or why not?
2.  Why do you think that neither of the characters in the story is given a name?

## Exploring the Author's Craft

In reading "Birthday Box" you learned that the climax or high point of a story is generally followed by a dénouement in which the plot winds down.

However, writers need not always follow this pattern exactly. Where do you find the climax in "First Love"? Why do you think it is in that location?

## Writer's Workshop

If "First Love" works for readers, it is because they have come to like both the boy and the girl and to root for their romance. Angela Patrick loads the story with specific things the couple does in their early days of infatuation. Following this model, create a scene of fiction that shows a couple having a wonderful time together. Try to capture the same feeling of exhilaration that Patrick did, and be sure to include dialogue that brings the couple alive.

## Alternate Media Response

This story could easily be made into a short film or video. But there would be the problem of communicating the ideas in the last two paragraphs. How would you solve that problem?

## Two Perspectives

### John Crowe Ransom

John Crowe Ransom was born in Tennessee in 1888. He taught at both Vanderbilt University and Kenyon College for many years and founded the famous *Kenyon Review* literary magazine. As a Southerner, Ransom was interested in the region's place in American literary tradition and wrote critical works analyzing it. Ransom's poems may be considered old-fashioned in that they follow tight structures of rhyme and meter, but they are always beautiful. Ransom died in 1974.

### Langston Hughes

Langston Hughes was born in 1902 and died in 1967. As a participant in the creative 1920s movement known as the Harlem Renaissance, Hughes became one of the major literary spokespeople for the African-American experience. His poems, written in the language of everyday speech and often sounding musical, advocate pride of heritage and determination to not give up. Some of his most famous poems include "The Negro Speaks of Rivers," "I, too [sing America]" and "Harlem" ("What happens to a dream deferred?"). He also wrote short stories, essays, song lyrics, and plays.

*As love brings togetherness, so it can also bring separation.*

# Janet Waking

**John Crowe Ransom**

Beautifully Janet slept
Till it was deeply morning. She woke then
And thought about her dainty-feathered hen,
To see how it had kept.

5   One kiss she gave her mother.
Only a small one gave she to her daddy
Who would have kissed each curl of his shining baby;
No kiss at all for her brother.

"Old Chucky, old Chucky!" she cried,
10  Running across the world upon the grass
To Chucky's house, and listening. But alas,
Her Chucky had died.

It was a transmogrifying[1] bee
Came droning down on Chucky's old bald head
15  And sat and put the poison. It scarcely bled,
But how exceedingly

And purply did the knot
Swell with the venom and communicate

---

1. **transmogrifying:** changing in a surprising or grotesque manner.

Its rigor! Now the poor comb stood up straight
20  But Chucky did not.

So there was Janet
Kneeling on the wet grass, crying her brown hen
(Translated far beyond the daughters of men)
To rise and walk upon it.

25  And weeping fast as she had breath
Janet implored us, "Wake her from her sleep!"
And would not be instructed in how deep
Was the forgetful kingdom of death.

# I Loved My Friend

**Langston Hughes**

> I loved my friend.
> He went away from me.
> There's nothing more to say.
> The poem ends,
> 5  Soft as it began—
> I loved my friend.

---

## Responding to the Poems

What aspect of love do both of these poems communicate? Which poem strikes you as more effective? Why?

## Exploring the Authors' Craft

1. "Janet Waking" uses a regular rhyme structure. What is the rhyme scheme of this poem?
2. Langston Hughes always writes in seeming simplicity. Does the plain and direct style of his poem fit its message? Explain.

## Writer's Workshop

Write a poem that parallels either Hughes's or Ransom's in terms of style. Aim for the simplicity of Hughes or the more complex structure of Ransom.

## Making Connections in
# PART FOUR

Complete one or more of the following assignments as your teacher directs.

1.  Write a five-paragraph essay that organizes the pieces of writing in Part Four into various categories of loving. Have each of the three middle paragraphs deal with a different aspect of this powerful topic. In these paragraphs be sure not just to mention the pieces but explain what each selection says about loving.

2.  In this section there are four pairs of selections: "The Picnic" and "Where Have You Gone?"; "Stop the Sun" and "Dear Sir"; "Those Winter Sundays" and "My Father's Song"; and "Janet Waking" and "I Loved My Friend." Which pairing seemed most effective to you? Which seemed least effective? Write an essay explaining not only your opinions, but the criteria you used for judging "effectiveness."

3.  Both "Snowfall in Childhood" and "First Love" depict infatuated teenagers. Discuss some of the similarities in the young couples' situations and reactions. Then point out any significant differences.

4.  The word *gamut* means a full range. The characters or speakers in Part Four experience a gamut of emotions in addition to love. Choose at least four selections that involve a different emotion besides love and write a brief summary of what goes on in them.

# PART FIVE

# Separating

One of the crucial tasks of adolescence is preparing to separate, to move away from parents and be able to function on our own.

In this last section of the book we meet characters facing separation in different ways. Sometimes the separations are forced, as when a parent dies or is hospitalized, as in "Our Lady of the Gentle Fingers." Other times, as in "Nights Away from Home," it is because there are bonds that are breaking of their own accord. And then there are cases, as in "Ex-Basketball Player," when people just can't make the separation that they need to make.

No matter the situation, separation from family, home, and the past are emotional issues for everyone.

# Richard Hartman

Richard Hartman was born in 1961. He says, "I wrote 'Rehearsal' in 1978. . . . I set out to create two very separate moods in the story—the quiet tension of a car ride and the raucous energy of a band room. After finishing my first draft, though, I felt there was something missing, a central image or theme that would somehow tie the two halves of the story together. I remember thinking, 'That's it!' when I reread one of my sentences that contained a description of windshield wipers moving across glass. With the new importance of this image firmly placed in my mind, I revised 'Rehearsal' several times and finally came up with the last line, which, I hoped, would help tie the story together.

"Writing 'Rehearsal' helped tie two parts of my own life together: a love of playing music and the loving but sometimes testy relationship I had with my father. Naturally, much has changed in the twenty years since I wrote the story. . . . However, I still work hard at making connections . . .

"I'm honored that 'Rehearsal' has been selected to appear in this collection."

*What can a music rehearsal show a person about his own life?*

# Rehearsal

**A** misty rain fell as the brown Cadillac penetrated the darkness. Windshield wipers chased one another streaking droplets of water aside. All that could be heard was the droning of the engine.

"There's probably no rehearsal tonight," Bradley's father said interrupting the silence. Bradley was annoyed by the comment but his father could not tell.

"There is a rehearsal," he said.

"I doubt it. How many times have we gotten to the school and nobody was there?" Bradley contemplated the best response so as not to give his father more to criticize.

"There is a rehearsal tonight, Dad." Silence. The car sped on until the school came into view. Bradley was relieved to see other cars in the parking lot. There was indeed a rehearsal. The big brown monster rolled up to the curb.

"Ten o'clock, Bradley?" The question annoyed Bradley for he knew that his father knew the answer.

"Yes, Dad, ten o'clock." He stepped out of the car.

"O.K. Be waiting for me. I don't want to sit in this car for an hour like last week."

"Yes, Dad, I'll be ready."

"Do you have your music and your trumpet?"

"Yes. Bye, Dad."

"Watch out for puddles. Don't get your feet wet."

"I'll be careful." Bradley slammed the door of the car and walked through the damp night air carefully and deliberately dodging the puddles of water on the pavement. When he heard the Cadillac drive away he found a big puddle, took one jump and splashed water in every direction. His feet were wet and cold.

He entered the lobby of the school. He was standing alone and listening when he heard it. At first, it was just the wandering notes of a clarinet. A faint smile formed on Bradley's face and he began walking toward the sound. Soon he heard a saxophone and then a trombone. As he moved closer, the sounds increased. A full smile was on his face as he opened the door to the rehearsal room. For a moment he stood enjoying the cacophony[1] of the band warming up. Then he went to his chair, took out his trumpet and began warming up himself.

Bradley looked at the clock. It read nine. The rehearsal was to begin shortly. Mr. Thompson, the conductor of the band, entered. He was a fine conductor and teacher. He had taught Bradley how to play trumpet in grammar school.

Mr. Thompson raised his hands. The room silenced. "Hello, once again," he said. "I hope we have another good rehearsal tonight. Let's start right away; we only have an hour. First we'll tune up." He pointed to each person in the room who responded with a B-flat concert. Looking around, Bradley saw all the people who were his friends.

There was Fred, the old bass trombone player. Eighty years of life had aged his body but not his music. His was that of a playful child. And there were the Fischer twins, Robert and Joseph, alike in appearance alone, their saxophone playing as distinct from one another as night and day. And Gene, the young clarinetist whose grace on her instrument equaled the grace of her own self. There were others, ranging in age from old to young. There were teachers and store clerks and college students. It was a friendly group of people from all walks of life who met every week to share their common interest—the love and enjoyment of music. This was Community Band.

"Okay," said the conductor. "Take out the Mozart Symphony." The members of the band took out the selection. Bradley watched the conductor as he raised his hands into the air. Each musician's eyes were fixed in anticipation on those hands. When the hands finally fell, it was as if a barrier had been broken, a dam had collapsed, a volcano erupted. Music was created, soothing the needs of each musician.

Bradley watched the conductor. A magician, he thought, waving his hands and creating melodies of the universe from simple instruments of brass and wood. His hands chased one another, causing the trumpets to call out the fanfare followed by the pounding of the timpani. The theme raced about the room, first to the flutes and then the French horns. The reeds picked up the fine melody. The trombones followed. The basses answered with powerful fortissimos.

---

1. **cacophony:** harsh, clashing sounds.

And still the hands of the conductor chased one another seeming to speak. "Softer, softer yet. Yes, that's it. Shhh. Now build slowly, slowly. Louder, louder. Now loud!" The room broke into a frenzy of tonal quality as the entire brass entered in thunderous glory, adding yet another dimension with each bold chord. And then the last. The symphony had ended.

No one spoke nor moved All the musicians sat, stunned by their own music. The echoing of the last chords could still be felt. The conductor was the first to speak. "Good rehearsal," he said. "Sorry we went over time a little. See you next week."

Slowly the people moved, putting away their instruments, getting their coats, and finally departing. Bradley walked as if in a trance. When he opened the door to the outside, he saw the brown Cadillac waiting. The cold, wet night hit his face and woke him up. It had not stopped raining. He opened the car door and climbed in to see his father.

"You're late."

"Sorry, Dad."

"Did you get very wet?"

"Not too wet."

"How was the rehearsal?"

"O.K." Silence. The monster pulled away from the curb and sped into the darkness. Bradley watched the windshield wipers as they chased one another, conducting the night rain.

---

## Responding to the Story

1. There are two clear worlds in this story, the world of the boy with his father in the car and the world of the boy at the rehearsal. How is each world characterized?
2. Where do you think the boy's life will be moving from this point onward? What in the story leads you to your conclusion?

## Exploring the Author's Craft

1.  Mood is the result of careful word choice in both description and dialogue. Give some specific examples of how this writer's word choice creates different moods for each of the two worlds of this story.
2.  Last lines are often crucial in prose writing. In this volume alone, "Checkouts," "Through the Tunnel," "Like Mexicans," "The Moustache," "Reunion," and "Snowfall in Childhood," among other pieces, have last lines that connect various elements of the work and end it with a significant statement. Explain how the last line in "Rehearsal" achieves Richard Hartman's intent of tying the story together.

## Writer's Workshop

Create a piece of short fiction using Richard Hartman's technique of contrasting two different worlds that one young person moves in. Be sure that the piece of writing communicates a point of view about the two worlds, as "Rehearsal" does.

## Alternate Media Response

This story seems suitable to adapting into a short script: there is good dialogue, good action, and only a couple of settings needed. Write a script and then videotape your version of "Rehearsal." Show the finished product to the class. If you wish, send the author of this book a copy for Richard Hartman; he'd be proud.

## Two Perspectives

## Gary Soto

For a biography of Gary Soto, see page 161.

## Frank Conroy

Frank Conroy was born in 1936. "Nights Away from Home" was published in *The New Yorker* magazine and was later a part of Conroy's autobiography *Stop-Time*. *The New York Times* called *Stop-Time* "a book whose honesty and evocation of youth is a triumph." Author William Styron said of the same work, "*Stop-Time* is in every way a distinguished book, distinguished by its freshness, its wisdom and, above all, . . . its almost total lack of self-pity." Conroy has also published a collection of short stories, *Midair*, and a novel, *Body & Soul*.

*What makes a teenage boy leave home? What makes him return?*

# Saturday at the Canal

Gary Soto

I was hoping to be happy by seventeen.
School was a sharp check mark in the roll book,
An obnoxious tuba playing at noon because our team
Was going to win at night. The teachers were
5  Too close to dying to understand. The hallways
Stank of poor grades and unwashed hair. Thus,
A friend and I sat watching the water on Saturday,
Neither of us talking much, just warming ourselves
By hurling large rocks at the dusty ground
10  And feeling awful because San Francisco was a postcard
On a bedroom wall. We wanted to go there,
Hitchhike under the last migrating birds
And be with people who knew more than three chords
On a guitar. We didn't drink or smoke,
15  But our hair was shoulder length, wild when
The wind picked up and the shadows of
This loneliness gripped loose dirt. By bus or car,
By the sway of a train over a long bridge,
We wanted to get out. The years froze
20  As we sat on the bank. Our eyes followed the water,
White-tipped but dark underneath, racing out of town.

# Nights Away from Home

Frank Conroy

As I walked across the George Washington Bridge toward New Jersey, the sun broke from behind the clouds. Bright rays caught the highest cables and slipped down along the long, sweeping curves like molten silver. Far below, the water was dark. A stiff breeze kept whipping my hair over my eyes, but I paid no attention. I was seeing a new world. Everything seemed special—a police call box, the surface of the walkway, the cables, the cars rushing by. All of it was super-real, each image sharply defined in space. The air itself was triple strength and seemed to clean out my lungs as I marched along.

Descending into New Jersey, I looked around at the public world—the sidewalks, empty lots, signs, diners, phone booths—conscious that these things were now the furniture of my life, that until I got to Florida they were all I had. I stood for a moment in front of a coin-operated milk machine, transfixed by its significance. Put a quarter in the slot and the milk would come out. No questions, no ramifications,[1] just the milk. One could live without words and without people.

Route 1 wasn't far away. I slipped across the traffic and turned south, walking steadily for a couple of miles before I found a long, open stretch of road where cars could stop easily. Then I turned (for some reason I remember this precisely), put my left hand in my pocket and my right thumb in the air. I didn't make the familiar long, sweeping gesture as the cars went by; I just held out my thumb. I was wearing khaki trousers, a light-blue shirt, and a leather jacket.

My first ride was a brand-new '51 Dodge. Running down the road to where it waited, I glanced at the license plates, only mildly disappointed to see they were New Jersey issue. (I'd been daydreaming of a single ride all the way to Florida as the cars went by.) I pulled open the door and jumped in quickly. "Thanks," I said, breathing hard. The driver, a man of about thirty, pulled back into the traffic. A briefcase lay on the seat beside him, and in the back I could see what looked like folded cardboard boxes, stacked flat and tied with string. A few loose papers lay beside the briefcase.

---

1. **ramifications:** consequences.

"How far are you going?" he asked.

"To Florida. Fort Lauderdale, Florida."

"Well, I can take you about thirty miles before I turn off."

"That's fine. Thanks a lot."

We rode in silence for some time. Now that I was on my way, I felt almost lighthearted. Inside the comfortable car, mile after mile falling behind me, I grew expansive. I glanced down at the papers and read a letterhead.

"How's the cardboard-box business?" I asked, pleased at my own cleverness.

"Not bad," he said. "It's a living. Gets a little dull sometimes."

"Do you make them?"

"No, I just sell them. Go around to factories and manufacturers and take their orders."

"I had a job working in a drugstore, but I got fired for sleeping in the stockroom."

He laughed. "Aren't you a little young to be going off to Florida?"

I watched the road, not turning my head. "No. I don't think so."

"Well, maybe not," he said slowly. "Maybe not."

"I'm fifteen."

"You don't look fifteen. I can tell you that."

"I know, but it's the truth."

"Well, I believe you. No reason why you should lie to me." He drove for a while without saying anything. "Florida's a long way. I guess you're going to hitch all the way down?"

"That's right. I'm hoping for long rides—maybe even someone going to Miami."

"You figure on coming back?"

"No."

"Not ever, uh?"

"Nope. Not ever."

"Well, there you are," he said, and gazed out through the windshield.

The flat, green Jersey Meadows slipped by outside, wiped every few seconds by the dark blur of a telephone pole.

"I ran away when I was seventeen," he said suddenly after miles of silence. "I never went back."

My head whipped around. "You did?" It seemed an incredible coincidence, but I believed him.

"My old man was a bastard." A faint smile appeared on his face. "He beat us up all the time. Best thing I ever did was leave."

"Where'd you go?"

"One morning he came at me in the barn, and before I knew it I laid him out with a pitchfork. Wham! Right on the ear." The smile was broader now. "He went down like a tree. I thought sure he was dead, but of course he wasn't. Just out cold." He laughed. "I didn't wait for him to come around. No, sir. I left immediately."

I laughed with him. "Where'd you go?"

"Well, I had a little money. Enough to eat for a while, anyway. I skipped the state on a freight train and moved around the country picking up work here and there. I was a big kid, so I didn't have much trouble. Then I got a job on a farm up in Iowa, and the people were really nice—best people I'd ever met—so I stayed on there. Every winter I thought about coming East, but somehow I'd wind up staying. Finally did leave when their boy came back from the Marines."

I sat silently for a while, absorbing the story. "When you got here you found a job and just"—I hesitated, unsure of how to phrase it—"just went on?"

"That's right," he said. "This same company, matter of fact. I started in the shop as a cutter."

His words were momentous.[2] I drank them in and stored them away, hoping they would somehow protect me from the dangers ahead. He'd run away, he'd started from nothing as I was starting, and there he was, looking like everyone else in a suit and tie, driving a car, holding down a decent job—living proof that one could bring it off. Perhaps I wouldn't have to live in the woods. Maybe I could get a job and begin a new life. I might even learn to laugh at the old days, as the man beside me had learned to laugh at the thought of his unconscious father. I began to see possibilities I hadn't considered in the heat of my escape. I could even get married in a few years and start a family of my own!

The car was slowing down.

"I have to turn off here," he said. "It's a good spot, though. They'll be able to see you from pretty far back."

---

**2. momentous:** significant; very important.

I felt a faint twinge at the sight of the deserted intersection. Somehow I'd forgotten that I'd ever have to get out. But I was ready as we came to a stop.

"Now, son," he said, turning to me. "If I were you, I'd stay away from trains and railroad yards. Just keep hitching, and don't get in with anybody who looks funny."

"All right." I nodded. "Why do you say that about trains?"

"Well, the bums and the winos. They get rough sometimes."

"Thanks for telling me. I'll be careful." I pulled back the handle and opened the door. . . . I stepped out into the sunshine. "Good-bye, and thanks a lot."

"So long," he yelled through the window. "Good luck!"

I watched the car pull away and head west, its rear end sinking slightly as the driver accelerated. There was a flash of brake lights as the car approached a curve and then the road was empty. A blast of air struck my ankles and neck as a big semi roared by behind me.

I was in the cab of an old Studebaker truck. The driver, an immensely fat man whose belly cleared the steering wheel by no more than an inch, had told me he was carrying a load of dental floss from a wholesaler in Jersey City to a warehouse south of Camden. "I've carried everything in my time," he said. He drove with his shoulders, his pudgy hands holding the wheel as if the palms were grafted on. "Pineapples, live chickens, paper clips, bathtubs—you name it. Even a little booze in the old days, but my wife made me stop. Yes, sir, nothing surprises me anymore. I just drive along and work on the old voice." He threw back his head and began to sing. "When that red red robin comes bob bob bobbin' along, a-LONG!" His voice rang out clearly over the whine of the engine. "How about that, kid? Pretty good, eh? Someday I'll go on the Ted Mack Amateur Hour.[3] I'll win in a breeze. Did you see that movie where Mario Lanza is a truck driver and he delivers this piano, you know, and he thinks he's alone and sits down and plays a little and makes with the old voice? Boy, what a terrific movie. It turns out the piano is for some knockout opera star and she hears him from the other

---

3. **Ted Mack Amateur Hour:** TV talent contest program of the 1950s, through which a number of famous performers got their first break into stardom.

room and he winds up a star too, you know, going around in those monkey suits and drinking champagne all the time. Dee-eep river, my home is O-ver Jordan! That guy can really sing. You gotta give it to him." He beeped the horn as we passed a car.

We rumbled on through town after town. I watched the sun sinking in the sky and realized I should have stolen some money at home. I had a dollar-fifty in my pocket, and the trip was going to be longer than I'd planned. It was afternoon already and I was still in New Jersey.

The truck slowed down and we pulled up in front of a roadside stand. "Come on, kid, let's eat."

I was hungry, but I hesitated.

"Come on," he said, descending from the cab. "It's on me."

"Thank you. I have some money, though." I opened my door and jumped to the ground.

"Don't be silly, kid," he said as we walked through the dust. "Keep it for later. You'll need it." He spoke softly, as if not to embarrass me. At the stand he slapped both hands on the counter. "Hiya, gorgeous! How ya been keeping since I saw you last?"

"What'll it be?" the waitress asked, smiling.

"Five hot dogs, coffee, and a big glass of milk for the kid here."

As she went off to prepare the food, he turned and leaned back against the counter, balancing his weight on his elbows. He winked at me, gave his belly a slap, and very delicately crossed one leg over the other. I could hear the hot dogs sizzle as they hit the griddle.

"Some enchanted evening," he sang in a full voice, "you will see a strange-ahh! You will see a strange-ahh, across a crowded room. . . ."

Night. I walked along the side of a road, my way lighted by the headlights of cars whipping past. I've been walking for a long time, not bothering to hitch since the sun went down. The rhythm of my body takes up my entire attention. I'm drunk with movement. Ahead I see the lights of a town. Suddenly there's a sidewalk under my feet. Houses, most of them dark, are set back behind hedges and lawns. A dog barks a block or two behind me.

Moving through the center of town, I am only dimly aware of my surroundings. The shops are closed and the streets nearly empty. I watch for the route signs. The state is Delaware. I don't know the town. I pass under the darkened marquee of a movie theatre. The street widens. More houses behind lawns. Tall trees above. My breath makes smoke in the damp air.

On the far side of town, I approach the intersection of two gigantic highways. There are lights everywhere—gas stations, restaurants, liquor stores. I stop in front of an all-night diner. A couple neck in a car in the shadows. I go in the diner. Sitting on a stool near the end of the counter, my legs prickling with a thousand minuscule pulse beats, I eat tomato soup and a cheese sandwich. Finished, I push the plates away and order a Coke and a piece of layer cake. On my way out I buy a nickel cigar from a machine near the door.

Outside, I regain my sense of direction and continue south. After a few steps the rhythm of walking takes hold of me again, and it's as if I'd never stopped. For mile after mile my mind is empty. (No, not empty exactly. Imagine a symphony orchestra responding to a suddenly paralyzed conductor by holding a single note on and on, forever, without change.)

I look up to see an immense building flooded with light in the near distance. A red neon sign on the roof says "STATE POLICE." I stop where I am and watch the sign. Then I look around. A path on my left leads away to a dark clapboard house. A shingle on the lawn says "HENRY FREEMAN, M.D." There are three concrete steps at the foot of the path. I sit down with my back to the house and take out the cigar. The cellophane falls away and I light up. Watching the red neon, I smoke slowly.

The cigar finished, I see a dark shape across the lawn. Moving closer, I can make out a small ornamental tree, no more than six feet tall, with broad, thick branches very low to the ground. Down on my hands and knees, I peer underneath. I can feel a bed of fallen needles. I crawl under carefully, the branches closing after me. There's just enough room as I curl myself around the thin trunk. No one will see me in the morning. I fall asleep with the scent of pine heavy in my head, thinking of the woods in Florida. . . .

Under the tree on the doctor's lawn, I woke early. Crawling out carefully, I stood up and brushed the pine needles from my clothes and hair. Everything was utterly still—the road, the houses, the damp air itself. I looked around at the town in the colorless dawn light, seeing it for the first time. It was smaller than I'd thought in the darkness. Not even a town, really—just a few houses strung along either side of the highway. I crossed the road and started south. As I approached the police station, the red neon sign went out. I went by quickly without turning my head.

My first ride of the day was a milk truck. The driver, a teen-aged boy, seemed to be standing behind the wheel in the tall, open cab. Then I realized there was a very high seat so he could jump in and out with a minimum of effort. I sat down on the corrugated-steel floor and lifted my face to the wind. Behind us, the bottles rattled in their wire cages.

"Go ahead," he yelled over the wind and the rattling glass. "Take a quart. I'll chalk it up to breakage."

I opened a bottle and drank in long, deep swallows. The milk was ice cold and delicious. Five or six miles up the road, the boy had to turn off to begin his rounds. At the corner, I jumped out the open door with a wave, absurdly pleased that he didn't have to stop. The sun was out and I took off my jacket, slinging it over my shoulder as I walked.

It was too early for much traffic. When a car passed, I'd turn around and walk backward, my thumb in the air, whipping my head to see the license plates. By never losing my forward momentum, I felt less dependent on the cars. Plowed fields stretched away on either side of the road. I measured my progress by sighting something far ahead—a group of mailboxes, a road sign, or a line of telephone poles—and making it my goal. Passing a huge girl drinking Coca-Cola (the sudden awareness of silence as I walked under her immense eyes, one of them bulging slightly where the paper had blistered), I had already picked my next target, an isolated gas station on the horizon.

I was sweating as I crossed the asphalt driveway and approached the office. Through the wide plate-glass window I could see an old man sitting with his feet up, staring out at the pumps. His head came around slowly as he caught sight of me. I pushed open the door. Hillbilly music blasted from a radio on the desk beside his feet.

"Can I use the bathroom?"

"What say?"

"Can I use the bathroom, please?"

"Around back." He waved his arm to indicate the direction.

I let the door fall shut and went around the corner of the building. The ground was littered with old oil cans, paper cartons, and fragments of auto bodies. Inside the men's room, I looked at myself in the mirror over the washstand, mildly surprised that except for a layer of dirt and messy hair I looked the same as usual. I ran hot water into the basin and pulled my shirt over my head. There wasn't any soap, only a can of Grease-Off, a gray powder that felt like sand between my palms. I scoured myself thoroughly—face, neck, shoulders, and arms—and bent over the small basin to rinse off when the paste began to sting too much.

Back out in front, I gathered my courage. I ran my fingers through my hair and went into the office. The old man was cleaning his nails with a penknife.

"Have you got any odd jobs you want done?" I asked, having rehearsed the question in the bathroom mirror. "Cleaning up or washing windows or something?"

He attacked his index finger with exquisite care. "Nope."

"I could clean up that junk around back."

He answered without raising his head. "This ain't my place. I'm just watching it."

"Will the boss be back soon?"

"Nope." He raised the knife to his mouth and blew something off the tip.

I stood by the door, reluctant to leave. "Well, thanks anyway," I said after a minute, and backed out. I knelt down for a drink from the water tap between the gas pumps, wiping my mouth and glancing back at the office as I finished. The old man hadn't moved. I turned away and crossed the black asphalt back up to the highway.

I was resting by the side of the road, my back up against a fence post, when a yellow school bus came around the bend and stopped directly in front of me. The folding doors crashed open and the driver stared down his extended arm at me. "Well, come on," he yelled, his hand opening and closing over the handle of the door lever.

I got up and advanced a step. "I'm not . . ." I began, unsure of how to explain.

"What?" he yelled. He squinted his eyes and, peering down at me, raised his upper lip in an expression of annoyance, exposing a quarter inch of red gums.

"I don't go to your school," I said, stepping back. "I don't ride the bus."

His mouth fell shut and he pulled the lever to close the doors, his whole body straightening with the effort. "Damn kids."

The children had crowded over to my side to see what was happening. They watched me from behind the glass, their mouths moving silently as they shouted. The bus began to move and they slipped away, pale faces turning into a white blur. I started walking.

As the morning sun rose higher in the sky, traffic picked up, but there were no trucks. It occurred to me that I'd taken a wrong turn somewhere. I was on Route 1, but there might have been an alternate, a truck route, that I'd missed. In any event, I knew that the thing to do was keep heading south. Eventually the roads would rejoin. I wiggled my thumb at a big De Soto. It went by at a good seventy miles an hour, rocking slightly on the poor road surface. About to turn away, I saw another car in the distance. A flash of sunlight caught something on its roof, and I froze in my tracks. A red beacon. The police. It was too late to hide. I turned my back on them and continued walking, my mind spinning in a sudden frantic effort to be ready for them if they should stop. I realized I should have prepared a story—something from a book I'd read, or a movie. I should have had a false personality at my fingertips, so they wouldn't be able to trace me back. No matter what happened, I couldn't let them send me back. Forcing myself not to turn around for a quick glance, I kept walking.

At first a faint sighing, like wind in the tops of distant trees. Then a kind of whine, almost imperceptible at first, growing steadily louder and higher until (at the very instant a shock wave of air slammed softly across my shoulders) it reversed itself and plunged down the scale to an even hum. I watched the black car racing away ahead of me. The tail-lights came on, a bright, burning red. The entire rear end lifted slightly.

After a momentary pause, the cruiser began to back up. I stood fascinated, rabbitlike, drinking in the image of the approaching car. When it arrived in front of me, so close I could have touched it, the image was unreal, like something from a dream. The window came down and a pair of blue eyes watched me calmly.

"What you doin' out here, boy?"

"I'm on my way to school. I missed the bus." (A certain tranquillity spreading like oil over the surface of my mind as I plunge into the lie.)

"We saw you hitching. Hitching rides is against the law," he said, his voice neither threatening nor reassuring, leaving me plenty of room to answer. He scratched his nose and watched me.

"Well, I'm sorry," I said, looking down. "I was getting awfully late."

He turned and stared out the windshield. A speck of shaving soap had dried just under his ear, very white against the red skin. "Where're your books?"

"In my locker," I said. "We didn't have any homework, so I left them."

He turned away and spoke to his partner at the wheel. I couldn't hear the short exchange.

"O.K. Get in," he said, staring straight ahead.

"What?" I felt the beginning of panic, like a giant hand squeezing my heart.

"Get in back. We go by the high school."

"Oh, that's great," I said, talking quickly to conceal my relief. "Thanks a lot. I sure appreciate it." I opened the back door and hesitated with one foot inside. The rear of the car was separated from the front by heavy wire mesh, and the handles had been stripped off the inside of the doors. I entered after a split second, surrendering myself to fate with the same delirious passivity the awkward diver feels as he springs off the board. My body fell back as the car pulled away, and I covered my mouth in a convulsive yawn. Through the black mesh, I could see the wide bristled necks of the two cops ramrod stiff above their neat gray shirt collars.

"You drive like an old lady, George."

"Uh-huh. Tell the governor."

"I might do that."

I slid forward on the seat and reached out to hold the wire mesh. Suddenly I wanted to tell them the truth. My name is Frank Conroy and I don't belong here. I opened my mouth to speak, but stopped as I felt tears starting in my eyes. My fingers tightened in the mesh and I waited for the emotion to pass.

The radio crackled and the driver reached down for the microphone, pressing it against the side of his mouth. "Twelve. Twelve," he said. "An assist. We got a kid who missed the school bus. It's on our way. Twelve out." A voice responded, talking in numbers. The driver leaned forward and replaced the microphone.

I ran over his words and decided that despite the mysterious word "assist" they were in fact going to do nothing more than drop me off at the local high school.

"I sure appreciate it," I said again. The urge to confess had disappeared. I watched the countryside go by.

That night I came upon a truck depot in Maryland. Hundreds of trucks were spaced out in long lines on the hard-packed earth like the vertebrae of some immense animal. A quarter mile down the line I could see the faint neon haze of the diner. The air was filled with a continuous rumbling as trucks pulled in and out in the distance, air brakes gasping, headlights flashing against the sky. I walked among the tall wheels, staring up at the gargantuan trailers, big as houses, admiring the shiny cabs with their chunky radiator grilles and fanciful decorations. Most of the rigs were dark, but every now and then one had been parked with the running lights left burning, small pinpoints of red, green, or amber light describing the huge mass of the trailers, high in the air, like magnified examples from a geometry book. I stopped behind each truck to check the banks of license plates. I ran through the Eastern Seaboard states in my mind, imagining the group of plates most likely to indicate a truck going to Florida. I found what I was looking for at the edge of the parking area—a sixty-foot semi with plates from Massachusetts to Florida. The barn-sized rear doors were locked. I went around to the front and examined the empty cab. Lettered on the red door were the words "FAVARIO TRUCKING, NORTH-SOUTH EXPRESS SHIPPING, BOSTON, MASS.," followed by a series of numbers and specifications. I stepped into the deeper darkness between the cab and trailer, in among the tanks, hoses, and hydraulic lines, and urinated invisibly.

I waited on the running board for an hour or so, dozing off and then waking with a jolt as my back began to slip on the smooth metal of the door. Once I stood up at the approach of voices, but the men passed unseen in the next corridor and continued up the line, their voices dying out after a burst of laughter. I moved away from the truck toward the long grass at the edge of the area. Where the grass began, an old cab had been put up on blocks, the wheels removed, umbilical cords[4] dangling on the ground. I climbed up on the running board and pulled open the door. It was dark inside, but as my eyes adjusted I could see the cab was empty. Kneeling on the seat, I spread the curtain hanging where the rear window should have been and looked into a small compartment. There were two small round windows at each end and a thin mattress to lie on. I climbed in and closed the curtains. . . .

Suddenly, in the cab of the truck, it was morning. The porthole at my feet threw a slanting bar of sunlight across my legs. I heard something

---

**4. umbilical cords:** the cords connecting the cab of a truck to the trailer and providing power from one to the other.

moving and opened the curtains in time to see a brown cat leap from the seat to the open window of the door and disappear. Climbing down carefully, I rubbed the sleep from my eyes, kicked the door open, and jumped to the ground. The field was empty. I took a few steps, looking around in astonishment. The flat earth spread before me, almost white under the blazing sun, an empty desert the size of a couple of football fields. On the other side I could see the diner, a small square building at the edge of the road. The cat loped toward it, moving in a straight line over the dusty ground, hindquarters jouncing smoothly and head held high. I followed in its tracks. And it was as I crossed the empty field that something entirely unexpected happened in my head—a sudden switch, a reversal of polarity, overwhelmingly strong and oddly mechanical, as if my brain were one of those old-fashioned treadle machines that start sewing backward if you catch the cycle wrong. I had to return to New York.

I remember quite precisely the single fact that I allowed myself to believe was the cause of my change of heart—that if I went on I'd never see my half sister again, the baby I'd taken care of for so long it seemed to me she couldn't get along without me. I followed the cat through the dust and allowed nothing else to exist in my thoughts—only the baby, as if *she* were forcing me to capitulate, as if I no longer had any choice. Thus works the mind of a child, always a bit behind itself, swamped with emotion, and innocent of its own cunning. I veered away from the cat, crossed the road, and started hitching north.

## Responding to the Selections

1. Why does the narrator in "Saturday at the Canal" want to leave home? Can you identify with his feelings? Explain.
2. How are Frank Conroy's motivations and situation differ from those of the boy in the poem?
3. Is it plausible to you that Conroy decided to return to New York? Explain your answer.

# Exploring the Authors' Craft

As has been discussed earlier in this book, naming tangible parts of a world can lead to vivid writing.

1. Gary Soto names specific things from the high school world that the narrator in his poem wants to escape from. What are some of these?
2. In the early hours of Frank Conroy's leaving, everything he sees and experiences is extremely vivid to him, since it's all new. What *are* the things that especially strike him in the early pages of this narration? Include the conversation with the driver of his first ride and why it inspires him.

# Writer's Workshop

In either poetry or prose, write about a time of either leaving home or thinking about it. Be sure to name specific things to bring the narration to life, just as, for example, Frank Conroy's reference to a "can of Grease-Off, a gray powder that felt like sand between my palms" adds authenticity to his story.

## Alternate Media Response

In any artistic form you choose, deal with the concept of leaving home. Your representation can be literal or abstract.

# Nancy Kern

Nancy Kern was born in 1969. After finishing college, she enrolled in the graduate program for creative writing at the University of South Carolina, studying for a short time under the poet James Dickey. Presently she teaches and resides in northern New Jersey.

Nancy Kern says, "'Our Lady of the Gentle Fingers' came into being while I was studying at U.S.C. One of my instructors there had given us an assignment which was actually a poetry exercise created by Rita Dove called 'Your Mother's Kitchen.' The idea was to set a poem in our mother's kitchen without including ourselves in the picture. Instead of taking the kitchen my mother has now, . . . I decided to imagine the one she had while she was a child. Going back, remembering my grandmother's oilcloth floor and Formica table, the plastic flowers and the chintz curtains, I re-visioned the past. I'd heard plenty of 'family myths' as a child, and this piece is filled with them. Though this story is by no means true, it definitely is connected to my own understanding of my ancestry."

*Sometimes separation comes before you're anywhere near ready for it.*

# Our Lady of the Gentle Fingers

### I

Our Lady of the Gentle Fingers[1] wore a veil of stars. She had soft, closed lips that I liked to run my hand across when nobody was around. Our Lady crushed a snake with feet you could not see. She was my real mother, Uncle Shank told me. She never answered me, though, or even looked at me, because her eyes were always looking at the ground.

We crowned Our Lady in the garden that week, Uncle Shank, Mama, and me. I put on my First Communion dress and party shoes, and Mama wove buttercups into a crown for Our Lady's head. It was hot, summertime hot, the hottest May since Aunt Ethel passed, Uncle Shank said. Mama smiled so quiet under the trees, I didn't know what was inside.

That was the week that the men took Mama away. She was kicking her feet and she wore no shoes, and the men held her like a rolled-up carpet when they carried her down the stairs. Mama was small. She didn't need four men to bring her down.

*That's how many there always is,* Uncle Shank said as he held onto the banister.

Uncle Shank knew, because he'd lived with Mama for all of his life. For a few years when Aunt Ethel was alive he lived on top of the Five and Ten and worked at the slaughterhouse behind the Pickens' pig farm, but after Aunt Ethel passed he began having nightmares about the pigs, and so Papa found him work at the brewery, doing something with the filters for the beer. Papa and he drove to work about an hour before the sun came up, and they came home an hour after the sun came down, when I was already in bed. Most of the time they made a lot of noise bumping their way up the stairs, and when they got to the top they always saw Mama there, framed by the doorway, holding the black pan in her hand. Even with the blanket and pillow over my head I heard the sound of the pan as it hit the wall and sometimes Papa. One time, Papa wore a toy army helmet that he found in the garden, and Mama aimed

---

1. **Our Lady of the Gentle Fingers:** a statue of the Virgin Mary, mother of Jesus.

at Uncle Shank instead. That was before Mama was taken away, though. When she came back she never threw anything, not even the black pan.

*This here's your supper,* Uncle Shank said after the men and Papa and Mama were gone. *Eat up.*

He gave me a fried bologna sandwich and sugar milk. He was wearing his work uniform, which was still brand new with stiff creases in the sleeves and pants.

*Mama has no shoes,* I said.

*Don't worry about your mama,* said Uncle Shank. *She'll be fine. Now look at me, Lizzie. I gotta go make sure Papa's alright. Eat up, and get to sleep soon as you're done.* Then he shoved a sandwich in his pocket and left.

Gogo was drinking out of the toilet, so I called to him and gave him the sandwich soon as I heard Uncle Shank's car pull away. Gogo swallowed it whole, and then I made him follow me out to the garden to sit with Our Lady. She was perfect, with her long, white fingers pressed softly together. I touched the folds in her robe and followed them all the way down to where the snake was, and I thought about the packet of photographs Uncle Shank had brought home from the fair that year. He'd gotten them from a fortune teller there who used to be a Sister of Mercy.[2] She'd told Uncle Shank that the different patterns of stars in each photograph were signs from Our Lady, who wanted to warn us what'd happen if we didn't pray to her.

*See this one?* Uncle Shank showed us. *This one says that California is going to have an earthquake and sink into the ocean. And this one here, where the stars are shaped like a fishing hook, this tells us that the anti-Christ has already been born.*

Papa gave a loud and rough laugh when Uncle Shank showed the pictures, but me and Mama looked on, blinking in the thick smoke of Uncle Shank's and Papa's cigars.

---

2. **Sister of Mercy:** member of a congregation of Catholic nuns.

## II

Mama was beautiful before she was taken away. She had long, yellow hair that she always wore on top of her head in twisted braids. She never let me see her with her hair down, but I could catch her sometimes brushing it out in the morning after Papa and Uncle Shank left for work. Papa used to say that Mama could've been a beauty queen in Atlantic City but that she was too shy and afraid of people. I did not think Mama was shy at all. She talked to me mostly every day when I came home from school, even while I did my homework. Usually she told me stories of how we came from German royalty, how my grandmother ran away from the castle when she was fourteen because she'd fallen in love with the stable boy, my grandfather. Sometimes Mama and me would close our eyes and pretend that we were Grandma, waiting for our stable boy to take us away. The day before they took Mama away it was so hot the two of us put cold cream all over our arms and legs and sat by the open icebox and made believe we were in Grandma's tower, feeling the cold air from the sea to the east.

*They were in love,* Mama told me. *So much in love that when Grandma died, Grandpa turned on the oven and closed all the windows and went to sleep forever. That's how you are to me,* she said. *Look at me, Lizzie. You are my life. You are the only reason I go on living.*

On some days, I would come home from school and find Mama sitting quiet at the front window, tracing the bubbles in the glass with her fingers. On those days, instead of doing my homework at the kitchen table, me and Gogo would go down to his doghouse and we would both crawl in and look through the door at Our Lady, who stood across the path, on a small hill of round, white rocks.

## III

We fell asleep in Gogo's house and I dreamt of Mama, only in the dream she had no hair. When I woke up it was almost dark, and the fireflies were blinking in the yard. In the shadows I saw the red dot of Uncle Shank's cigar getting closer. Our Lady glowed in the darkness.

*Quick Lizzie,* Uncle Shank said. Gogo lifted his ears and poked his head out to sniff Uncle Shank's big shoes. *Where does Papa keep his money?*

I wasn't sure where Papa kept his money, but I knew that Mama hid a jar of coins in the cabinet where we kept the black pan, because that's where she'd reach whenever she sent me to the corner store to get her cigarettes. I never got more than two at a time, because Mama was always afraid Papa would find out.

*Never let a man see you smoke,* she'd say. *Royal women do not smoke.*

I didn't really want to show Uncle Shank the place, but he held my arm hard and took me upstairs to show him. He wasn't real happy when he counted up the coins, either, because when he was done he went into Mama's and Papa's room and began opening drawers and bumping things around in the closet. He came out a few minutes later and grabbed my hand.

*Come on,* he said. Then he looked at my pants. *Now wait a minute. You can't go all wet like that. Go change into a nightie or something.*

Uncle Shank waited in the kitchen while I went into my room.

*What's wrong?* he called in.

*I can't reach,* I said.

He shook his head and went into the bureau and pulled out my nightie and then went into the kitchen while I changed.

*Good girl,* he said when I came out. *You're a good girl.* Then he held my hand and we went to the car. He smelled sour and smoky.

While we were driving my favorite Elvis song came on, the one about the blue shoes.

*We going to get Mama?* I asked.

*Not Mama,* Uncle Shank said. *Papa.*

I sat back and watched the lights of all the other cars on the highway. We were coming up on a giant bridge, and it looked like a big red and white snake in front of us, snaking up and down the highway, and I thought of Our Lady and how she might have crushed this snake with her feet you could not see. Then I looked up at the stars and wondered what she was trying to say just then.

We drove up a ramp and Uncle Shank pointed to a building with lots of lit windows and said, *That's where Mama is, where the doctors are taking care of her.*

I looked up and tried to find Mama.

We pulled up to another building which had no windows at all and Uncle Shank opened my door. Inside, there was a policeman behind a counter who made Uncle Shank fill out forms and give him money.

*It's fifty,* said the man. *This is only thirty-three.*

*Help me out, brother,* said Uncle Shank. He looked towards me and the man looked at me and shook his head and left. When he came back he brought Papa, whose eye was purple and bloody. As we walked to the car, Uncle Shank had to half-carry Papa.

*How many times I told you not to mess with that new sheriff?* Uncle Shank said. *How many times I told you?*

*You a piglover?* Papa asked. *Cause you sound an' you smell like one.*

Papa snorted and laughed into Uncle Shank's neck like he just told a real funny knock-knock and Uncle Shank dropped him onto the pavement and kicked him in the leg.

*Now you listen here, Willy. That boy got a shiny new thirty-eight he just itching to use. And he won't have no qualms about using it on your drunk hide. You gonna get yourself killed one of these days, you don't watch it.*

*I know,* said Papa, looking up. *'Swhat I'm aiming to happen.*

*Don't be a fool, Willy,* said Uncle Shank. *You got a child. Come hell or high water you gotta stick around long enough to raise her.*

Uncle Shank helped Papa to his feet then, and when we got to the car he put him in the back seat with the window rolled open.

IV

The black pan was Mama's favorite to cook with because it had tall sides and was big enough to hold all the bacon at once. On Sundays, she would cook breakfast for us in less time without having to warm any in the oven on a plate while she finished cooking the rest. Now Papa was sitting on the living room floor with the pan between his legs. He was crying.

*Lizzie, your Papa's going to die tonight,* he said. *I'm going to kill myself, just like your grandaddy did.*

*Willy you drunk bastard,* yelled Uncle Shank. *Don't do this to the girl.*

He grabbed the pan from between Papa's legs and lifted it high. Papa put his arms over his head and shrunk to the floor, then he made sick all over the rug. *Now get your drunk ass to bed,* Uncle Shank said. *Get to bed!*

Papa didn't move. He lay there slumped on the floor like a flour bag. Uncle Shank put down the pan and dragged Papa by the shoulders into the bedroom and slammed the door. He took my hand then and walked me into the bedroom.

*Hot in here, in'it?* he said as lifted me on the bed. *Don't you worry about nothing, Lizzie. Mama'll be alright. Soon as the doctors make her happy she'll be home again.*

Mama once told me that her happiness was a handkerchief, and that when she was born it had been crumbled up and put into her pocket, and it was never clean again.

*Tomorrow we'll go down the corner store and get you some black licorice,* he said. He pulled the sheets over me but not the blanket, and then he leaned over me and kissed my cheek. *Now don't forget to say your prayers.*

I lay there and listened as Uncle Shank went into the kitchen and rinsed off the black pan in the sink. Then I heard the scratch of a match, and, after a few minutes, I smelled the heavy smoke of the cigar, right when I was about to begin a prayer for Our Lady.

---

## Responding to the Story

1. How much of what is going on around her do you think Lizzie actually understands? Explain your answer.
2. What part does Our Lady of the Gentle Fingers play in the story? What does she mean to Lizzie?

## Exploring the Author's Craft

In this story Nancy Kern uses a young, unsophisticated character as a first-person narrator. Employing this kind of storyteller, sometimes called a **naive narrator,** allows her to tell a story in which the reader realizes more than the character does. Name three things that the reader understands that the narrator doesn't.

## Writer's Workshop

Try your hand at creating a first-person voice quite different from your own. Make your narrator naive about certain aspects of life. Write the story in such a way that the reader understands more than the narrator does.

## Alternate Media Response

Do an illustration of any of the settings in this story. Have your illustration—a drawing or painting—capture the mood of the story.

## James D. Houston

James D. Houston, who was born in 1933, lives in Santa Cruz, California. He has written several novels and nonfiction works as well as cultural documentary films. One of his best-known efforts is *Farewell to Manzanar*, which he coauthored with his wife, Jeanne Wakatsuki. In it they relate the story of her years in a Japanese internment camp during World War II. In the following selection Houston relates a story from his own youth.

*Can you really get rid of a person by throwing out his possessions?*

# Elegy Written at the County Junkyard

At the county dump I am throwing away my father. His old paint rags, and stumps of brushes. Color catalogues. The caked leather suitcase he used for so many years carrying small tools and tiny jars of his trade, suitcase so cracked and bent and buckle-ripped it's no good for anything not, now even what he used it for. I start to toss it on top of the brushes and the rags, but hesitate, toss instead the five-gallon drums that once held primer. He stacked them against one wall of his shop, for nothing, kept dozens more than he'd ever use. Around these fall the ointments from his medicine chest. And cracked galoshes, filled with dust, as if in his closet it's been raining dust for years. And magazines. His fishing hat. Notes to himself.

*Fix window*
*Grease car*
*Call Ed*
*Call Harlow about job*

Bent nails in a jar, rolls of old wire, pipe sections, fiddle he always intended to mend, embossed cards some salesman left, old paid bills, check stubs, pencils his teeth chewed.

Ragtaggle bits of this and that he touched, stacked, stored, useless to anyone but him, and he's gone now, so toss it all out there among the refrigerators and lettuce leaves and seven hundred truck tires, busted sofas, flower pots, and grass from the overgrown gardens of every household. Into it I throw my father, saving for last that suitcase of his, first seen twenty years back, and old then, the first day he took me out on a job, pair of his spattered overalls to wear, rolled thick at the cuff, and Sherwin-Williams white billcap, and us two squatting while he unbuckles the case and touches dark labels of pigment tubes, deciding something.

Crusted with splats of seventy colors now, lid corners split as if somebody sat on it. The ragged straps dangle. One shred of leather holds the chromium buckle, yet the buckle itself hasn't worn much at all, still catches the sun, where paint doesn't cover it, relic from those days before things tarnished in a week.

One last glance. By five tonight it'll be gone for good, when the bulldozer comes around to shove it over the side with the rest of today's arms and toes and parts of hearts.

"What're ya gonna do, dad?"

He doesn't answer. He never answers, as if it offends him to be interrupted. And I always wait, as if all those previous silences were exceptions, and this time he will turn and speak. It's a big reason for coming along this morning, the chance that out here on the job something might pass between us. I would never have been able to describe it ahead of time, but . . . something.

I wait and watch two minutes of puckering lips and long slow blinks while he studies the labels, then selects one tube, smudged and wrinkled, unscrews its top and squeezes out a little on his fingertips.

Five feet away a canvas dropcloth covers a few square yards of hardwood floor. I follow him to a five-gallon drum he's mixing paint in. A narrow stick of plywood holds the color he's shooting for—pale pale green. He's proud of his eye, his knack for figuring just how pale this green will be when it's dry. Squeeze a green strip from the tube and stir it in, wide easy stirs while the green spreads out like taffy strips. Stir and stir. Then test: dip another stick in. Pair it. Stir.

"Okay, Jim. Take half this green paint and git that wall there covered."

He hands me a clean brush, black bristles glistening with yesterday's thinner. He pours a gallon bucket full, deft tilt, and cuts the fall off clean.

"I'll be back in a minute," he says.

It's the first time I've painted anything away from home. I do not yet know that this wall is the beginning of the end, that before the summer is out I will dread the look of yet another long, unpainted wall and wince at the smell of thinner. I want this one to be a good job. I want to live up to the paint he's just mixed. I start by the living room door, taking my time, keeping the molding clear for a white trim later.

Ten minutes pass, and this first wall becomes my world, each piece I cover is a quadrant[1] on my map of it. I am moving across the wide-open middle country—working my brush like dad told me to the time we painted the back side of our house, using the wrist, lapping strokes over—when I feel compelled to turn around.

In the far doorway the lady of the house stands glaring at me, her eyes a blend of terror and hate. I realize how dangerous I must look to her: next to the wall of her priceless living room she finds Tom Sawyer with his cuffs rolled thick, whitewashing away an afternoon.

Under green freckles my face turns scarlet.

She disappears.

From the hallway comes her loud whisper. "Mr. *Hous*ton! That boy painting my living room wall couldn't be over fifteen!"

"He's thirteen, ma'am."

"He's what?"

"It's my boy, Jim. He's giving me a hand this summer."

"I just wonder if he knows what he's *doing* in there."

"I painted my first house when I was ten."

"Well . . . I . . . if . . . I'd certainly be keeping an eye on him if I were you."

"Don't worry, ma'am, he knows what to do."

Behind me I hear her walking slowly across the room. I keep painting, don't look at her this time. Plenty of paint on the brush. But don't let it run. Feather it at the overlap. Cover. Cover.

---

1. **quadrant:** one fourth of the world on a map.

Dad comes in and fills up another gallon bucket and helps me finish the wall. He catches my eye once and winks at the fast one we have pulled on Mrs. So-and-so. Then we are covering the middle country together, in a curiously enclosed stillness, broken only by the whish of bristles and cluck of brush handle against the can. Somewhere in the back of the house a radio is playing, but its faraway music doesn't penetrate our territory.

We finish the room by quitting time. Dad looks over the sections I've painted, finds a couple of holidays[2] along the baseboard and has me fill these in before we clean the brushes, saying only, "Keep an eye out for them holidays," and then a little later, when the sash tools are thinned, and the pigment tubes lined up the way he wants them, next to the knives he uses for cutting linoleum and spreading putty and spackling cracks, he drops the lid shut on his kit of a suitcase, snaps the buckle to, straps it, says, "Might as well take that on out to the truck."

I have never paid much attention to his kit. Now I know just enough about what's inside for its contents to be mysteries. A year from now I will know too much about what's inside, and I will be able to read his half smile, already on the verge of apologizing for having only this to reward me with. But today it is an honor. No one has ever carried that kit but him. It has mysterious weight, with gypsy daubs of ivory, burnt umber, and vermilion all across the ancient leather. A fine weight for carrying from the house downstairs to the curb.

At the county dump I am throwing away my father, hefting this suitcase to toss the last of him onto the smoking heap, when that shred of leather gives and the buckle breaks. The kit flies open. As if compressed inside, waiting to escape, the pungent smell of oil and rare pigments cuts through smoke and rot and fills the air around me. The few tubes still in there begin to topple. My throwing arm stays. My other hand reaches. I'm holding the suitcase, inhaling the smell that always surrounded him, even after he had scrubbed. It rose from the creases in his hands, from permanent white liners rimming his fingernails, from the paint-motes he sometimes missed with thinner, at the corners of his eyes.

I breathe deep. Close the suitcase slowly. Prepare to heave it once and for all. This time with both hands. Out among all those things you only

---

2. **holidays:** places a painter mistakenly left unpainted.

find by losing them. Out and up. And onto the truck bed. Where it lands with a thunk. And sits solid. Those aromatic tubes give it density. I wait for him to tie his ladder on the overhead rack, and we climb into the cab. He winks once more, as we prepare to leave Mrs. So-and-so behind. Reeking of paint and turpentine, billcaps shoved back, we are Sherwin and Williams calling it a day, with no way to talk much over the stuttering engine of this metal-floored Chevy, and no need to talk. The sticky clutch leaps. Wind rushes in, mixing paint and gasoline fumes, and all you need to do is stay loose for the jolts and the whole long rumble ride home.

---

## Responding to the Memoir

1. What kind of feelings does the narrator have about his father? How can you tell?
2. Name some of the objects that bring back memories of the father. What do you learn about the man from these objects?
3. What is your favorite line in this story? Why?

## Exploring the Author's Craft

1. An **elegy** is a funeral song, a tribute to someone just dead. An elegy is usually written in poetry form. What elements are in this memoir that make it deserving of being called an elegy?
2. A **flashback** is an interruption in the flow of a story to show something that happened at an earlier time. James D. Houston moves in and out of flashbacks throughout this memoir of his father. Identify at least two places where the story goes into flashback. What effect does this moving back and forth in time have on the effectiveness of the story?

## Writer's Workshop

Write a short memoir of someone who was close to you, either someone who died or a person you rarely see anymore. Use two or more specific incidents in your memoir, and present them in the form of flashbacks.

## Alternate Media Response

A videocamera can reproduce extraordinary images of the real life around us. Still, given that fact, is there any way a video can be made of "Elegy Written at the County Junkyard" that conveys the same emotion as the story itself? Take on as a challenge the task of creating such a video.

## John Updike

John Updike, one of America's most famous writers of the last 40 years, was born in 1932. In addition to literary criticism and other nonfiction, Updike regularly publishes novels, short stories, and poems that portray aspects of small-town, middle-class American life; he has won both the Pulitzer Prize and the National Book Award for his work. Several of his best-known novels deal with Harry "Rabbit" Angstrom, a star student athlete who could never recapture his success in later life. Notice how Updike picks up on this same theme in "Ex-Basketball Player."

*What happens to those of us who cannot break with the past?*

# Ex-Basketball Player

Pearl Avenue runs past the high-school lot,
Bends with the trolley tracks, and stops, cut off
Before it has a chance to go two blocks,
At Colonel McComsky Plaza. Berth's Garage
5   Is on the corner facing west, and there,
Most days, you'll find Flick Webb, who helps Berth out.

Flick stands tall among the idiot pumps—
Five on a side, the old bubble-head style,[1]

---

**1. the old bubble-head style:** gasoline pumps at one time were topped with glass spheres.

Their rubber elbows hanging loose and low.
10  One's nostrils are two S's, and his eyes
An E and O. And one is squat, without
A head at all—more of a football type.

Once Flick played for the high-school team, the Wizards.
He was good: in fact, the best. In '46
15  He bucketed three hundred ninety points,
A county record still. The ball loved Flick.
I saw him rack up thirty-eight or forty
In one home game. His hands were like wild birds.

He never learned a trade, he just sells gas,
20  Checks oil, and changes flats. Once in a while,
As a gag, he dribbles an inner tube,
But most of us remember anyway.
His hands are fine and nervous on the lug wrench.
It makes no difference to the lug wrench, though.

25  Off work, he hangs around Mae's luncheonette.
Grease-gray and kind of coiled, he plays pinball,
Smokes those thin cigars, nurses lemon phosphates.
Flick seldom says a word to Mae, just nods
Beyond her face toward bright applauding tiers
30  Of Necco Wafers, Nibs, and Juju Beads.

## Responding to the Poem

1. Explain how the description of Pearl Avenue in lines 1–3 also works as a description of Flick Webb's life.
2. What contrasting pictures of Flick are presented in stanzas 3 and 4?
3. Why is this poem in a section of the book called Separating?

## Exploring the Author's Craft

In this poem John Updike puts words together very carefully to present a strong picture of Flick and his life. Sometimes he uses figurative language—similes, metaphors, and other constructions making imaginative comparisons. He also uses **imagery**—word pictures that appeal to one or more senses. Find and discuss the effectiveness of the following constructions.
a. the personification in line 16
b. the simile in line 18
c. the imagery in line 26
d. the imagery in lines 29–30

## Writer's Workshop

It's commonplace to read stories about athletes who have succeeded. Create a story or poem that deals with both of the following: an athlete, male or female, who hasn't succeeded; and some aspect of the topic of separation.

## Sharon Olds

Born in 1942, Sharon Olds is one of America's most accomplished poets. Her writing, drawn intensely from her family life both as a child and now as a parent and wife, is frank, vivid, and often very touching. In addition to writing poems, she teaches creative writing at New York University in New York City and gives many poetry readings. Her collections include *The Gold Cell* and *The Wellspring*.

*The children are ready to move on. Is their mother ready to let them?*

# High School Senior

For seventeen years, her breath in the house
at night, puff, puff, like summer
cumulus above her bed,
and her scalp smelling of apricots
5   —this being who had formed within me,
squatted like a bright tree-frog in the dark,
like an eohippus[1] she had come out of history
slowly, through me, into the daylight,
I had the daily sight of her,
10   like food or air she was there, like a mother.
I say "college," but I feel as if I cannot tell

---

1. **eohippus:** small, extinct horse, an ancestor of the modern horse.

the difference between her leaving for college

and our parting forever—I try to see

this house without her, without her pure

15 depth of feeling, without her creek-brown

hair, her daedal[2] hands with their tapered

fingers, her pupils dark as the mourning cloak's

wing,[3] but I can't. Seventeen years

ago, in this room, she moved inside me,

20 I looked at the river, I could not imagine

my life with her. I gazed across the street,

and saw, in the icy winter sun,

a column of steam rush up away from the earth.

There are creatures whose children float away

25 at birth, and those who throat-feed their young

for weeks and never see them again. My daughter

is free and she is in me—no, my love

of her is in me, moving in my heart,

changing chambers, like something poured

30 from hand to hand, to be weighed and then reweighed.

---

2. **daedal:** skillful; ingenious.

3. **mourning cloak's wing:** the purplish brown wing of a type of butterfly.

# Solo

Our son shrugs into his macho jacket
with the swollen shoulders, he swings his sports bag
over his shoulder, runs his fingers through his
blown-dry feather-cut, raises an eyebrow,
5   tosses his keys, flips a token and is
out the door to karate—in the bag
his *gi*[1] and belt lie coiled.
I turn the lock, I lean on the door
and hear him joggle the old elevator button and then
10   kick it with a flying kick,
and then I hear it, for the first time,
and the last time, I hear him sing
five or six pure, slow
soprano notes, like part of a Mass,
15   Mass for the end of a man's childhood.
Just those few, clear tones
in the hall narrow as an echo chamber,
A, B-flat, C, F,
whole, isolated, sweet, that voice
20   which has not changed since it first sounded,
his throat opens, and he breathes a low O.

---

1. *gi*: loose-fitting white outfit worn in karate and other martial arts.

## Responding to the Poems

1. What is surprising about the lines, "I had the daily sight of her,/like food or air she was there, like a mother"?
2. Which of these poem portraits most appeals to you? Why?

## Exploring the Author's Craft

The strength of these two poems is in Sharon Olds's ability to convey, with just a few words, a vivid picture of or insight into the narrator and her children. Find at least one example of a phrase or line that helps you form a clear impression of the mother, the daughter, and the son.

## Writer's Workshop

In a poem create a portrait of, and tribute to, someone you know and love vividly, the way the narrator in these poems clearly loves her daughter and son. As always, it will be the specific words you use and details you include that will make the poem come to life.

## Alternate Media Response

Do an illustration of either of the two subjects of these poems. Base it on the way Sharon Olds portrays the character.

## Sandra Cisneros

Sandra Cisneros was born in Chicago in 1954. The publisher of her imaginative work *The House on Mango Street* describes her in this way: "The daughter of a Mexican father and a Mexican-American mother, and sister to six brothers, she is nobody's mother and nobody's wife." The stories that follow are from *The House on Mango Street;* Cisneros has also published collections of short stories and poems.

*Once you make a separation, will you ever really be able to return?*

# from The House on Mango Street

### The Three Sisters

**T**hey came with the wind that blows in August, thin as a spider web and barely noticed. Three who did not seem to be related to anything but the moon. One with laughter like tin and one with eyes of a cat and one with hands like porcelain. The aunts, the three sisters, *las comadres,*[1] they said.

The baby died. Lucy and Rachel's sister. One night a dog cried, and the next day a yellow bird flew in through an open window. Before the week was over, the baby's fever was worse. Then Jesus came and took the baby with him far away. That's what their mother said.

Then the visitors came . . . in and out of the little house. It was hard to keep the floors clean. Anybody who had ever wondered what color

---

1. *las comadres:* the godmothers; the gossipy neighbors. [Spanish]

the walls were came and came to look at that little thumb of a human in a box like candy.

I had never seen the dead before, not for real, not in somebody's living room for people to kiss and bless themselves and light a candle for. Not in a house. It seemed strange.

They must've known, the sisters. They had the power and could sense what was what. They said, Come here, and gave me a stick of gum. They smelled like Kleenex or the inside of a satin handbag, and then I didn't feel afraid.

What's your name, the cat-eyed one asked.

Esperanza, I said.

Esperanza, the old blue-veined one repeated in a high thin voice. Esperanza . . . a good good name.

My knees hurt, the one with the funny laugh complained.

Tomorrow it will rain.

Yes, tomorrow, they said.

How do you know? I asked.

We know.

Look at her hands, cat-eyed said.

And they turned them over and over as if they were looking for something.

She's special.

Yes, she'll go very far.

Yes, yes, hmmm.

Make a wish.

A wish?

Yes, make a wish. What do you want?

Anything? I said.

Well, why not?

I closed my eyes.

Did you wish already?

Yes, I said.

Well, that's all there is to it. It'll come true.

How do you know? I asked.

We know, we know.

Esperanza. The one with marble hands called me aside. Esperanza.

She held my face with her blue-veined hands and looked and looked at me. A long silence. When you leave you must remember always to come back, she said.

What?

When you leave you must remember to come back for the others. A circle, you understand? You will always be Esperanza. You will always be Mango Street. You can't erase what you know. You can't forget who you are.

Then I didn't know what to say. It was as if she could read my mind, as if she knew what I had wished for, and I felt ashamed for having made such a selfish wish.

You must remember to come back. For the ones who cannot leave as easily as you. You will remember? She asked as if she was telling me. Yes, yes, I said a little confused.

Good, she said, rubbing my hands. Good. That's all. You can go.

I got up to join Lucy and Rachel who were already outside waiting by the door, wondering what I was doing talking to three old ladies who smelled like cinnamon. I didn't understand everything they had told me. I turned around. They smiled and waved in their smoky way.

Then I didn't see them. Not once, or twice, or ever again.


## Alicia & I Talking on Edna's Steps

I like Alicia because once she gave me a little leather purse with the word GUADALAJARA stitched on it, which is home for Alicia,[1] and one day she will go back there. But today she is listening to my sadness because I don't have a house.

You live right here, 4006 Mango, Alicia says and points to the house I am ashamed of.

No, this isn't my house I say and shake my head as if shaking could undo the year I've lived here. I don't belong. I don't ever want to come from here. You have a home, Alicia, and one day you'll go there, to a

---

1. **home for Alicia:** Guadalajara is a city in west-central Mexico.

town you remember, but me I never had a house, not even a photograph . . . only one I dream of.

No, Alicia says. Like it or not you are Mango Street, and one day you'll come back too.

Not me. Not until somebody makes it better.

Who's going to do it? The mayor?

And the thought of the mayor coming to Mango Street makes me laugh out loud.

Who's going to do it? Not the mayor.

## A House of My Own

Not a flat. Not an apartment in back. Not a man's house. Not a daddy's. A house all my own. With my porch and my pillow, my pretty purple petunias. My books and my stories. My two shoes waiting beside the bed. Nobody to shake a stick at. Nobody's garbage to pick up after.

Only a house quiet as snow, a space for myself to go, clean as paper before the poem.

## Mango Says Goodbye Sometimes

I like to tell stories. I tell them inside my head. I tell them after the mailman says, Here's your mail. Here's your mail he said.

I make a story for my life, for each step my brown shoe takes. I say, "And so she trudged up the wooden stairs, her sad brown shoes taking her to the house she never liked."

I like to tell stories. I am going to tell you a story about a girl who didn't want to belong.

We didn't always live on Mango Street. Before that we lived on Loomis on the third floor, and before that we lived on Keeler. Before Keeler it was Paulina, but what I remember most is Mango Street, sad red house, the house I belong but do not belong to.

I put it down on paper and then the ghost does not ache so much. I write it down and Mango says goodbye sometimes. She does not hold me with both arms. She sets me free.

One day I will pack my bags of books and paper. One day I will say goodbye to Mango. I am too strong for her to keep me here forever. One day I will go away.

Friends and neighbors will say, What happened to that Esperanza? Where did she go with all those books and paper? Why did she march so far away?

They will not know I have gone away to come back. For the ones I left behind. For the ones who cannot out.

## Responding to the Stories

1. What do you think Esperanza means when she refers to the "sad red house, the house I belong but do not belong to"?
2. What do the aunts mean when they say, "When you leave you must remember to come back for the others"?
3. What impact do the aunts have on Esperanza? How do you know?

## Exploring the Author's Craft

Although a complex and deep topic—separating—is being explored, the language of these four brief scenes is simple. What does Sandra Cisneros do to create a young, "simple" voice? How can you tell that the voice is one of a person who "like[s] to tell stories"? Cite specific lines.

## Writer's Workshop

What attitude would you have about leaving a place you lived in for at least a year, as Esperanza lived on Mango Street? Convey that attitude in a piece of fiction—not an essay—adopting a younger person's vocabulary and simple narration.

## Making Connections in
# PART FIVE

Complete one or more of the following assignments as your teacher directs.

1   Write an essay that organizes the pieces of writing in Part Five into various categories of separating. Have a different supporting paragraph for at least three types of separating, and make it clear how each piece of writing fits into the category you've placed it in.

2.  Explain in a short essay which piece of writing most expresses thoughts that you have felt. Be sure to include why you made the connection.

3.  Many of the selections in Part Five are told through a first-person narrator. Choose two selections in which you think that first-person voice is very different, and write a paper contrasting the two narrators. Show how, even though they are different, they are still going through the process of separating.

4.  Consider the five sections of this book: Searching, Competing, Realizing, Loving, and Separating. Find three pieces of writing *from three different sections* and show how they are similar in the way they treat some aspect of growing up. Make connections. Point out the differences among the pieces, too.

# Acknowledgments

## FRONT MATTER

**x** "I Didn't Want to Be Me" from *Jules Feiffer's America: from Eisenhower to Reagan*, edited by Steven Heller. Copyright © 1982 by Jules Feiffer, published by Alfred A. Knopf, Inc.

## PART 1

**2** "Memorial Day" by Peter Cameron from *The Half You Don't Know* published by Plume Penguin. Copyright © 1986 by Peter Cameron. Reprinted by permission of the author and the author's agent, Irene Skolnick Literary Agency. **9** "Boy at the Window" from *Things of This World*, copyright 1952 and renewed 1980 by Richard Wilbur, reprinted by permission of Harcourt Brace & Company. **12** "Journal: My Freshman Year in College" by Scott Margolin. Reprinted by permission of the Margolin Family. **22** "My First Conk" from *The Autobiography of Malcolm X* by Malcolm X, with the assistance of Alex Haley. Copyright © 1964 by Alex Haley and Malcolm X. Copyright © 1965 by Alex Haley and Betty Shabazz. Reprinted by permission of Random House, Inc. **27** "My Parents Kept Me from Children Who Were Rough" from *Collected Poems 1928-1953* by Stephen Spender. Copyright © 1934 and renewed 1962 by Stephen Spender. Reprinted by permission of Random House, Inc. **28** "We Real Cool" by Gwendolyn Brooks, © 1991, published by Third World Press, Chicago, 1991. **30** "Checkouts" from *A Couple of Kooks and Other Stories about Love* by Cynthia Rylant. Copyright © 1990 by Cynthia Rylant. Reprinted by permission of Orchard Books, New York. **35** "Michael Egerton." Reprinted with the permission of Scribner, a Division of Simon & Schuster from *The Collected Stories* by Reynolds Price. Copyright © 1993 Reynolds Price. **43** "The 'Black Table' Is Still There" by Lawrence Otis Graham. Copyright © 1991 by The New York Times Co. Reprinted by Permission. **48** "Snake's Daughter." Reprinted from *Snake's Daughter: The Roads In and Out of War* by Gail Hosking Gilberg by permission of University of Iowa Press. Copyright 1997 by University of Iowa Press. **60** "Follower" from *Poems 1965-1975* by Seamus Heaney. Copyright © 1980 by Seamus Heaney. Reprinted by permission of Farrar, Straus & Giroux, Inc.

## PART 2

**66** "Cut." Reprinted from *Cheeseburgers: The Best of Bob Greene* by permission of Sterling Lord Literistic, Inc. Copyright © 1985 by Bob Greene. **73** All pages from "Through the Tunnel" from *The Habit of Loving* by Doris Lessing. Copyright © 1955 by Doris Lessing. Originally appeared in *The New Yorker*. Copyright renewed. Reprinted by permission of HarperCollins Publishers, Inc. **84** "Baseball" by Bill Zavatsky. Copyright © 1985 by Bill Zavatsky. Used by permission of the author. **89** "Waiting" from *The Leaving and Other Stories* by Budge Wilson, published by Philomel Books, New York. **104** "Of My Friend Hector and My Achilles Heel" by Michael T. Kaufman. Copyright © 1992 by The New York Times Co. Reprinted by Permission. **107** "Flash Cards" from *Grace Notes* by Rita Dove. Copyright © 1989 by Rita Dove. Reprinted by permission of the author and W. W. Norton & Company, Inc. **109** "Priscilla and the Wimps" by Richard Peck, copyright © 1984 by Richard Peck. From *Sixteen: Short Stories* by Donald R. Gallo, ed. Used by permission of Dell Books, a division of Bantam Doubleday Dell Publishing Group, Inc. **114** "Fourth of July" by Robin Brancato.

Publishing Corporation. **253** "My Father's Song." Permission granted by the author, Simon J. Ortiz. Poem originally published in *Woven Stone*, The University of Arizona Press, 1992. **256** "Birthday Box." Copyright © 1995 by Jane Yolen. First appeared in *Birthday Surprises: Ten Great Stories to Unwrap*, published by Morrow Junior Books. Reprinted by permission of Curtis Brown, Ltd. **261** "First Love" by Angela Patrick from *Literary Cavalcade*, October 1975. Copyright © 1975 by Scholastic Inc. Reprinted by permission of Scholastic Inc. **267** "Janet Waking" from *Selected Poems* by John Crowe Ransom. Copyright 1927 by Alfred A. Knopf, Inc. and renewed 1955 by John Crowe Ransom. Reprinted by permission of the publisher. **269** "I Loved My Friend" from *Collected Poems* by Langston Hughes. Copyright © 1994 by the Estate of Langston Hughes. Reprinted by permission of Alfred A. Knopf, Inc.

## PART 5

**273** "Rehearsal" by Richard Hartman. Reprinted by permission of the author. **278** "Saturday at the Canal" is used by permission of the author. Copyright © 1991 by Gary Soto. **279** "Nights Away from Home" by Frank Conroy. Reprinted by permission of Donadio & Ashworth, Inc. Copyright 1966; originally published in *The New Yorker* magazine, October 22, 1966. **293** "Our Lady of the Gentle Fingers" by Nancy Kern. Reprinted by permission of the author. **300** "Elegy Written at the County Junkyard" from *Three Songs for My Father* by James D. Houston. Copyright © 1974 by James D. Houston. Reprinted by permission of Capra Press. **306** "Ex-Basketball Player" from *The Carpentered Hen and Other Tame Creatures* by John Updike. Copyright © 1960 by John Updike. Reprinted by permission of Alfred A. Knopf, Inc. Originally appeared in *The New Yorker*. **309** "Solo" from *The Wellspring* by Sharon Olds. Copyright © 1995 by Sharon Olds. Reprinted by permission of Alfred A. Knopf, Inc. **311** "High School Senior" from *The Wellspring* by Sharon Olds. Copyright © 1995 by Sharon Olds. Reprinted by permission of Alfred A. Knopf, Inc. **313** "The Three Sisters," "Alicia and I Talking on Edna's Steps," "A House of My Own," "Mango Says Goodbye Sometimes" from *The House on Mango Street*. Copyright © 1984 by Sandra Cisneros. Published by Alfred A. Knopf, a division of Random House, Inc., New York in 1994. Reprinted by permission of Susan Bergholz Literary Services, New York. All rights reserved.

# Index of Authors and Titles